SCIENCE FICTION CINEMA IN THE TWENTY-FIRST CENTURY

Recent films are increasingly using themes and conventions of science fiction such as dystopian societies, catastrophic environmental disasters, apocalyptic scenarios, aliens, monsters, time travel, teleportation, and supernatural abilities to address cosmopolitan concerns such as human rights, climate change, economic precarity, and mobility. This book identifies and analyses the new transnational turn towards cosmopolitanism in science fiction cinema since the beginning of the twenty-first century.

The book considers a wide selection of examples, including case studies of films such as *Elysium*, *In Time*, *2012*, Andrew Niccol's *The Host*, *Codependent Lesbian Space Alien Seeks Same*, and *Cloud Atlas*. It also questions the seeming cosmopolitanism of these narratives and exposes how they sometimes reproduce social hierarchies and exploitative practices.

Dealing with diverse, interdisciplinary concerns represented in cinema, this book in the Studies in Global Genre Fiction series will be of interest to readers and scholars working in the fields of science fiction, film and media studies, cosmopolitanism, border theory, popular culture, and cultural studies. It will also appeal to fans of science fiction cinema and literature.

Pablo Gómez–Muñoz is Assistant Professor of English and Film at the University of Zaragoza (Spain). His research interests are transnational cinema, science fiction, borders, cosmopolitanism, globalization, precarity, and spectacle. His work has been published in journals such as *Geopolitics*, *Journal of Transnational American Studies*, and *Atlantis* and volumes such as *Making Sense of Popular Culture* and *Frontières au Cinéma*.

Studies in Global Genre Fiction

Series Editors: **Bodhisattva Chattopadhyay**, University of Oslo, Norway
and **Taryne Jade Taylor**, Embry-Riddle Aeronautical University, USA

Studies in Global Genre Fiction offers original insights into the history of genre literature while contesting two hierarchies that constrain global genre fiction studies: (1)
Anglophone literature and other global language literatures and (2) literary fiction and
genre fiction. The series explores the exchanges between different literary cultures that
form aesthetic concerns and the specific literary, sociopolitical, geographical, economic,
and historical forces that shape genre fiction globally. A key focus is understudied genre
fictions from the 'global South' — where geographical location or language often con-
fines works to the margins of the global publishing industry, international circulation,
and academic scrutiny, even if they may be widely read in their own specific contexts.

Contributions to this series investigate the points of disruption, intersection and flows
between literary and genre fiction. The series analyses cross-cultural influences in literary
classifications, translation, transcreation, localization, production, and distribution while capturing the rich history of world and global literatures.

Editorial Advisory Board

Books in this series

The Making of *The Wandering Earth*
A Film Production Handbook
Edited by Jiaren Wang and Regina Kanyu Wang (STORYCOM)
Translated by Guo Qi and Revised by John Shanahan

Burning Down the House
Latin American Comics in the 21st Century
Edited by Laura Fernández-González, Amadeo Gandolfo and Pablo Turnes

For more information about this series, please visit: https://www.routledge.com/
Studies-in-Global-Genre-Fiction/book-series/SGGF

SCIENCE FICTION CINEMA IN THE TWENTY-FIRST CENTURY

Transnational Futures, Cosmopolitan Concerns

Pablo Gómez-Muñoz

 Routledge
Taylor & Francis Group

LONDON AND NEW YORK

Cover image: Getty Images

First published 2023
by Routledge
4 Park Square, Milton Park, Abingdon, Oxon OX14 4RN

and by Routledge
605 Third Avenue, New York, NY 10158

Routledge is an imprint of the Taylor & Francis Group, an informa business

British Library Cataloguing-in-Publication Data
A catalogue record for this book is available from the British Library

Library of Congress Cataloging-in-Publication Data
A catalog record has been requested for this book

ISBN: 978-0-367-71532-8 (hbk)
ISBN: 978-0-367-75906-3 (pbk)
ISBN: 978-1-003-16451-7 (ebk)

DOI: 10.4324/9781003164517

Typeset in Bembo
by Deanta Global Publishing Services, Chennai, India

For my parents

CONTENTS

FIGURES

ACKNOWLEDGMENTS

Research towards this book has been funded by the Spanish Ministry of Education, Culture, and Sport (research grant FPU-2013-00316), the Spanish Ministry of Science and Innovation (research projects FFI2013-43968-P and FFI2017-83606-P), and the Government of Aragón (research projects H23_17R and H23_20R).

Apart from these institutions, many people have helped in the process of writing this book. First of all, I would like to express my gratitude to Celestino Deleyto. He has provided invaluable feedback and advice at different points in the development of this monograph. His motivation and academic excellence have also been a major source of inspiration. I am also immensely grateful to Marimar Azcona for her kindness, constant encouragement, and support. I extend my gratitude to the members of the Cinema, Culture, and Society research group and the Department of English and German at the University of Zaragoza. Beatriz Pérez also deserves special mention. I would like to thank her for her friendship and for the many experiences we have shared since graduate school.

A research stay at the Eaton Collection of Science Fiction and Fantasy at the University of California, Riverside was essential in the process of writing this book. My heartfelt thanks to Sherryl Vint for welcoming me in Riverside and discussing some initial ideas related to this book. I am also grateful to Mark Bould and Marianne Kac-Vergne for their observations on an early version of the manuscript. The anonymous reviewers have also offered extremely valuable insights and suggestions. Dean Allbritton and Miriam Borham invited me to give talks at Colby College in Salamanca and the University of Salamanca which helped me develop some specific ideas included in the book. I would like to thank them for these fruitful opportunities to discuss my work.

I am particularly indebted to the series editors, Bodhisattva Chattopadhyay and Taryne Taylor, for their enthusiasm about this project from the beginning and their understanding and help along the way. I am also very grateful to Shoma Choudhury, Shloka Chauhan, and Hannah Champney at Routledge and to Narayanan Ramachandran at Deanta for their help at different stages in the publication process. Special thanks to Javier Calvo for sharing his passion for cinema and for countless conversations about many of the films mentioned in this book. Finally, I would like to thank my parents, María Teresa and José Antonio, for their boundless love and support.

INTRODUCTION

Transnational Futures, Cosmopolitan Concerns

Borders between rich and poor regions, multinational corporations exploiting natural resources in far-flung places, transnational couples, large-scale environmental disasters, and global interconnectivity are all common phenomena in the world we live in. In the cinema, they are also part of the worlds of *Elysium* (Blomkamp 2013), *In Time* (Niccol 2011), *2012* (Emmerich 2009), *The Host* (Niccol 2013), *Codependent Lesbian Space Alien Seeks Same* (Olnek 2011), and *Cloud Atlas* (The Wachowskis and Tykwer 2012), among many other movies. These science fiction (sf) films combine such 'real' situations and events with not-so-real elements like global elites living in a giant wheel floating in outer space, people using time as currency, alien body snatchers, the sinking of the world, reincarnations, and futuristic cities such as Neo Seoul. Even though the universes that these films create are imaginary, they work as metaphors of our social context. In this book, I discuss a growing number of recent science fiction (sf) films (2000–present) that use their extrapolative power to reflect on the cosmopolitan dimension of several contemporary issues. Although sf has regularly shown interest in international matters, in the last two decades, the genre has begun to overly exploit the possibilities of its generic conventions to examine transnational phenomena and cosmopolitan concerns. This shift coincides with the marked transnational character of both present-day societies and cinema. Sf, because of its traditional relationship with technology and borders and its ability to imagine alternative worlds and to combine spatiotemporal dimensions, is one of the best-equipped genres to deal with phenomena related to globalization. Approaching sf films from a cosmopolitan perspective, this book argues that many twenty-first-century sf films combine seemingly cosmopolitan discourses that question borders with ambivalent narrative elements that reinforce them.

   The turn to the twenty-first century has witnessed a proliferation of discourses on cosmopolitanism. In the late 1990s and early 2000s, a series of scholars started

DOI: 10.4324/9781003164517-1

to resort to cosmopolitanism to reflect on the social reality that they observed (Nussbaum; Beck 1996, 1998, 2002; Harvey 2000; Vertovec and Cohen). Rather than speaking of "a cosmopolitan age," "an age of cosmopolitanism" (Fine 2007, 19), or even "an age of cosmopolitanization" (Beck 2012, 304), it may be more appropriate to refer to the present as an age of cosmopolitan struggles. Our time is characterized by tensions between the impacts of globalization and cosmopolitan and anti-cosmopolitan reactions to them. In other words, we live in an age of transnational changes and global challenges that call for cosmopolitan answers. New technologies facilitate faster and safer travel, instant communication, and the movement of capital, while traditional and new technological borders and surveillance systems control the movement of people. At the same time, economic decisions in one country can have a direct impact on other societies, ignoring national boundaries, just as CO_2 emissions and viruses do. Several other factors such as geopolitical and economic measures, lack of opportunity, corruption, violence, repression, and changes in the environment affect local populations who are forced to move elsewhere to live decently or to survive. Jobs also move around in search of cheap labor or tax benefits, while workers from different parts of the world move to Western countries to look after Western children and elders in order to support their families back home. Meanwhile, industries, companies, and services traditionally owned by the state or national investors now have multiple owners around the world and international institutions like the International Monetary Fund tell national governments what they should do in order to keep their economies afloat and not make stock markets nervous or unhappy. Along similar neoliberal lines, undeclared fortunes jump from one tax haven to another in order to reenter the 'real' economy in a laundered form. Not everything revolves around money: cultural trends also move rapidly across borders and social movements replicate and forge alliances across countries. At the other side of the coin, fundamentalist, terrorist attacks from transnationally connected individuals and organized groups also hit countries across the globe, such as Nigeria, France, Iraq, Syria, the USA, Spain, the UK, or Australia. All of these realities may be best addressed and understood from a cosmopolitan point of view that considers their transnational dimension and the cosmopolitan challenges that they pose.

Migration, borders, travel, intercultural communication, transnational influence, international trade, and top-down control have existed for centuries. Cosmopolitanism is not new either: there have been at least three major cosmopolitan moments (apart from the present one) characterized by the theories of the Greek Stoics, Immanuel Kant, and Hannah Arendt (Fine and Cohen 1–22). What is new in today's world is a heightened awareness of transnational and global social phenomena (Beck 2006, 21). Such a perception is due to the intensification of globalization processes and their impact on individuals. Sf cinema has a unique ability to articulate discourses on a social context characterized by transnational processes and cosmopolitan challenges like the present. Barry Grant argues that, since the late 1960s and early 1970s, sf has taken the place of the western as the dominant film genre. Grant explains that the rise of sf is due to its ability to deal with technological developments in the last decades (2013, 1–2). What Grant does not mention is the central role of technology in globalization processes and cosmopolitan struggles. For instance, recent advances in technology allow faster and more efficient movement and control of people, information, and goods (although, at the same time, the development of technologies in some places pushes some areas and many people further into the margins). The central role of technology in globalization processes is not the only reason for the prevailing position of sf within the current transnational context. Borders—one of the main places where transnational phenomena take place—are inscribed in the genre's identity: many sf films fall between the real and the imaginary and they often deal with different kinds of borders (human/ non-human, Earth/outer space, upper class/lower class, humanity/technology, body/mind, physical/virtual). Like globalization, science fiction often jumps and combines spatial scales. Sf also makes connections across time: it speculates on the future of transnational interactions and explores their relationship with the present and the past. The ability of sf to incorporate rare, novel concepts, images, and narratives also grants it a matchless and almost boundless freedom to explore social concerns and establish compelling parallels with the 'real' world. In sum, sf is a well-equipped genre to deal with the current proliferation of transnational connections, disruptions, and cosmopolitan challenges. However, I do not argue that the films that I analyze here are necessarily cosmopolitan. Films, like other media, may generate empathy and solidarity, but they may also adopt anti-cosmopolitan stances or ambiguous positions that allow disparate readings.

This book proposes that some of the main trends in twenty-first-century science fiction cinema revolve around the construction of alternative worlds that offer opportunities to reflect on cosmopolitanism. Adopting a cosmopolitan perspective, I analyze a significant number of science fiction films from 2000 onward that deal with borders, transnational phenomena, and globalization. More specifically, I focus on the ways in which the genre relies on a series of themes and conventions such as dystopian societies, unbelievable natural disasters, apocalyptic scenarios, aliens, monsters, time travel, teleportation, and supernatural abilities to address cosmopolitan concerns. Most of the films that I analyze were released after 2007. Yet, I set the limit in 2000 to include other films worthy of mention or analysis such as *What Planet Are You From?* (Nichols, 2000), *Code 46* (Winterbottom 2003), *The Day After Tomorrow* (Emmerich 2004), and *The Fountain* (Aronofsky 2006), to name a few. Obviously, there are many pre-2000 films that develop narratives that connect with the cosmopolitan imagination, including *High Treason* (Elvey 1929), *Island of Lost Souls* (Kenton 1932), *The Day the Earth Stood Still* (Wise 1951), *Planet of the Apes* (Schaffner 1968), *Star Trek: The Motion Picture* (Wise 1979), *Enemy Mine* (Petersen 1985), and *Starship Troopers* (Verhoeven 1997). Despite these earlier instances, I have chosen to focus on films produced after the turn to the twenty-first century because the number of sf films that explore cosmopolitan conflicts and their investment in such issues has multiplied in recent years. As I have mentioned before, the aim of this book is not to label a group of films as cosmopolitan. Rather, I intend to explore, through the analysis of these movies, some of the conflicts, tensions, and struggles around which discourses on cosmopolitanism revolve. Through formal and sociocultural film analysis, I argue that a large number of twenty-first-century sf films adopt ambivalent positions towards cosmopolitan concerns. These films articulate a type of cosmopolitanism that both questions and reinforces social borders, hierarchies, inequalities, and environmental exploitation: an ambivalent cosmopolitanism. Close formal analysis allows me to test this hypothesis by concentrating on how a variety of twenty-first-century sf films use film techniques to develop wondrous concepts, spatiotemporal connections, spectacular elements, or an abundantly or sparsely detailed mise-en-scène.

Before further delving into the transnational and cosmopolitan dimensions of this book, it is worth clarifying what I understand by such closely related but semantically different terms as globalization, global, international, transnational, and cosmopolitan(ism). I use the term 'globalization' mostly in an economic sense. Globalization makes it easier for world capital to penetrate markets, building systems of commercial and financial dependency. It also facilitates the movement of goods and some kinds of qualified labor and makes it possible for companies to produce wherever labor is cheaper or taxes lower. Globalization also describes technological developments (mostly in transportation and telecommunications) that connect people, goods, and places and spread information and cultural products across the world. Yet, as Robert Holton notes, globalization also includes a series of cultural, political, and religious processes that are not necessarily dominated by technology and the economy (2008, 7–8). I use the term 'global' in a broader sense to refer to events that affect many parts of the world, for example, in the case of climate change or financial decisions that have an impact on many countries. The word 'international' often alludes to relations between nation-states. Steven Vertovec also uses the term 'international' to describe the movement of people or goods "from one nation-state […] to another" (3). International connections, unlike transnational interactions, do not necessarily challenge state borders (Vertovec 3–4). Transnational phenomena, for their part, are not necessarily global in scope, but they often transcend bilateral relations (Vertovec 3). Although transnational formations in many cases derive from the economic and logistic structures of globalization, the adjective 'transnational' refers to a wider range of social phenomena and relations, including (but not limited to) migration, intimate relationships, kinship, informal and underpaid labor, access to and exploitation of natural resources, environmental degradation and protection, cultural connections, and violence.

'Cosmopolitanism' describes an ideal, desirable horizon characterized by sociocultural connectivity, sustainability, and respect for human rights on a global level. Some of the key elements that define cosmopolitanism are the right to work, migrate, or seek asylum; decent work conditions; access to water, food, and healthcare; sensible resource management; environmental protection; global institutions grounded on people's sovereignty; the regulation of markets; and the eradication of tax evasion (Appiah 163; Beck 2006, 9, 89; Delanty 2009, 7, 41; Harvey 2009, 93–4). Reality is not necessarily becoming cosmopolitan, but films and other cultural forms incorporate discourses on cosmopolitanism. In this book, I use cosmopolitanism as a critical perspective to interpret transnationalization processes at multiple scales (local, regional, national, transnational, global) and the cosmopolitan challenges, tensions, and struggles that such processes create.

Beyond the Nation: Transnational Science Fiction Film

Although movies have always reflected transnational influences and collaborations, in the last two decades transnational story elements and filmmaking practices have become more and more common for both economic and social reasons. As far as the industry is concerned, contemporary studio ownership, funding, casts, crews, creative labor (visual effects, digital compositing, etc.), audiences, and box office sales are part of transnational ecosystems (Chung 7, R. Davis 74). An obvious example of this trend is the changes that US cinema is currently undergoing in order to meet the expectations of its growing Asian audiences, especially Chinese audiences. Films that perform poorly at the US box office can be top ticket-sellers in other countries. One example is *Jupiter Ascending* (The Wachowskis 2015), which flopped in the US but was number one at the Chinese box office (McClintock 2015). Sf movies like *Pacific Rim* (del Toro 2013), *Looper* (Johnson 2012), *Transformers: Age of Extinction* (Bay 2014), or *Godzilla vs. Kong* (Wingard 2021) include locations like Hong Kong or Shanghai, while the Chinese-US co-production *The Great Wall* (Zhang Yimou 2016) takes place at the Chinese fortification that gives title to the film. *Big Hero 6* (Williams 2014), for its part, even imagines a new city: San Fransokyo, a combination of San Francisco and Tokyo. While the inclusion of these locations in films may be a commercial decision, these choices undoubtedly affect the development of the storylines and lead films to address questions about mobility, transnational connections, and intercultural negotiations, even if they sometimes do so in superficial ways.

Other films like *The Martian* (Scott 2015) and *Arrival* (Villeneuve 2016) explore alternative geopolitical scenarios in which the US and China need to collaborate to solve problems. The prominence of East Asia in recent US films is in many cases probably due to the attempt of US studios to get a bigger share of the Chinese box office, which is in the course of becoming the top film market in the world (Lim 2–4). Yet, the relevance of Asian characters in most of these and other films is still limited, as Astria Suparak suggests in the 2021 video essay "Virtually Asian," in which she draws on examples from *Ghost in the Shell* (Rupert Sanders 2017), *Blade Runner 2049* (Denis Villeneuve 2017), and earlier films. At the same time, the Chinese film industry is also transforming and exerting its own kind of soft power in other film markets, as Chinese films increasingly include foreign spaces and nations in their narratives (Lim 3). For example, the part set in the future in *Mountains May Depart* (Zhangke 2015) takes place in Australia and, in the last scene of *The Wandering Earth* (Gwo 2019), China gathers different nations around its initiative to save planet Earth and they appear in the same order in which they offered help after the 2008 Sichuan earthquake (Santirso). Yet, even if the transnationalization of these film narratives is sometimes part of attempts to access certain film markets, these changes have a direct impact on the development of film narratives and their discourses. Obviously, transnational connections do not only spring between the US and East Asian countries. These are just some examples of the variety of transnational collaborations, influences, and references that characterize contemporary filmmaking.

Since this book looks at transnational narratives in sf cinema from a cosmopolitan perspective, Maria Rovisco's notion of "cosmopolitan cinema" may seem an ideal point of departure (153). Yet, Rovisco's notion of cosmopolitan cinema is based on a pre-defined set of characteristics that exclude a variety of contemporary filmmaking practices. Her notion of cosmopolitan cinema is similar to Hamid Naficy's "accented cinema" (111–2). As Rovisco explains, both cosmopolitan and accented cinema focus on the experiences of exilic and diasporic subjects, "[have] a recognizable self-reflexive and multilingual style," and "often [stem] from an artisan and collective mode of production that seeks to resist the mainstream" (153). A key difference between the two is that, unlike accented films, cosmopolitan films are not necessarily made by "exilic and diasporic filmmakers" (Rovisco 154). Even though Rovisco attempts to make her approach broader than Naficy's, her notion of cosmopolitan cinema also refers to a very specific kind of film. In the case of science fiction at least, it is not productive to establish such a division between mainstream and artisanal films. Neill Blomkamp and Gareth Edwards are clear examples of directors who started making transnational films or short films with few resources (*Alive in Joburg* [Blomkamp 2005], *Monsters* [Edwards 2010]) and have later employed their skills in transnational higher-budget Hollywood films (*Elysium, Godzilla* [2014], *Chappie* [2015], *Rogue One* [2016]). Apart from the fact that transnational films explore connected sociocultural phenomena that involve two or more countries, the term 'transnational cinema' does not necessarily refer to a specific set of characteristics shared by a group of films. Mette Hjort (16, 21) and Deborah Shaw (294), respectively, identify up to nine and fifteen different kinds or categories of transnational cinema, of which accented or diasporic cinema is just one. Transnational films include a variety of themes dealing with social life beyond the scope of the nation. They are often concerned with borders, global cities, migration, (in)hospitality, interconnectivity, networks, mobility, legal loopholes, transnational kinship, power relations, global economic actors, neoliberalism, (neo)colonialism, the environment, global risks, and cultural influence. Taking this heterogeneity into account, this book uses cosmopolitanism as a perspective or approach to transnational cinema rather than as a predefined set of characteristics to look for in films.

Although sf films have engaged with issues that transcend the scope of the nation since the inception of the genre, the transnational orientation of sf cinema has seldom been emphasized. Jay Telotte offers a clear example of the early transnational investment of the genre through his analysis of the film *F.P.1 Doesn't Answer* (Hartl 1932) and its British, French, and German versions. This is a significant film from an industrial point of view, as parts of it were remade to suit the cultural expectations of different national audiences (Telotte 115). At the same time, it is a film that explores how the construction of a platform in the middle of the Atlantic Ocean would help develop a fruitful relationship between the American and European continents (Telotte 103). The interest of *F.P.1 Doesn't Answer* in transnational dynamics is not an exception: other films like Maurice Elvey's *High Treason* (1929) and *Transatlantic Tunnel* (1935) also tapped into both social anxieties and hopes about transatlantic relations, linking them to the construction and fear of destruction of transnational infrastructure bridging geographical obstacles and divides. Telotte's analysis of *F.P.1 Doesn't Answer* not only draws attention to the fact that science fiction film has looked beyond national borders since its early days, but also illustrates that scholarly interest in this dimension of the genre is relatively recent. Indeed, Telotte's chapter on *F.P.1 Doesn't Answer* was published in 2015. It is not until the turn of the twenty-first century, and especially since the 2010s that studies on the transnational dimension of the genre have bloomed. This relatively new interest seems no coincidence, as it can be connected to the fact that twenty-first-century sf films seem more prone to represent transnational concerns and many of them do it more overtly than previous sf films due to the intensification of globalization processes in the last two decades.

Although, traditionally, scholars have rarely referred to the notion of transnational sf, they have often drawn a connection between the figure of the alien and that of the foreign other. For example, Peter Biskind, among others, has associated 1950s alien invasions with Cold War fears (136). From a broader perspective, Charles Ramírez Berg has noted that aliens often stand in for migrants. More specifically, he has argued that alien characters can often be read as Latino migrants in the context of US cinema (402–32). In the early 2000s, some analyses (mostly literary) started to underline the genre's ability to engage with phenomena across borders and to develop discourses on imperialism and colonialism. Csicsery-Ronay highlights the interest of science fiction in "post-national structures," particularly since the 1960s (2002, 237). He notes the tendency of the genre to develop discourses that reach beyond the scope of the nation but also acknowledges that such discourses have often projected the point of view of empires. Pursuing a similar line of analysis, in *Colonialism and the Emergence of Science Fiction* (2008), John Rieder develops new readings of science fiction literary classics, considering the centrality of colonialism to their narratives. For example, Rieder offers an original interpretation of the relationship between the Morlocks and the Eloi in *The Time Machine* (H.G. Wells 1895). He suggests that, apart from representing class conflict in British society, the relationship between both groups in the novel also captures the relationship between Great Britain and its colonies (86–9). Yet, even though colonialism, imperialism, and otherness are related to transnational interactions and continue to be relevant in contemporary sf cinema, they do not account for the variety of transnational interactions, influences, and connections in today's world.

More recently, sf critics have begun to directly address and exploit the critical possibilities that sf's transnational orientation offers. In a special issue of *Science Fiction Studies* (*SFS*) on globalization published in 2012, Csicsery-Ronay explains how many of the technological, economic, environmental, and social changes that the world is experiencing are related to traditional sf motifs such as environmental disasters, alien attacks, dystopian settings, technological, cybernetic, and biological developments, and transnational criminal schemes (480). In the same *SFS* issue, Lysa Rivera focuses on sf texts set on the Mexico-US border region. Two examples mentioned by Rivera are of special interest here: Alex Rivera's short film *Why Cybraceros?* (1997) and the feature film *Sleep Dealer* (2008). These films imagine systems of virtual labor which make physical migration a thing of the past. As Rivera notes, *Why Cybraceros?* and *Sleep Dealer* invite viewers to consider the relationship between transnational capital and labor after the implementation of the North American Free Trade Agreement (NAFTA) in 1994. While doing so, these films also draw attention to the replication of previous colonial structures in the region (Rivera 423–7). From a slightly different angle, the editors of the volume *Alien Imaginations* emphasize the metaphorical connection between the figure of the alien and migrants and, like Rivera, point to borders as a prominent element of contemporary sf (Küchler et al. 6). Similarly, in the volume *Simultaneous Worlds: Global Science Fiction Cinema*, Everett Hamner identifies *Sleep Dealer, Code 46, District 9*, and *Monsters* as part of "a growing body of twenty-first-century science fictional immigration narratives that are rethinking assumptions about geopolitical boundaries and transnational spaces" (154–5). Hamner's chapter shows perceptive awareness of the proliferation of transnational interactions in sf cinema. Yet, immigration is but one of the many issues that sf films explore through the multiple border configurations that they imagine.

Mark Bould's *Science Fiction* (2012) offers a slightly broader scope, looking both at and beyond colonialism, migration, and borders. In the last part of the book, he shows how sf films have dealt with colonialism, imperialism, and globalization from the early twentieth century until the present. Yet, Bould also identifies neoliberal capitalism, labor, and (im)mobility as some of sf cinema's growing concerns since the 1980s and as some of its main topics in the twenty-first century (177–95). More specifically, he notes that films such as *Africa Paradis* (Amoussou 2006), *Transformers* (Bay 2007), and *Sleep Dealer* "illustrate the relationship between global, networked, neoliberal capitalism and the varieties of labour upon which it is built" (189). Following a similar path, this book seeks to develop the aforementioned debates on borders, migration, neocolonialism, capital, and labor and explore how they work in a larger corpus of recent sf films. At the same time, there are several other ways in which the transnational and the

cosmopolitan appear in contemporary sf film. Biometrics, territorial transformations, militarization, networks of power, and greed and its connection to the
aspirations for global expansion of economic and political agents are recurrent
topics, particularly in narratives that revolve around borders and labor. Many
twenty-first-century sf films such as *Code 46*, *G.O.R.A.* (Sorak 2004), *Transfer*
(Lukačević 2010), or *Upside Down* (Solanas 2012) also explore transnational
romance and kinship in their various guises. Films often rely on biotechnological innovations, aliens, interspecies bonding, and interplanetary adventures
(among other things) to address the transnational dimension of adoption, surrogate motherhood, couples, families, care, affection deprivation, and obstacles
and opportunities for certain kinds of relationships (e.g., interracial, queer). The
transnational is also prominent in sf films that revolve around ecological themes
such as *Snowpiercer* (Bong 2013), *Geostorm* (Devlin 2017), or *Godzilla: King of
the Monsters* (Dougherty 2019). In recent years, the transnational scope of disaster has received more attention in sf cinema. Storylines also feature extreme
weather, ecosystem disruption, and resource exploitation and imagine new social
structures and alternatives to life on Earth while developing narratives that often
transcend national borders. While time travel has been a staple of science fiction
from the beginning, recent films frequently rely on connections across time and
space to explore the cosmopolitan dimension of personal connections. Among
these, random links, networks, reincarnation, and the transnational implications
of the butterfly effect stand out. Clear examples of this trend are *The Man from
Earth* (Schenkman 2007), *I Origins* (Cahill 2014), and *X-Men: Days of Future Past*
(Singer 2014).

Towards a Cosmopolitan Turn in the Study of Science Fiction Cinema

Although Ulrike Küchler, Silja Maehl, and Graeme Stout suggest that many
recent Western sf works challenge common "Western hegemonic discourses"
and project a critical outlook (6) and David Higgins has also rightly highlighted
the cosmopolitan possibilities of sf literature (331–2), this book argues that sf is
not necessarily critical or cosmopolitan. Starting from this premise, I examine
some strategies that sf films employ to present cosmopolitan ideas and the ambivalent side of the discourses that these films develop. A cosmopolitan approach
to sf contributes to the articulation of a critical interpretation of transnational
sf narratives. Gerard Delanty's approach to cosmopolitanism locates the term's
critical orientation in the interplay between the concept's methodological and
normative dimensions (2009, 1–2). He holds that what differentiates cosmopolitanism from purely empirical approaches to globalization and transnationalization is its normative horizon (Delanty 2009, 82). By projecting a desired horizon,
cosmopolitanism allows us to look at the present, the past, and the future critically. Methodological cosmopolitanism is based on the study of the conflicts and
struggles that develop from the transnationalization of society, while normative

cosmopolitanism draws on an imagination that includes markers such as rights, social and environmental responsibility, well-being, conviviality, mobility, and mutually beneficial cultural exchange. Critical cosmopolitanism constitutes a particularly suitable framework to analyze sf, as both sf and critical cosmopolitanism base their imaginations on discourses about otherness, (neo)coloniality, borders, global events, and transnational impacts related, for example, to environmental deterioration and disasters.

Although normative and methodological cosmopolitanism are defined separately here, in practice, they are intertwined and part of the same critical cosmopolitan perspective. The methodological dimension of critical cosmopolitanism is based on the study of struggles related to cosmopolitan projections of society. Ulrich Beck posits methodological cosmopolitanism as the analysis of the relationship between "cosmopolitan developments and movements" and "the resistances and obstructions to which they give rise" (2006, 94). In this way, Beck draws attention to the centrality of conflicts in the process of analyzing social reality from a cosmopolitan perspective. Similarly, Delanty refers to cosmopolitanism as "a site of tensions" (2009, 15). Conflicts, tensions, and struggles problematize social reality and facilitate the exercise of critical cosmopolitan analysis: their contradictory nature calls for a reflexive interpretation of convergence and divergence. Such an approach highlights the analytical possibilities of the sf genre, as its critical potential is inscribed on the conflict between the reality from which it extrapolates and the alternative worlds that it builds. This book investigates the strategies that sf films use to incorporate cosmopolitan concerns, how they deal with struggles, and how they generate (in)consistent and (in)coherent discourses about cosmopolitanism.

From the perspective of critical cosmopolitanism, normative considerations should complement a methodological focus on cosmopolitan struggles. When examining the normative side of critical cosmopolitanism, this book approaches cosmopolitanism as an imagination. The cosmopolitan imagination projects a horizon characterized by the desirability of a global recognition of rights, access to natural resources and foodstuffs, decent work conditions, welfare, and quality of life in general. In addition, this imagination revolves around the interrogation of social, economic, and cultural borders, a sense of transnational responsibility and accountability, and a predisposition to focus on what cultures have in common rather than on what makes them different (Beck 2006, 89, Delanty 2009, 7, 86–7). The last point refers to what Beck calls the "both/and" logic of cosmopolitanism, which contrasts with the "either/or," "us/them," and inside/outside logics of nationalism (2006, 32–3). Another key trait of the cosmopolitan imagination is its dialogic character.[1] The cosmopolitan imagination challenges divisions and celebrates "exchange, encounter, and *dialogue*" [my emphasis] (Delanty 2009, 8). Cosmopolitan dialogue entails considering, from a reflexive position, how different cultures may influence each other in a mutually beneficial way. Last but not least, the awareness of the global interrelation of societies is also part of the cosmopolitan imagination: risks and catastrophes related to climate change, terrorism, epidemics, business practices, and economic crises sometimes produce globe-spanning impacts that can cultivate a planetary consciousness and transnational solidarity (Beck 2006, 22). Like the cosmopolitan imagination, sf often addresses the relationship between self and other, relying on the figure of the alien, other species, or the human inhabitants of imaginary geopolitical entities. Many sf films negotiate borders of some kind. Some sf narratives also revolve around large-scale planetary events or connect actions and consequences across different spatial and temporal contexts. The genre is particularly fond of presenting environmentally degraded landscapes and natural disasters that open paths for reflection about global ecological challenges. Like cosmopolitanism, sf also projects horizons: imagined futures and alternative pasts and presents that open a dialogue between the viewer's reality and the world depicted on screen.

Science Fiction Film from a Border Perspective

Science fiction often relies on conceptual borders to structure discourses around cosmopolitan conflicts. This is hardly surprising, as borders are prime sites to observe cosmopolitan tensions. They have, as Étienne Balibar points out, a "world-configuring function" (79). Recently, Celestino Deleyto has proposed a cosmopolitan approach to cinema, situating borders at its center. Drawing on Ian Woodward and Zlatko Skrbiš' work, Deleyto invites us to see films as "performers of cosmopolitanism" which "may [or may not] activate and enact a series of cosmopolitan strategies" (2017, 98). He argues that borders, as central elements of the cosmopolitan imagination, constitute a privileged viewpoint from which to analyze the ways in which films perform cosmopolitanism. Translating Chris Rumford's sociological work to film studies, Deleyto suggests looking at films "from the border" (99-100). That is, he proposes examining the ways in which film narratives rely on borders to articulate their discourses and how borders configure cinematic spaces. Following Deleyto's approach, this book explores some of the main ways in which recent sf films perform cosmopolitanism through borders. In this sense, the applicability of the approach that this book proposes is not limited to narratives that deal with transnational or cosmopolitan topics in an explicit manner. The potential of this approach lies in its ability to offer a vantage point from which to analyze sf media or texts which may not seem to engage with such discourses at first sight. A critical cosmopolitan approach that pivots on borders brings to the surface discourses and narrative strategies that would otherwise go largely unnoticed. One such example is the film *In Time*, which speculates on the idea of time becoming an actual currency to explore the diametrically opposite lifestyles of precarious workers and almost-immortal wealthy elites in a near-future Los Angeles. Yet, seen through a cosmopolitan lens, the film offers a unique portrait of the role of finance and local borders in the operation of transnational systems of economic exploitation.

The sf genre has a longstanding relationship with borders. Sf narratives typically negotiate male/female, human/machine, virtual/real, rich/poor, powerful/

helpless, human/monster, technology/nature, science/savagery, or inside/outside borders. Yet, these borders are not necessarily transnational and, hence, they do not necessarily channel cosmopolitan discourses. Elena dell'Agnese and Lysa Rivera have pointed at the more geographical side of borders in sf by drawing attention to the ways in which *Men in Black* (Barry Sonnenfeld 1997), *The Day After Tomorrow*, and *Sleep Dealer* comment on geopolitical and socioeconomic relations in the Mexico–US borderlands. Cosmopolitan discourses in twenty-first-century sf fall somewhere between these two kinds of symbolic and territorial borders.[2] That is, seemingly cosmopolitan narratives in sf film do not exclusively revolve around physical borders or the territories that surround them, nor do they just incorporate any kind of social border (e.g. virtual/real or rich/poor). The relationship between cosmopolitanism, borders, and sf on which I focus in this book concerns the *transnational* physical, symbolic, spatial, and temporal borders that sf uses to construct seemingly cosmopolitan discourses. This approach to transnational borders coincides with recent developments in the conceptualization of borders. For many scholars, borders are not just the walls or fences that separate countries. In fact, borders appear in multiple places, sometimes hundreds or thousands of miles away from border walls (Balibar 79; Cooper and Rumford 263; Popescu 16; Mezzadra and Neilson 2013, 2–3). In consonance with these observations, contemporary sf films tend to organize cosmopolitan tensions around transnational borders that sometimes spread throughout countries.

Borders are one of the most prominent places where cosmopolitan conflicts ravel and unravel: they mediate transnational interactions between cultures, economies, social models, environmental impacts, and people with different socioeconomic statuses. Sandro Mezzadra and Brett Neilson propose using borders as a method to understand the contemporary world. Even if they do not address theories of cosmopolitanism directly, Mezzadra and Neilson do put critical cosmopolitanism into practice in an oblique way. They explain:

> The border is for us not so much a research object as an *epistemological viewpoint* that allows an acute critical analysis not only of how relations of domination, dispossession, and exploitation are being redefined presently but also of the struggles that take shape around these changing relations. The border can be a method precisely insofar as it is conceived of as *a site of struggle*." [my emphasis]
>
> (2013, 18)

As a viewpoint or perspective, the border offers valuable critical possibilities. Mezzadra and Neilson's concern over "relations of domination, dispossession, and exploitation" coincides with the normative/critical backbone of the cosmopolitan imagination and, at the same time, avoids the construction of an exterior/interior binarism (18). Mezzadra and Neilson's conceptualization of the border as "a site of struggle" recalls Delanty's emphasis on tensions and connects with the focus on cosmopolitan conflicts in this book. In addition to this, the employment of borders as method is based on the constant revision and reconfiguration of concepts. Using borders as method also entails questioning the treatment of "the objects of knowledge [here, seemingly cosmopolitan sf films] as already constituted and [investigating] instead the processes by which these objects are constituted" (Mezzadra and Neilson 2013, 17). To employ this method is then to problematize and approach social reality in a reflexive manner, a strategy that Delanty also proposes as a function of critical cosmopolitanism (2009, 8). This means that this book interrogates the cosmopolitan discourses that twenty-first-century sf films develop and looks for inconsistencies in them, drawing attention to the ambivalence of some of their narratives. In sum, the notion of borders as method deploys critical cosmopolitanism by focusing on border struggles, adopting a normative critical stance, and favoring problematization and revision.

A critical cosmopolitanism based on the use of borders as method shares several traits with sf. This approach focuses on one of the genre's greatest strengths: its ability to reflect on borders. Organizing its narratives around borders allows sf to deal with struggles and to negotiate tensions between the inside and the outside. In addition, sf films problematize the worlds that they build: while the universes that sf films create cannot escape the context in which they are produced, they dislocate 'reality' and produce alternative perspectives on it. Sf films also introduce viewers to unfamiliar models of social and natural organization and thereby encourage them to explore less-traveled routes. Studying sf through a critical cosmopolitan/border perspective implies that sf does not only require suspending disbelief. Seen from the border, sf films also ask viewers to suspend their beliefs: to examine their perception of the world in which they live. Yet, in some cases, even when sf films interrogate viewers' perceptions of society, they may do so only to reinforce the state of things as they are (e.g. the perception of aliens/migrants as a threat). It is precisely in this tension between the problematization and the strengthening of un- or anti-cosmopolitan forces that science fiction and the notion of borders as a method offer critical cosmopolitan possibilities.

Scope and Case Studies

Since this book aims to map some of the key themes and discourses in contemporary sf cinema, I have adopted a comprehensive approach when selecting the films on which I focus. This entails that Hollywood and, more generally, Western productions predominate in my selection of examples. However, I have also attempted to include films made from the margins and in non-Western contexts. In spite of this, the prominence of Western films may sometimes seem at odds with the cosmopolitan framework of the book. Yet, Will Higbee and Song Hwee Lim (10) and Deborah Shaw (296) have also warned about the incongruity of presenting mainstream commercial texts as less transnational or worthy of study than other more alternative productions. Indeed, as Lucia Nagib points out, when we approach cinema from an inclusive world perspective, Hollywood (and Western cinemas in general) may "receive major, minor or no attention depending on the object in question" (34). In this sense, this book confronts the paradox that it is often US American movies, major productions, and films from other affluent countries that tend to address cosmopolitan conflicts. Taking this context into account, I argue that such films are optimum material on which to apply a critical cosmopolitan/border perspective. Like any film that may draw from the cosmopolitan imagination, they depict cosmopolitan conflicts and, as Western(-ized) products, they offer abundant opportunities to problematize and interrogate their discourses. Even though many recent sf films appear to imagine cosmopolitan responses to contemporary challenges, this book attempts to make the ambivalence of cosmopolitan discourses visible by pointing at the ways in which film narratives reproduce social hierarchies and exploitative practices.

When selecting the key films on which I base my analysis, I have tried to choose examples that draw attention to both prominent and often-overlooked cosmopolitan concerns and which, at the same time, allow me to make connections to other films from a variety of geographical locations and filmmaking backgrounds. This book looks beyond the examples that typically come to mind when we think about transnational sf cinema: *Code 46*, *The Day After Tomorrow*, *Children of Men* (Cuarón 2006), *Sleep Dealer*, *District 9*, *Avatar* (Cameron 2009), and *Snowpiercer*. Scholars have already paid a lot of attention to these films and so this book aims to draw attention to a wider variety of examples and narratives. This does not mean that these films are excluded from this study. Rather, I do not place them at the center of my analysis. I draw connections between the main films I analyze closely and these and other less familiar examples. Most of the key examples I have selected (*Elysium*, *In Time*, *2012*, and *Cloud Atlas*) are relatively popular sf films with medium or large budgets and wide global distribution. However, in some cases, I have chosen to focus on lower-budget, lesser-known films that look at relevant transnational issues that the film industry typically ignores (*Codependent Lesbian Space Alien Seeks Same*) or that are representative of a larger trend despite being somewhat overlooked (Andrew Niccol's *The Host*).

The chapters in this book present four groups of films in which the cosmopolitan concerns of twenty-first-century sf cinema are particularly evident. In the first section of each chapter I point out the key features of each strand and discuss multiple films that participate in the trend. In the remainder of each chapter, I offer close readings of one or two films, drawing connections between the main film(s) and other sf narratives. Chapter 1 focuses on the proliferation of transnational dystopias and their interest in exploitative economic systems. The chapter explores this trend through the notion of systemic dystopias: films that critically engage with imagined models of socioeconomic organization. In the first two decades of the twenty-first century, such films have often directed viewers' gazes towards unrestrained neoliberalism, the militarization of the economy, generalized surveillance, precariousness, and the decreasing value of human lives—which sometimes entails the biotechnological modification of bodies for profit. Films typically address these topics by looking at the role of physical and symbolic border regimes in the operation of socioeconomic systems. Although these discourses have proliferated and gained prominence in the genre in the last few years, they are not entirely new. Consequently, the chapter also looks at earlier examples of systemic dystopias and their emerging interest in transnational dynamics. In the first case analysis, I examine *Elysium* and the ways in which it explores the interrelationship between public and private actors in the framework of transnational neoliberalism. The second film I analyze closely in this chapter, *In Time*, provides an opportunity to investigate the connection between urban borders and the interests of transnational financial actors—a topic that sf films tend to ignore and yet is a core element in the economic systems currently in place. Both *Elysium* and *In Time* address issues that appear regularly in other twenty-first-century systemic dystopias such as economic divides, borders, and biometrics while offering a unique focus on territorial reorganization and the power of corporate and financial agents.

The second chapter pays attention to the proliferation of eco-conscious sf discourses, concentrating on films that articulate transnational environmental concerns through spectacle-ridden narratives. The first part of the chapter considers the relationship between the genre and ecology, focusing on the kinds of environmental concerns that it has channeled in the last two decades and the main strategies employed to do so. The range of films discussed goes from those that imagine extreme weather scenarios and nightmarish ecological landscapes to those that speculate about space exploration and alternatives to life on Earth to those that revolve around powerful natural forces, monsters, or aliens that challenge humans' hegemonic role as a species and our generalized carelessness towards natural resources and ecosystems. The chapter highlights the tendency of science fiction disaster films to incorporate transnational threads and the worthiness of analyzing spectacle and how it intertwines with narrative. The main case study in this chapter is *2012*, a film which may not appear to be about climate change at first sight, but actually engages with contemporary discourses on this phenomenon at multiple levels. Indeed, the analysis of *2012* brings to the surface several patterns that also appear in other recent films such as *The Day After Tomorrow*, *Wall-E*, *The Day the Earth Stood Still* (2008), *Snowpiercer*, *Godzilla* (2014), and *Interstellar*. Through the example of *2012*, I show that seemingly mindless spectacles of disaster can be an effective means of representing the impacts of climate change. More specifically, the film develops an eco-cosmopolitan sense of planet[3] by hinting at the relationship between different kinds of environmental disruption and their interconnectedness across borders. *2012* also points at the unpredictable, imminent, and wide-reaching character of climate impacts. Lastly, my analysis of *2012* addresses the biopolitical implications of the apocalyptic scenario that the film depicts. That is, it considers the role of a range of status markers in establishing the worth of certain kinds of lives over others in a context of limited chances for survival.

The third chapter examines transnational/transcultural romance and kinship, arguing that the alien can be a particularly useful vehicle to reflect on cosmopolitan questions. The first part of the chapter offers an overview of recent discourses of the genre around love, sexuality, and reproduction. Romantic relationships receive special attention throughout the chapter, which first focuses on couples formed by two humans and then on alien-human couples. In addition, the chapter points both at the predominance of white heterosexual aliens and at the importance of critically analyzing this phenomenon. Despite such a racial and sexual homogeneity, several of the films analyzed in this chapter suggest that the development of intimate relationships between beings from different planets encourage attitudes of cosmopolitan openness in their societies. The chapter first looks at *The Host* (2013) as a film that is representative of the proliferation of sf young adult love stories at the turn of the twenty-first century. The analysis of *The Host* suggests that, despite its clichéd representation of love, the film presents a nuanced image of the development of cosmopolitan sensibilities in a context of interspecies/transnational tensions. The analysis of *The Host* brings to the fore the lopsided nature of cosmopolitanism, its intermittent and reluctant character, and the importance of developing mental spaces of openness. Then, the chapter questions the lack of queer sf films that deal with cosmopolitan issues and offers a close reading of the zero-budget, B-movie *Codependent Lesbian Space Alien Seeks Same*. My analysis of this film focuses on its coupling of its camp aesthetics and premise with a love story that revolves around sexual and alien otherness. My reading of the film also highlights the importance of envisioning and desiring other realities, spaces, and ways of being both from a queer and a cosmopolitan point of view. The section on this film ends by arguing that, despite its whiteness, *Codependent Lesbian* envisions a queer utopia that is not necessarily Western.

Finally, Chapter 4 deals with films that draw connections between people across time and space, often emphasizing characters' shared humanity. Although all the films in this chapter engage in one way or another with the notion of cosmopolitan networks, the group of films that form this fourth trend within early twenty-first-century sf cinema is more heterogeneous than previous ones. As the first part of the chapter shows, some films use spatiotemporal connections to address the interrelation between transnational networks and a range of phenomena including neoliberalism, fundamentalism, and epidemics. Several films also channel cosmopolitan concerns through time travel and time loop storylines. Others explore the transnational implications of the butterfly effect, the mutation of spaces through time, the interconnectedness of time, and even topics such as reincarnation and connections between different species. In general, these films attest to the growing interrelatedness between temporal and transnational connections in contemporary sf films dealing with cosmopolitan issues. After offering a glimpse into the main narrative and thematic strategies that this heterogeneous group of sf films offers, the chapter focuses on *Cloud Atlas*, a multi-protagonist film with six storylines that bring characters together across five centuries, four continents, and two planets. The close analysis of this film draws attention to the relationship between cosmopolitan struggles and different iterations of coloniality through time. *Cloud Atlas* explores a variety of intersecting lines related to oppression, race, greed, sexuality, age, sentience, beliefs, and environmental exploitation. In this sense, *Cloud Atlas* engages, to varying degrees, with most of the cosmopolitan concerns that typically appear in contemporary sf cinema. This film is a particularly relevant case study. It not only engages with a variety of cosmopolitan issues but also experiments with the borders of narrative conventions and editing while weaving together the different storylines. The chapter also considers the limitations of the film's discourse, which sometimes avoids exploring thorny cosmopolitan conflicts and tends to privilege Western locations and characters. The book concludes by arguing that contemporary science fiction films tend to articulate a type of cosmopolitanism that both questions and reinforces social borders, hierarchies, inequalities, and environmental exploitation: an ambivalent cosmopolitanism.

Notes

1 See Beck (2002, 18) and Delanty (2012, 42).
2 I am borrowing the notion of physical/territorial and symbolic borders from Gabriel Popescu. Although Popescu distinguishes between them, he also points out that borders usually combine their physical and symbolic dimensions (8, 84).
3 On the notion of an eco-cosmopolitan sense of planet, see Heise 51–62. This notion is also discussed at the beginning of chapter 2.

1

SYSTEMIC DYSTOPIAS THROUGH A COSMOPOLITAN LENS

Contesting Global Neoliberalism

Dystopias have always worked as social thermometers of their time.[1] They typically project grim visions of alternative spaces and times to address contemporary concerns. For example, *Alphaville* (Godard 1965), *Blade Runner* (Scott 1982), and *The Terminator* (Cameron 1984) register anxieties over the development of technology, computers, and artificial intelligences. *Soylent Green* (Fleischer 1973) and *They Live* (Carpenter 1988) point at the ever-increasing influence of large corporations and economic neoliberalism accompanying the progressive neoliberalization of the US and world economy from the 1970s onwards. *Strange Days* (Bigelow 1995), for its part, reflects racial tensions surrounding the 1991 Rodney King beating in Los Angeles. As these examples suggest, dystopias typically address issues such as authoritarian power, class/income inequality, biotechnological advances, and otherness. At the turn of the twenty-first century, a substantial number of dystopian film narratives have begun to add a further layer to their traditional discourses by showing greater interest in the transnational dimension of socioeconomic borders and hierarchies. *Code 46* (Winterbottom 2003), *Sleep Dealer* (Rivera 2008), *In Time* (Niccol 2011), *Upside Down* (Solanas 2012), the 2012 *Total Recall* remake (Wiseman), *Elysium* (Blomkamp 2013), and *Snowpiercer* (Bong 2013), among others, are some of the most representative examples of this trend.

This chapter focuses on *Elysium* and *In Time*, two films that travel often-uncharted paths in science fiction cinema. They explore the form and role of physical and symbolic borders of global economic structures at multiple scales, focusing on aspects such as territorial organization, sovereignty, markets, finance, and lifespan. For example, *Elysium* imagines life in the year 2154, when the affluent elites live in a space wheel to which no one else is allowed access. Meanwhile, the rest of humanity remains on an over-populated Earth that is running short of natural resources and whose infrastructures have severely deteriorated. In this

DOI: 10.4324/9781003164517-2

world, borders have been relocated and multiplied for the benefit of political and corporate elites, leaving Earth inhabitants practically destitute. The analysis of *Elysium, In Time,* and other dystopias from a cosmopolitan perspective sheds light on what Sandro Mezzadra and Brett Neilson call "operations of capital," that is, the logics and workings of "dispossession, exploitation, and accumulation" and also "incorporation" into the system (2015, 4–5). Seen from this perspective, *In Time* and *Elysium* draw attention to societies governed by neoliberal expansion, the financialization of the economy, and the individualization of the benefits that technological advances and modernity bring about. At the same time, these movies seem to struggle to imagine alternative modes of socioeconomic organization. *In Time, Elysium,* and similar films often picture worlds that eventually reproduce the same circumstances and hierarchies that they seemingly criticize.

The recent proliferation of dystopian films revolving around transnational socioeconomic matters is not surprising: the last five decades have borne witness to a series of technological, economic, and social changes that have contributed to a major leap in the scope and scale of globalization. A progressive financialization of the economy has been developing since the mid-1970s and early 1980s (Epstein 4; Marazzi 28–31; Mezzadra and Neilson 2013, 81–2). Such financialization entails the growing influence of finance in the production and commercialization of services and goods and an increasing control of the economic system by globally connected financial elites (Marazzi 28–9). Apart from this, societies have experienced a gradual neoliberalization, that is, a transfer of the control of economies and social services from the state/the public to global corporate hands (Harvey 2009, 56–7; Sassen 2014, 84). In this context, private interests and profit growth predominate over citizens and their well-being. The recent development of communication technologies has also contributed to the growth and consolidation of the global economy. Information technologies such as the internet and telecommunication systems have enabled instant modes of communication that allow finances to operate smoothly. Finance and logistic technologies such as containers, mega trucks, and drones also facilitate the planning of commodity routes and networks, cost efficiency, and the maximization of profitability (Mezzadra and Neilson 2015, 3). Such developments are providing prime narrative material to a genre that, as Istvan Csicsery-Ronay notes, has always been drawn to the exploration of the darker side of socioeconomic models and global designs (2002, 218).

From a cosmopolitan perspective, it is essential to investigate the dystopian dimension of the aforementioned developments. As Kwame Anthony Appiah notes, cosmopolitanism is often not "the name [...] of the solution but of the challenge" (xiii). Processes of economic globalization produce a range of precarious, unequal, and destabilizing circumstances that are directly related to cosmopolitan concerns. Cosmopolitan challenges are evident in contemporary realities such as transnational tax evasion, the undermining of the welfare state, public services, and workers' rights, lack of access to healthcare, extreme poverty, uneven access to resources (e.g. water), brutal re-localizations of capital and labor, forced mobilities, unwelcome migrations, land-grabs, and the erosion of sovereignty.[2] In general, the workings of global neoliberalism affect a central dimension of cosmopolitanism: well-being and the possibility of having "decent lives" (Appiah 163, 167). As David Harvey argues, in order to imagine cosmopolitan alternatives, it is necessary to "unpack" the abstract character of neoliberal globalization and examine the actors behind it, their background, their intentions, and how they operate (2009, 57–8). In an attempt to do so, my analysis in this chapter relies heavily on theories of borders, the economy, and finance. Such theories are crucial to unpack neoliberal globalization from a cosmopolitan perspective based on the aforementioned concerns. In this sense, this chapter uses cosmopolitanism in a predominantly methodological fashion.

Since the number of films covered by the term dystopia is too large to be considered in one chapter, here I focus on what I call 'systemic dystopias.' Other chapters in the book also include reflections on different kinds of dystopia, although in a more tangential way. Systemic dystopias often deal with models of socioeconomic organization and their impact on the lives of citizens. These gloomy narratives often examine the role of class, social hierarchies, government, corporations, and other social or economic actors in the configuration and operation of a given system. Apart from addressing concerns about systems of social organization, contemporary dystopias also focus on other themes such as epidemic or viral threats and environmental risks. Obviously, films about robots, cyborgs, AIs, and new technologies continue to be a staple group of dystopias, but their investment in discourses on transnational interactions is not as clear as in the case of other dystopias, so I pay little attention to them in this book.

Outbreak (Petersen 1995), *28 Days Later* (Boyle 2003), *Children of Men* (Cuarón 2006), *I Am Legend* (Lawrence 2007), *Contagion* (Soderbergh 2011), *World War Z* (Forster 2013), and *Maze Runner: Scorch Trials* (Ball 2015), among others, reflect on the epidemic risks of the ever-increasing connectivity of contemporary societies and the role of borders in viral crises. They often register how the intensively mobile lifestyles of the (pre-COVID-19) present can contribute to the global spread of viruses and diseases. Indeed, as the famous scene of zombies climbing a wall in *World War Z* suggests (geopolitical readings aside), not even the highest and most impenetrable borders are capable of containing the spread of pathogens. In the first 12 minutes of *Contagion*, the film intersperses scenes set in Hong Kong, London, Minneapolis, Tokyo, Atlanta, San Francisco, Geneva, the Guangdong province, and Chicago (in most cases, displaying a subtitle with the name of these cities and the size of their population). These opening scenes— which include a global montage of images of people feeling unwell connected by the same non-diegetic music track—provide viewers with background information on the development of the sanitary crisis while linking the fates of these distant places. Sometimes, epidemic films show the potential consequences of exploiting other species and ecosystems. *Outbreak*, for example, presents deforestation in Zaire (now Congo) and the transportation of a wild monkey from a jungle in this country to the US to be sold as a pet as the root causes for the spread of the virus. In general, epidemic films tend to engage with concerns about connectivity, mobility, and shared global risks. In *World War Z*, however, certain kinds of mobilities and knowledge sharing seem to be part of the solution rather than the problem, as the protagonist travels from Philadelphia to different world locations (NYC, South Korea, Jerusalem, and Wales) in search for ideas to mitigate the zombie pandemic. Although epidemic films capture paramount transnational risks and challenges of our increasingly interconnected world (even in the times of COVID-19), in this book I have chosen to focus on other kinds of films that engage with cosmopolitan concerns more clearly. Also, Dahlia Schweitzer has recently analyzed the global dimension of these films in her book *Going Viral: Zombies, Viruses and the End of the World* (2018) and these kinds of narratives are also the main objects of study of the forthcoming book *Pandemic Cinema*, written by Julia Echeverría.

Environmental dystopias such as *The Day After Tomorrow* (Emmerich 2004), *Wall-E* (Stanton 2008), *The Road* (Hillcoat 2009), *2012* (Emmerich 2009), *Snowpiercer, Elysium, The Rover* (Michôd 2014), and *Mad Max: Fury Road* (Miller 2015) emphasize the grim ecological landscapes of the age of climate change. These environmental dystopias are discussed in the second chapter of this book. Chapter 2 looks at the transnational dimension of environmental issues in sf, focusing on climate change and the use of spectacular images and scenes to address this phenomenon. Of course, the boundaries between the aforementioned categories are not clear-cut. For example, *Children of Men* and *Maze Runner: Scorch Trials* rely on both viral and systemic plot lines. Similarly, *Snowpiercer, Elysium,* and *Mad Max: Fury Road* draw on systemic and environmental motifs.

Throughout their history, systemic dystopias have dealt with authoritarian human and technological powers, oppression, and violence. *Metropolis* (Lang 1927), *The Time Machine* (Pal 1960), *Planet of the Apes* (Schaffner 1968), *Zardoz* (Boorman 1974), *Parts: The Clonus Horror* (Fiveson 1979), and *Gattaca* (Niccol 1997) use class, status, species-belonging, biological traits, and genetic profiles to pose questions about highly stratified societies, economic exploitation, hierarchies, and (under)privilege. *Alphaville, Fahrenheit 451* (Truffaut 1966), *THX 1138* (Lucas 1971), *Logan's Run* (Anderson 1976), *Nineteen Eighty-Four* (Radford 1984), *Brazil* (Gilliam 1985), and *The Handmaid's Tale* (Schlöndorff 1990) focus specifically on authoritarian governments that suffocate their own citizens. Among these, *Alphaville* and *Logan's Run*, along with other films such as *Colossus: The Forbin Project* (Sargent 1970), *The Terminator,* and *The Matrix* (The Wachowskis 1999) attribute oppressive powers to computers, AIs, and machines in general. Coinciding with the rise and expansion of neoliberalism since the 1970s, *Soylent Green, Rollerball* (Jewison 1975), *Blade Runner, Robocop* (Verhoeven 1987), and *They Live,* to name a few, concentrate on the excesses of corporate control and its search for ever-rising profit. Similar social scenarios also appear in *A Clockwork Orange* (Kubrick 1971), *Mad Max* (Miller 1979), *Dead-End Drive-In* (Trenchard-Smith 1986), and *The Running Man* (Glaser 1987). These films imagine times of economic crisis and unrest, linking these situations to crime, violence, and gangs on the rampage. Twenty-first-century systemic dystopias continue to organize their narratives around these themes and concerns, although their emphasis on some of them has decreased. Economic stratification and exploitation stand out as major concerns in contemporary systemic dystopias, while authoritarian states or machines and civilian violence are not as prominent and, when they appear, they are often connected to other socioeconomic considerations (as in the case of films such as *The Hunger Games* [Ross 2012] or *Elysium*).

As previously mentioned, a clear difference between classical dystopias and contemporary ones is the latter's focus on transnational interactions and global designs. Although global concerns are not exclusive to twenty-first century sf films, earlier films tend to overlook the global contexts in which they set their narratives or develop transnational narratives that barely reflect on transnational issues. *Colossus: The Forbin Project, Mad Max, Total Recall* (Verhoeven 1990), *Blade Runner, The Terminator, and The Matrix* are either set in a context of global or even galactic economic unrest or of presumably global totalitarian machine domination but do not include explicit evidence of transnational connections and economic influence. An illustrative example is *Blade Runner*, which is set in an interplanetary context but fails to explore the role of 2019 futuristic Los Angeles in the larger system. The film emphasizes the racial and cultural mix at street level, yet it barely gives any information about the—presumably global—elites that live in off-Earth colonies. Viewers do not even get a glimpse of the off-world colonies and there is no direct evidence of the influence of Dr. Eldon Tyrell (Joe Turkel)—the owner of the transplanetary corporation that produces replicants—in the urban environment that the film presents. In spite of this, *Blade Runner*'s mise-en-scène provides a bleak depiction of urban growth, material waste, and all-encompassing corporations. The opposite happens in the 158-minute cut of *Until the End of the World* (Wenders 1991). The film opens with several shots of Earth from outer space and has its protagonists move from Italy to France, then Germany, Portugal, Russia, China, Japan, the US, and finally, Australia. Apart from this, the film also reports on an Indian nuclear satellite going out of control. Yet, *Until the End of the World* barely provides any specific information on how the society that it presents works and it pays little attention to the socioeconomic system in which its characters live. In contrast to twenty-first-century dystopias, the aforementioned examples tend to either foreground socioeconomic/systemic aspects of specific locations or, in some cases, transnational connections, but they rarely focus on both at the same time. In this sense, more recent films like *In Time, Upside Down*, and *Elysium* develop the imaginaries of the aforementioned films and provide more elaborate portraits of global elites, their relationship with other social actors, and the transnational impact of their activities.

Rollerball and *They Live* are probably the two pre-2000 films that most closely resemble the transnational orientation of twenty-first-century systemic dystopias. Both films make explicit what the films mentioned in the previous paragraph just imply: they show the role of aspiring global agents in the socioeconomic system. *Rollerball* presents a world in which nations no longer exist and a handful of corporations control everything. Although *Rollerball* focuses mostly on US American characters and on a game that is part of corporate strategies to shape citizens' personalities, the film also highlights transnational communication and coordination among corporate elites. For example, it includes a scene of a video call among managers from different places and shows Madrid, Tokyo, Houston, and New York executives sitting closely in stadium boxes. In this world dominated by secretive corporations, the protagonist wants to find out who makes corporate decisions and how. In spite of this, viewers do not see what the socioeconomic impact of absolute corporate control is. The film concentrates instead on a series of seemingly illogical personal/moral demands of a group of corporate leaders on the protagonist, an experienced sports player who defies corporate logic with his outstanding performance on the rollerball track. In this sense, the film's concerns seem closer to the authoritarian states of *1984* or *THX1138* than the economic nightmares of *In Time*, *Upside Down*, or *Elysium*.

They Live initially presents a realistic portrait of LA and the US in 1988. Yet, as the film progresses, two construction workers, George (Roddy Piper) and Frank (Keith David), gradually find out that aliens, along with an elite group of humans, control their society and manipulate their perception of it. Towards the end of the film, Frank and George walk into a gala dinner where a group of business people and aliens celebrate having taken over the whole US and having plans to do the same on a planetary scale by 2020. A few minutes later, a businessman tells George and Frank: "There ain't no countries anymore. No more good guys. They're running the whole show. They [aliens] own everything. The whole goddamn planet. They can do whatever they want." Through these two moments, the film acknowledges the global aspirations of neoliberal capital. Despite *Rollerball*'s lack of criticism of the socioeconomic impact of corporate operations, both films prove to be forerunners of the current tendency towards film narratives that explicitly point to the growing control of economies and societies around the world by a handful of neoliberal actors.

Situating their narratives in an often explicit transnational context, many twenty-first-century sf films combine previous dystopian motifs such as economic exploitation, stratification, class hierarchies, and corporate control with other themes such as borders, (im)mobility, territoriality, sovereignty, transnational networks of power, capital flows, profit-making practices, and even life extraction. By addressing these topics, recent sf films often bring to the fore concerns that are central to the cosmopolitan imagination (e.g. rights, access to resources, welfare). Although little attention has been paid to these themes as recurring motifs in contemporary sf cinema, Mark Bould identifies non-places, mobility, confinement, and the relationship between different kinds of labor and global capital as common concerns in contemporary sf films (2012, 184–94). Bould mentions several twenty-first-century films that feature characters living in isolated spaces that range from business lounges and offices to ghettoes and refugee camps. The examples that Bould mentions include, among many others: *Demonlover* (Assayas 2002), *Code 46*, *District 13* (Morel 2004), *Children of*

Men, *Eden Log* (Vestiel 2007), *District 9* (Blomkamp 2009), and *Attack the Block* (Cornish 2011). Bould's extensive selection of films shows the prominence of borders and border-related issues in contemporary sf. Apart from focusing on borders, mobility, and lack thereof, contemporary sf films also deal with other transnational issues. *Babylon A.D.* (Kassovitz 2008), *Sleep Dealer*, *In Time*, *Captain America: The Winter Soldier* (The Russo Brothers 2014), *Elysium, Robocop* (Padilha 2014), *Code 8* (Chan 2019), and again *Code 46* imagine worlds in which biometrics, surveillance, and dataveillance play a key role in organizing humans within and beyond the nation state. Another sub-trend that is equally central to the analysis of globalization processes, but has attracted little attention so far is that of films that picture alternative territorial organizations or project current territorial changes at larger scales or in an intensified manner. *Code 46*, *Children of Men*, *Africa Paradis* (Amoussou 2006), *Sleep Dealer*, *District 9*, *Captain America: The Winter Soldier*, *Branded* (Bradshaw and Aleksandr Dulerayn 2012), *Upside Down*, *World War Z*, *Elysium*, and *Downsizing* (Payne 2017) consider how these territorial schemes affect norm-making, sovereignty, individual rights, spatial integration, and market expansion. In addition, they often point at the extraterritorial actions of specific social actors.

Despite the recent proliferation of sf films that explicitly point to the global context of the events that they portray, some contemporary films—like films from previous decades—continue to portray transnational interactions and influences in an implicit manner. Although this chapter focuses on those films that deal with globalization in a more explicit manner, less explicit films also provide valuable material to be analyzed through a cosmopolitan lens. This is the case of films that only apparently deal with borders at local, regional, national, or unspecified levels such as *District 13*, *The Island* (Bay 2004), *Aeon Flux* (Kusama 2005), *Daybreakers* (The Spierig Brothers 2009), *Dredd* (Travis 2012), *The Hunger Games*, *The Maze Runner* and the *Divergent* franchises, *The Purge: Anarchy* (DeMonaco 2014), and *The Giver* (Noice 2014), to name but a few.

Several of the films mentioned in this chapter are also related to labor: they feature workers who are rarely allowed to move from their run-down areas and visit—let alone live in—wealthier neighborhoods, cities, regions, or countries. Conversely, those with economic and/or political power manage the industries where poorer people work, the areas where they live, and their resources. In these films, globally connected elites attempt to maximize profits and turn a blind eye to the consequences of their money-making activities. Apart from the films on which Mark Bould focuses his analysis of contemporary labor—*Africa Paradis*, *Transformers* (Bay 2007), and *Sleep Dealer* (2012: 189–195), films such as *Code 46*, *Eden Log*, *Cargo* (Engler and Etter 2009), *Transfer* (Lukacevic 2010), *In Time*, *Cloud Atlas*, *Upside Down*, *Snowpiercer*, *Elysium*, *Jupiter Ascending*, and also (although less pointedly) *The Island*, *Moon* (Jones 2009), *Repo Men* (Sapochnik 2010), *Self/less* (Singh 2015), *Maze Runner: Scorch Trials* constitute an additional branch of films that present systems in which those who rule society tend to take advantage of transnational/galactic asymmetries to extract value, health, or lifetime from other people's bodies, not only through physical activity, but also through the body itself, its organs or its life. These films point directly to the social implications and the personal costs caused by the operations of global corporate players and the privileges that only exclusive groups of people enjoy. They throw light into the logics, actions, and actors of global neoliberalism. In sum, contemporary systemic dystopias seem mainly concerned (sometimes explicitly, sometimes ambiguously and metaphorically) with geopolitical and biopolitical issues beyond national frameworks and borders.

Before turning to the analysis of *Elysium* and *In Time*, several other films deserve special mention. *Children of Men* illustrates a common concern in contemporary sf cinema about the proliferation of borders and other mechanisms of mobility control in a myriad places. The film imagines a grim world in severe crisis in which people are physically unable to conceive any more babies. Apparently, only Britain "soldiers on" while other countries are immersed in even bigger crises—a propaganda video informs train passengers and viewers at the beginning of the film. Yet, *Children of Men* portrays London and other English locations as heartless places in which people are subject to compulsory fertility controls, constant mobility controls, terrorist attacks, and humiliation and arbitrary executions by the British military. In spite of this, the country appears to be constantly receiving large numbers of migrants and refugees. Although several films register a multiplication of borders throughout space, they are remarkably pervasive in the society that *Children of Men* depicts. Borders can be found wherever the protagonists go: at various checkpoints, detention centers, cages where people are temporarily locked, and refugee camps. Even stations, buses, and trains with fenced windows have been secured and, in effect, bordered to favor or prevent the mobility of specific groups of people.

Another film that is particularly concerned with boundaries is *Code 46*, which imagines an Earth divided into bordered global cities such as Seattle, Shanghai, and New Delhi, desert regions populated by outcasts on the fringes of the system, and in-between spaces like Jebel Ali, near Dubai—a place that, unlike the ones I mentioned previously, people can easily visit and leave without a travel authorization. Drawing on this geographical model, the film addresses a variety of concerns related to labor, genetics, biometrics, norm-making, citizenship, mobility, and the environment. From the very beginning, *Code 46* presents a regime of highly controlled mobilities and, at the same time, a culturally blended society in which people naturally mix several languages in their daily conversations, although English seems to be the core language in this mix. In this society, mobility is controlled by the Sphynx Corporation and nation states seem to be eroding. When someone gets a pass to cross into a different area, they get "cover" from Sphynx, suggesting that they get health coverage—though the film never clarifies the meaning of this term. Despite the common references to the Sphynx throughout the film, it remains a faceless corporation. The film does not direct its attention towards the individual corporate actors that keep such a system running, actually replicating the obscurity around private sector giants that exert a strong influence on society.

Something similar happens in *Sleep Dealer*, which presents a world where Latinos no longer migrate to the US because they send their labor there by plugging their bodies to a computer and working through a virtual reality program. On US soil, robots receive the information sent by the workers in Mexico and perform the job for them. Even though *Sleep Dealer* offers a critical portrait of US-Mexico border relations, its almost exclusive focus on the Mexican side of the border prevents the film from exploring the role of foreign corporate managers and policy makers in the development of such a system. Nonetheless, the film develops an acute critical portrait of cross-border economic and resource exploitation. Apart from its sharp criticism of the exploitation of the asymmetries of transnational labor, the film shows that while workers are prevented from crossing the border, US companies have managed to take control of natural resources at the other side of the border. Indeed, the beginning of the film features a water dam protected by military force which has dramatically altered the way of life of the inhabitants of the neighboring area, some of whom have little choice other than migrating north to join the transnational workforce that keeps the US economy going right at the Mexican side of the border. Both *Code 46* and *Sleep Dealer* provide detailed portraits of the transnational impact of decisions presumably made by elites. They do so through their depiction of landscapes of surveillance and economic extraction and by pointing at the reliance of such systems on geographical differentiation. However, *Code 46* and *Sleep Dealer* produce abstract representations of power that do not illuminate the role of global elites and their ways of life in such systems.

The 2012 *Total Recall* remake also engages with concerns about the exploitation of transnational labor markets. The film imagines the geopolitical aftermath of global chemical warfare. In the scenario that the film projects, life on Earth is only possible in two areas: the United Federation of Britain (UFB) and the Colony, located in present-day Australia (which was originally meant to be called New Asia [Belloni and Siegel]). Both regions are connected through a shuttle tunnel built through Earth. *Total Recall* presents the UFB as a thriving region largely populated by white-collar workers who drive flying sedans. Meanwhile, many of the inhabitants of the slums in the Colony have no option but to take a 17-minute shuttle to the UFB every day and go through identity checkpoints to work in manual jobs for a low pay. Through this division, the film alludes to the precarious, highly policed job markets and tough life conditions that migrants often have to navigate and endure. The Colony, despite being located in Australia, clearly emulates the techno-orientalism of *Blade Runner*'s Los Angeles, although, in this case, Asian elements (signs, red paper lanterns, hats, boats, dragon statues, roofs) are even more prominent and the film features signs written in East Asian languages, Slavic languages, and English. Startlingly, Asians feature in several scenes, but do not receive any attention as individual characters. Despite the potential of the concept that the film presents, its action-packed scenes drive the film away from exploring this world in more detail. This is not to say that action scenes generally prevent films from doing so. Indeed, a car chase in *Total Recall* (2012) actually serves as an excuse to show viewers through the multi-layered cityscapes of the UFB, displaying vertical and horizontal transit systems and streets built on different levels over historical London and highlighting the difference between this carefully planned urban environment and the decaying, chaotic, and cramming maze of buildings in the Colony. Ironically, the film presents the destruction of the transportation system that ties both regions physically and economically as the solution to the Colony's problems. The elimination of this link suggests that economic exploitation comes to an end with it, a sort of cosmopolitan call for decent life and work conditions which contrasts with earlier cosmopolitan calls for connectivity through infrastructure in earlier films such as *Transatlantic Tunnel* (Elvey 1935) or *F.P.1 Doesn't Answer* (Hartl 1932).

Developing a similar concept to the one in *Total Recall* (2012), *Upside Down* presents two radically different portraits of two neighboring planets with different gravities that are connected through a skyscraper. The two planets are not only separated by gravity but by heavily policed borders. Even though there are some natural contact zones at the top of certain mountains from which inhabitants of the two planets may come into contact, access to these areas is forbidden. The film establishes a clear distinction between the two planets by depicting completely dissimilar spaces: the sleek high-rise buildings and pristine streets on one planet contrast with the substandard housing and urban landscapes of waste of the other. Through this setting, the film metaphorically explores and negotiates the economic divide between the global North and South or, more specifically, between the US and Latin America. In contrast to the *Total Recall* remake, *Upside Down* does not present the obliteration of transnational connections as a solution for the radical inequality between both spaces. Rather, the development of interpersonal connections acts as a catalyst for a more egalitarian relationship between both parts. *Upside Down* also revolves around a love story between two inhabitants of the two planets, and it is indeed this initially impossible relationship that leads to the development of a more fluid border system. The very ending of the film imagines the transformation of the neighboring area of both planets into a contact zone in which new buildings bridge the space between the two planets, multiplying connections.

Like *In Time* and *Elysium*, *Snowpiercer* and *Jupiter Ascending* show how those in power influence and even direct the lives of others across borders. *Snowpiercer* transplants class hierarchies and conflicts to a train that travels around a post-apocalyptic Earth without ever stopping. Those living in the overcrowded, multiracial, and multinational back of the train survive on the bare minimum at the mercy of those who live in the middle and front parts of the train and enjoy luxurious lifestyles. The film shows the attempt of the people living at the back of the train to start a revolution. Yet, their aim is not just to cross the multiple sealed doors that separate both worlds inside the train, that is, to cross to the other side and start enjoying a different lifestyle, but rather to reprogram a system based on fallacies around preserving the train ecosystem, managing resources, and keeping balance—a balance that benefits "the precious few." Also tapping into the animosity that economic elites seem to have attracted after the Great Recession, *Jupiter Ascending* imagines a scenario of transplanetary economic activity, in which a royal corporate family spread out across the galaxy breeds and harvests humans on Earth to make a rejuvenating product that expands the lives of those who can afford it. For the aristrocratic family that runs this industry in the film, capital accumulation has literally no ethical, spatial, or temporal boundaries. More recently, films like *Bacurau* (Mendonça Filho and Dornelles 2019) and *The Hunt* (Zobel 2020) have taken this trope of voracious elites to a new level by depicting elites who go on vacation to literally hunt other human beings but end up being the ones being chased. In *Bacurau*, a group of white US and European supremacists visit a Brazilian village with the aim of hunting its inhabitants. In turn, the people from the village draw on their traditions and local knowledge to counter the foreigners' attack and restore peace in their community. As in *Sleep Dealer*, the village is also under the threat of neocolonial/neoliberal agents who have gained control of the water resources.

Elysium and *In Time* are even more directly concerned with transnational socioeconomic systems: they address common themes in contemporary sf such as biometrics, borders, and economic extraction, and rarer topics such as finance and territoriality. They do so at different scales (particularly *Elysium*) and they explicitly point to the impact of corporate and governmental practices. As I mentioned earlier, *Elysium* imagines a seemingly new border regime by exploring the socioeconomic gap between a destitute Earth and a space wheel to which global elites have moved. Through this scenario, the film explores what Anne Laure Amilhat-Szary and Frederic Giraut call "the superposition of vast sets of technologies of control" (2). In addition, the spatial organization that the film presents invites reflection on reterritorialization processes, extraterritorial actions, and sovereignty. *In Time*, for its part, focuses on the impact of financial global designs at a local level. The film depicts a world where time is the new currency and cities are divided into "time zones" (income/money zones). *In Time* differs from the rest of the aforementioned films in its ability to connect border-making practices with the interests of a specific sector of neoliberal globalization: finance. While all the films surveyed in the previous pages imagine worlds that call for close analysis, *In Time* constitutes a unique case study due to its interest in the proliferation of borders in cities and the relative absence of science fiction films dealing with the financial sector. In addition, both films share an interest in the relationship between economic extraction and the shortening of specific kinds of lives and call for an analysis of the biopolitical implications of this reality. They also draw attention to a variety of processes that accentuate the divide between those who enjoy unprecedented levels of well-being and those who barely have access to food or shelter. By approaching these issues from a critical perspective, both films situate the cosmopolitan imagination at the center of their narratives.

When considering the role of borders, I bear in mind the notion of 'net-worked borders,' a term that accounts for the variety and interconnection of borders that appear in the films analyzed in this chapter. Building on previous elaborations on the notion of the networked border by William Walters and Chris Rumford, Gabriel Popescu explains that networked borders proliferate in multiple places, that is, they are not simply the lines that divide countries. They are part of a larger web of global borders that spread deep inside national ter-ritories (81). Popescu also notes that networked borders are mobile: they move along with flows of people and goods (82). My approach to borders is influenced by two more notions. First, Popescu distinguishes between physical or territo-rial borders and symbolic borders, which he also calls boundaries (8). At the same time, he notes that most borders partake in both categories (8, 84). Given this observation, I use the word 'border' to refer to both cases. Secondly, Henk van Houtum and Ton van Naersen note that borders are mechanisms of "spatial differentiation" that "order" and "other" people (126). Since the films included in this chapter present divided societies and suggest that borders are often sys-tems of differentiation and segregation, I consider how these borders "order" and "other." Yet, towards the end of the chapter, I also ponder how borders can be used as mechanisms of contestation in films and in the 'real' world. In sum, the the remainder of the chapter examines networked borders, how they order and other people, and how people may challenge such structures.

Elysium: Incorporating Markets, Bordering Benefits

Elysium revolves around the interactions between Los Angeles/Earth and the wheel where human elites live, focusing on the control that the latter exercises on the former. In visual terms, the Elysium wheel stands out due to its dimen-sions, some establishing shots that direct viewers' attention towards it, and several aerial shots and close-ups that allow viewers to inspect it. The wheel and the technocultural specificities of its society are also the central conceptual elements of the novum that *Elysium* develops. Darko Suvin defines novum as a plausible "novelty" or "innovation" that "determines the narrative logic" of the story (63). The wheel is indeed the greatest novelty in the system that the film depicts, as it is a new spatial formation. As such, it produces estrangement in viewers and draws attention to itself and the new spatial and social dynamics that it generates. This allows *Elysium* to capture many of the multiple bordering processes that take place nowadays: reterritorialization and rebordering practices, the network-ing, personalization, and mobility of borders, and the growing use of biomet-rics.[3] The film takes advantage of the privileged viewpoint that these borders offer to shape a discourse that denounces the growing socioeconomic inequali-ties that global capital generates. This is an aspect that *Elysium* shares with other recent sf movies such as *Code 46, Sleep Dealer, In Time, Total Recall* (2012), and *Upside Down.* From a broader geopolitical perspective, *Elysium* engages in debates on recent international trade agreements such as TTIP or TPP and older ones such as NAFTA, the economic annexation of territories in the historical and present development of capitalism, the expansionist logics of neoliberalism, the proliferation of special economic zones (SEZs), extraterritorial concessions, foreign land acquisitions, and the automation and privatization of violent force.[4] As different as these issues may be, *Elysium* elucidates how they are governed by a set of neoliberal logics in which borders play a key role.

Beyond the Fence: Dispersed, Mobile, and Embodied Borders

Border walls feature prominently at the beginning of *Elysium*, as the camera appears to fly over a fence topped with barbwire at the edges of the space wheel and an extreme long shot shows the dimensions of the fence. Yet, borders do not only appear at the limits of Elysium. As Étienne Balibar notes, borders are "wherever selective controls are to be found" (84). Migrants in *Elysium* find borders in the homes of the space wheel, as the advanced healing beds that the elites own only heal those who have an Elysium ID printed on their wrists. In addition, police robots automatically single out those passengers whom they deem suspicious at a local bus stop. A similar scene also appears in *Sleep Dealer*, where a security guard uses a hand-held scanner to check passengers before they get on the bus. In this sense, borders are, as Popescu writes, "dispersed through society" (27). The scenario that *Elysium* presents may seem futuristic, yet many borders are already dispersed hundreds of miles inside and sometimes also outside national territories. Examples of this can be found around the world. For instance, Australia has processed migrants, refugees, and asylum seekers in offshore centers outside its national territory in Bintan Island, Indonesia, or Manus Island, Papua New Guinea (Mezzadra and Neilson 2013, 167; Gibson 83). Since the drastic rise in the number of refugees who arrived in Europe in 2015 (mostly but not only because of the war in Syria), the borders of the European Union seem to have moved from countries in its edges such as Greece or Bulgaria to countries well inside its territory (such as Hungary and Austria) and outside of it (such as Turkey). These countries conduct additional controls and have built new fences to manage the arrival of refugees in their territories (Castle and Surk; Langley). Similarly, the US Border Patrol has set up interior checkpoints up to a hundred miles away from the borderline with Mexico or Canada (Ortega). In this sense, *Elysium* reflects a global tendency towards border dispersal.

The use of drones, satellites, and the data they gather in *Elysium* also show that, apart from being dispersed, some borders are also mobile. Satellites track the course of the three unregistered shuttles that carry migrants to Elysium and, as soon as migrants land there, a Homeland helicopter carrying robot border agents comes to their location. Homeland efforts no longer concentrate right at the border but wherever migrants are or go. In this sense, borders move around and follow migrants. Mobile border technologies such as satellites and drones do not only facilitate Elysium's control over its territory, they also help Elysium to carry out extraterritorial actions that aim to protect its citizens and its political/

economic interests on foreign soil. Satellites locate the place where the shuttle of John Carlyle (William Fichtner) crashes on Earth and allow Elysium to send a group of mercenaries to fight those who plan on attacking the Elysium CEO and stealing the sensitive information that he carries on a device in his brain. Satellites also reveal the identity of the protagonist, Max Da Costa (Matt Damon), as he and some other people who assault John Carlyle are identified by satellite. Later, drones manage to identify Max when he hides in the streets of Los Angeles. Satellites and drones obtain information on the go that helps Elysium's authorities to protect its territory, its privileged status and the well-being of its citizens in almost real time. Similar concerns about the mobile bordering capabilities of drones also appear in *Code 8*. This film presents a world where a new kind of humans with superpowers called "psykes" engage in manual labor for a low pay and often without the necessary official permits. Despite the whiteness of the protagonist psyke (Robbie Amell), this premise establishes a parallel between the situations in which both psykes and migrants often find themselves. Six minutes into the film, a drone scans the bodies of several people working in the construction of a house. Shortly after, a police car arrives and officers tell workers to line up and look at the sky so that the drone scans their faces in order to identify those with special abilities and without a permit. A few overhead shots from the point of view of the drone turn people into data, showing their status ("registered" or not, "enabled" or not), the group or category of citizen to which they belong (a "class" number), and whether they have any criminal records. In a similar way to *Elysium*, this scene highlights the mobility of borders: they follow people wherever they are, re-(b)ordering them according to their supposed place or position in society.

Elysium—like *In Time*, *Code 46*, and *Code 8*—goes even further and suggests that borders are not only dispersed and mobile, but also embodied. Through its depiction of embodied borders, the film shows that borders can be anywhere and may build on other borders. Gabriel Popescu explains that embodied borders "are highly mobile and utterly individual, allowing constant and accurate movement control at the smallest spatial scale" (2012, 107). Embodied borders in *Elysium* (and often also in real life) are also biometric borders: they use a subject's unique physical or behavioral traits to establish their identity. Common examples of biometric markers are iris, facial features, fingerprints, keystroke, or movement patterns (Amoore 342; Popescu 108; Potzch 105). The beds that heal citizens in the film work or not depending on the body that lies on them and are designed to heal Elysium citizens only. In order to determine whether someone is from Elysium, they read a tag that is inscribed in the patient's skin. Similarly, satellites and drones can identify Max because his biometric information is part of the database that they use. A brief glimpse of his facial features is enough for a drone to identify him. Apart from pointing to the use of physical features to sort individuals, *Elysium* shows that behaviors can also be used to produce information about bodies. In the film, robots acting as police and parole officers automatically read bodies: they do not only single out Max and instantaneously have access to his criminal history, but also track and respond to his reactions (knocking him down when he uses sarcasm, or offering him a pill when his heart rate rises). The robots' reliance on such behavioral markers resonates with Holger Potzch's argument that biometrics serve to identify "abstracted patterns of life" that are deemed to require disciplining (105–6, 114–5). As several scholars have noted, the growing use of biometric information and the subsequent embodiment of the border that comes with it entails that the border is wherever a human body goes (Amoore 347–8; Popescu 107; Potzch 106). Whether in their physical or behavioral form, *Elysium* makes clear that biometric borders are everywhere, as the information that bodies provide can be accessed and deployed wherever Max is. In general, the use of biometric information makes borders dispersed, mobile, and embodied at the same time. The combination of different modalities of borders indicates that they superpose and form networks. For example, the healing beds in the film constitute a dispersed border mechanism and also depend on the embodiment of the border at a personal level through the use of biometric information.

Re-(b)ordering Norms and Sovereignty

The multiplicity and superposition of borders in *Elysium* point to three current socioeconomic processes: the reconfiguration of norms and sovereignty, market incorporation, and the individual bordering of economic benefits. To begin with, the superposition of borders allows certain actors (such as Elysium ministers and mercenaries) to skirt around sovereignty. Border policing both in the film and in the real world takes place beyond a nation's territory and its borders. The mercenaries in the film are an illustrative example. One of them, Kruger (Sharlto Copley), receives an order to launch three missiles towards three "undocumented" shuttles from Earth transporting migrants headed towards Elysium. Kruger launches the missiles from Earth and, by doing so, he circumvents Earth's sovereignty. He executes an order on foreign soil, where he and Elysium would have, in theory, no authority. Even though Kruger's action is more of an extraterritorial than a cross-border shooting, this scene recalls other cross-border shootings that have occurred, among others, at the Turkey-Syria, Spain-Morocco, and US-Mexico borders during the last decade (Ortega and O'Dell; Nielsen; Human Rights Watch). Such actions are not only criminal offenses, but they also disregard sovereignty. As in real life, extraterritorial/cross-border shooting is not legal in the film. Elysium officials note: "we are unauthorized to use our assets on Earth." In this case, the Elysium government calls the person who is ultimately responsible for this action—Delacourt (Jodie Foster)—to a hearing. Yet, it is a hearing without consequences for her. She keeps her political position and rebukes other government members for their "weak" approach to the protection of Elysium's borders. The only measure that the Elysium government takes is to discharge the mercenary who actually executed Delacourt's order to shoot. As in the film, governments and judicial powers often allow these actions to go unchallenged, delaying investigations and eventually failing to take actions against those who are supposed to see to the compliance with the law but actually break it. In doing so, they also trample over the people and the government of the border territory affected by such violations (Ortega and O'Dell).

Sleep Dealer, Upside Down, and *Captain America: The Winter Soldier* present similar scenarios in which armed services deploy force on foreign soil to 'defend' their borders or to protect their economic interests. *Upside Down* shows patrol agents shooting anyone who ventures into the border area that allows the inhabitants of two neighboring planets to interact in person. The agents open fire even if those who step into this area are still in their own planet/country. *Sleep Dealer* extends the range of action of the US border forces with regard to dams owned by US companies in Oaxaca (southern Mexico) and Vaupes (Colombia). The film includes two scenes in which drone pilots attack so-called "water terrorists," that is, those whom they deem a threat for the water company. *Captain America: The Winter Soldier* envisions a global surveillance system comprising satellites and military-like flying ships capable of shooting anyone who poses a threat to the economic and political powers anywhere on Earth. *Elysium* participates in this dialogue around extraterritorial armed forces with other contemporary sf films and develops a cosmopolitan critique of the advance of neoliberalism in terms of territorial scope.

At the same time, *Elysium* presents a more nuanced picture of current geo-political trends than the aforementioned films by capturing the proliferation of private armies and mercenaries since the 1990s, a process that contributes to increasing the volume of private economic activity and to the consolidation of neoliberalism (Singer; Tonkin; Mc Fate; Varin). In the film, Kruger retrieves the missiles that he is asked to launch from a container displaying the words "Elysium Corporate Authority" and "*Civil* Cooperation Bureau" [my emphasis], hinting that he is not part of the military. When he and two other mercenaries chase Max and his colleagues, there is nothing in their gear, equipment, or ship that links them to Elysium. Indeed, the ship carries a South African flag (a country and government that does not appear in the film), thus suggesting that these private mercenaries may have bought it from the no-longer-existing (in the film) government of South Africa. In addition, Kruger's operations are not officially authorized by Elysium's government, thus recalling the covert nature of many of the operations carried out by mercenaries and private military firms in real life (Singer 48). By introducing private military actors in its narrative, the film enables a reading of military privatization as one of several steps towards the incorporation of activities with the aim of increasing private sector profits.

Production models and technologies of screening and control in *Elysium* show a wide network of extraterritorial economic influence designed to cater to the needs of corporations and the extreme neoliberal system in place in the film. Armadyne is a company managed by an Elysium citizen, John Carlyle, and it manufactures its products (robots) for the orbiting community. The government of the space wheel then decides how to deploy the robots both on Earth and Elysium. The large dimensions of the facility and the workers' precarious conditions point to Armadyne's resemblance to a maquiladora or a factory in a SEZ (special economic zone)—both examples of extraterritorial concessions. As Michael Strauss points out, extraterritorial concessions consist of a company or country operating activities in a delimited area on foreign soil in which special norms or laws apply (63). He also notes that "a leased territory can be a potential target of military attack" (66). Armadyne adopts security measures such as scanning workers to assure that they do not carry any weapons into the factory. This invites a reading of Armadyne as an extraterritorial concession. A similar way of depicting an extraterritorial concession appears in *Sleep Dealer*, where armed guards, automatic firearms, and drones protect dams owned by US capital in Colombia and Mexico. Extraterritorial concessions such as SEZs in China, India, Latin America, some African countries (often with China as a mediator) or maquiladoras in Mexico adapt their national legal framework to specific areas so that companies may benefit from a set of norms that meet their needs (Ong 19, 77, 106; Mezzadra and Neilson 2013, 216–7). In this sense, corporations indirectly alter legislation to suit their interests. Elysium's power to alter norms is also evident in its ability to designate Los Angeles as a no-fly zone as they see fit, temporarily banning any flights to and or from the city. Such configurations indicate that Elysium re-orders and re-borders norms and evince the malleability of Earth's sovereignty.

Territorial Integration and Market Incorporation

Elysium also presents a world of territorial and economic integration. Even though it focuses on a specific area—a sprawling LA in ruins—the film suggests that this area represents the state of most of the planet. This is evident from the very first shots. Elysium opens with a series of aerial tracking shots that show several identical sprawling urban areas in decay. The speed of these shots, the substantial range of space that they cover, and the almost-identical landscapes that they show indicate that the view that they offer is a generalized reality. In addition, the captions that accompany these initial shots introduce the film's geographical premise by referring to Earth as a whole. The fact that the parts set in LA were actually shot near Mexico City and that LA visually recalls, as Celestino Deleyto points out, a "Middle East war-wrecked town" (2013) also contribute to the effect of making this fictional LA look as if it could be set almost anywhere on Earth. After these glimpses of urban spaces, an establishing shot of the planet suggests that Earth has become a single territory. The film further reinforces this image of a unified global space through additional establishing shots of urban areas in decay without specifying their location at different points in the film. This is indeed an aspect that other films also hint at, although perhaps in more subtle ways, through their mise-en-scène. Several films present large global cities as perfectly interchangeable spaces: they could be anywhere. They could belong to any country. These cities present combinations of sleek glass façades, towering skyscrapers, decaying urban areas, and sometimes slums. Such films sometimes render US cities with a strong presence of Asian elements and Asian cities with a strong architectural influence of the primarily Western International Style and Neo-Futurism. That is the case of the arid landscapes and the urban scenarios of Shanghai in *Code 46*, the two cities in the 2012 *Total Recall* remake, Neo Seoul in *Cloud Atlas*, and the fictional cities of Up Top and Down Below in *Upside Down*, although this phenomenon can be traced back to earlier films such as *Blade Runner* or *The Fifth Element*.

Such territorial integration on Earth, along with Elysium's extraterritorial power, indicate that Elysium has set up a large scheme of economic extraction in which those who live in the space station benefit from the generation of value from Earth as a whole. Free trade with Earth satisfies one of the biggest concerns for Elysians (apart from border security): the maximization of revenue. In a conversation with Armadyne CEO John Carlyle, other managers show their concerns that "a clear path to upside" (to higher profits) may be compromised. Relying on different narrative techniques, other sf films such as *They Live* and *Jupiter Ascending* have shown similar cosmopolitan concerns by having civilizations from distant planets come to Earth to incorporate its economic activity into their system. Similar market enlargement and integration patterns can be observed around the world at the moment.

Apart from trade and market integration agreements that have been in place for several years such as the one regulating the European Economic Area and NAFTA (which was replaced by the United States-Mexico-Canada Agreement in 2020), several national governments have tried to develop similar agreements at an even larger scale in the last years. Two of the most prominent examples are the Comprehensive and Progressive Agreement for Trans-Pacific Partnership (CPTPP, formerly TPP), which is in effect since December 30, 2018, and currently includes Australia, Brunei, Canada, Chile, Japan, Malaysia, Mexico, New Zealand, Peru, Singapore, and Vietnam and the failed Transatlantic Trade and Investment Partnership (TTIP) between the USA and the European Union, whose negotiations were halted by the Trump administration in 2016. Before the United States' retreat from both the TTIP and the TPP, these agreements entailed a major leap in scope. They were forecast to regulate economic zones that account for 50% and 40% of the world's GDP respectively. Together, however, they were expected to comprise 60% of the world's GDP, as the US initially participated in both agreements (Oxford Analytica). These agreements guarantee(d) an easier mobility of capital and goods, but do/did not envisage the free mobility of people, nor do/did they protect their welfare. TTIP would have created advantageous normative frameworks for transnational business players, giving them a say in public policy-making and granting them the right to sue governments if their policies harmed their profits—however beneficial such policies may have been for the environment or society (Strange 86; De Ville and Siles-Brügge 130–1). In short, such agreements seek to expand the scope of corporate power and profits. While the idea of a homogeneous, completely integrated Earth that *Elysium* sketches is deceiving, it hints at the role of scale in the current development of neoliberalism.

The current trend towards the enlargement of the scope of economies by territorial means that *Elysium* presents is not entirely new: it is part of a larger historical context of territorial incorporation that is likely to keep developing in the future, as the film suggests. Aníbal Quijano and Immanuel Wallerstein argue that the Americas were essential in the growth and establishment of the modern world system, which they trace back to the sixteenth century. They note that one of the key factors in the development of the world system was that the Americas provided a large extension of land (549–50). Similarly, Walter Mignolo observes that the first Christian mission that incorporated the Americas into a world system subsequently gave way to what he calls the civilizing, developmental, and neoliberal missions (2000, 724–5), all of which have been ways of reorganizing world geopolitics to expand the economic scope and influence of capital-hoarding elites. Opportunities for profit enlargement are not limited to Earth: Peter Dickens and James Ormrod have noted the relevance of outer space in current economic systems and its central role in future economic growth. In their work on the galactic expansion of the economy, Dickens and Ormrod point to current realities such as the role of satellites in the functioning of communication systems and their relevance in sectors such as the media and finance (533–4). They also mention the plans for expanding the tourism industry in outer space and the economic potential of setting mines in other planets and finding new ways of using solar energy in outer space (535, 541). *Elysium* captures this ongoing development of the neoliberal mission in outer space through the spatial concept that governs the narrative, by filtering some events through satellite information screens, and through the camerawork that the film uses to present the space station. This last aspect is evident in an establishing shot at the beginning of the film in which the camera pans from Earth to the Elysium wheel as the music increases slightly in volume (Figure 1.1). Apart from showing the location of a

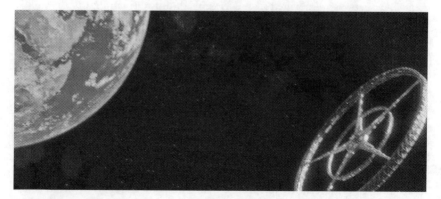

FIGURE 1.1   Earth is not enough: a socioeconomic system in need of perpetual growth has no choice but to enlarge its scope to outer space in *Elysium* (Blomkamp 2013).

new economic frontier, this shot captures the radical expansion of the system in a visual and aural way.

(De)bordering Benefits: Elysium's Ambivalent Cosmopolitanism

The expansion, integration, and accumulation processes described above are accompanied by the bordering of the profits and benefits that Elysium generates (a clean environment, advanced technologies, fast transportation, comfort, leisure, and premium healthcare). Of all these benefits, the film puts special emphasis on access to medical treatments and the de-bordering of this 'privilege' at the end of the story. *Elysium* juxtaposes an overcrowded and deteriorated hospital with scarce resources in LA with the individual healing beds that every Elysium citizen seems to have at home. Advanced technologies also check health risks and life threats for Elysians and provide them with instant information about their health anywhere on Earth or the space station. For example, when John Carlyle's shuttle crashes in LA, a computer lets him know that he is not harmed and provides Elysium with updates on his condition. The networked, dispersed, embodied, mobile, and extraterritorial character of borders guarantees restricted access to such Elysian privileges while allowing the expansion of borderlands and of the neoliberal economic system that Elysium relies on. The film suggests that borders do not only delimit (rich) countries but also protect the individual property, benefits and security that a few enjoy. When a shuttle with migrants heads towards the space station, Elysians treat it as a "security breach." This breach does not pose a violent threat to Elysians. Rather, for them, it threatens their privatized and personalized security (which reflects a reversal of the social security schemes that some countries built in the second half of the twentieth century and are now being privatized and thus, individualized). The film reflects what William Walters, in his analysis of British security policies, calls the "reordering and [...] re-hierarchicizing of political priorities" in favor of border security and to the detriment of social welfare (244). Elysians deem the inclusion of more citizens an obstacle to the growth of their income and privileges. In the hidden logic of this system, more people equals less share. However, at the end of the film, Max and Spider (Wagner Moura)—the leader of the gang that sends unauthorized passenger shuttles to Elysium—hack Elysium's computer and reset it so that everyone on Earth is recognized as an Elysium citizen. By doing so, they de-border Elysium's health privileges. Some of the last shots of the film show people of different ethnicities running towards medical shuttles sent to Earth and, in this way, the film celebrates the cosmopolitan ideal of global access to decent healthcare.

Yet, even though *Elysium* appears to develop a cosmopolitan discourse through its celebration of universal healthcare and its critical portrayal of borders, extraterritorial operations, and market incorporation, it is more ambiguous in other respects. The ending hints that the divide between both worlds vanishes as every person on Earth gets Elysian citizenship and access to healthcare. Without doubt, healthcare is an important issue, but it does not guarantee the creation of a series of circumstances that allow people to have a decent life (although it contributes to it). In spite of the changes that occur at the end of the film, a gulf still exists between the former citizens of Elysium and those who live in resource-depleted areas, those who have poor job conditions or do not even have a job, and presumably also other groups who do not explicitly appear in the film such as the homeless and families without income. At the end of the film, the systemic circumstances that lead most people to live in shanty towns and to subsist through informal economic activities do not change. Although many borders in *Elysium* disappear or weaken, the film's ending overlooks the central role of the economic model (extraterritorial concessions, market integration and expansion, corporate cultures of profit maximization, and resource exploitation) in creating the harsh life conditions that most people on Earth endure throughout the narrative. Echoing Giorgio Agamben, the authors of "The antiAtlas of Borders, A Manifesto" note that "neoliberal thinking [...] sees addressing the root causes of various issues as more costly than dealing with their effects" (Parizot et al. 3). This is precisely what *Elysium*'s ending does: it presents the mitigation of some effects of Elysium's neoliberal economic practices (the lack of healthcare) as a solution for people on Earth. It proposes a patch on the system rather than its reformulation. *Elysium* also reflects what Mark Fisher calls "capitalist realism": the inability to imagine alternatives to neoliberalism (2009, 2). Conforming to this notion, *Elysium* generates contradictions and makes the alternative (a global healthcare scheme) part of the mainstream (a savage neoliberal system) (Fisher 2009, 5, 9). In the end, *Elysium*'s cosmopolitan dreams fall prey to the capitalist-realist environment that permeates contemporary life.

Another aspect that contributes to the ambivalent character of *Elysium* is the role of race in the film. *Elysium* includes characters of different ethnicities: LA is a largely Latino area where some Spanish can be heard; the "undocumented" shuttles that travel towards Elysium carry Asian, Latino, and black characters; Carlyle has a video call with other managers who are a black man, a blonde Anglo woman, and an Asian man; and the last name of Elysium's Prime Minister is Patel, suggesting that he may be of Indian descent. Yet, except for nurse Frey (Alice Braga), Max's friend Julio (Diego Luna), and perhaps also Spider, most of the main characters (Max, Delacourt, Carlyle, Kruger) are white. More importantly, the end of the film emphasizes Max's role as a Christ-like (and white) savior, pushing other racial and systemic debates to the side. In this sense, *Elysium* develops a similar racial discourse to *The Matrix*. Nicola Rehling observes that "despite the trilogy's obvious effort to include a multicultural cast [...], Western racial norms are reinscribed" by presenting Neo as a white messiah (126). In one of the last scenes of *Elysium*, Max gives his life—that is, he dies—so that the rest of humanity may be granted citizenship and have access to healthcare. The last moments of the film pay tribute to Max's heroism by recreating some moments from his childhood. Previously, the film celebrates universal healthcare through several shots of non-white people running towards the health shuttles that are landing on Earth.

The inclusion of moments from Max's childhood at the end of the film shifts attention from the actual changes that the world is about to go through to focus on the white savior. In fact, the very last shot of the film is an image of Max as a kid running on the street as a thin halo of light glows in the middle of the frame. In addition, the shuttles and the robots that come to heal people are also white and their color fills the frame in several of the last shots. Although white is a color that is commonly used in medical contexts, such whiteness is non-existent in the LA hospital that appears earlier in the film. These images thus reinforce the image of the white savior and the strong dichotomy between the whiteness of the saviors and the blackness of the saved, a trope that Matthew Hughey has identified as a common practice in cinema (2). Despite the potential that *Elysium* has shown in this section for the analysis of contemporary global phenomena from a cosmopolitan perspective, the film fails not only to imagine systemic reinvention, but also to envision non-whites participating in the construction of their future.

In Time: Connecting Borders and Global Finance

In Time invites viewers to reflect on the role of borders at a local level and their relationship with the transnational interests of financial corporations. By exploring these issues, the film draws attention to a series of cosmopolitan concerns related to working conditions, quality of life, mobility, and the right to live. Despite the relevance of finance in bordering processes, theories of cosmopolitanism have generally overlooked its role in shaping situations that pose cosmopolitan challenges. Here, I attempt to bring to the surface some of these challenges. *In Time* imagines a near future in which time has replaced money as currency. In this world, people have been genetically engineered to stop aging at 25, so, when they reach that age, they have to earn time or else they die within a year. The film, shot in Los Angeles, portrays a world divided into "zones" and focuses on two of them: Dayton, a working-class area, and New Greenwich, a financial district. Through this setting, *In Time* explores the roles of borders in the processes by which the latter territory extracts value from the former. In order to investigate such processes, I consider the different kinds of borders that appear in the film, including not only fences and walls but also other borders related to wealth, time, behavior, race, and surveillance. Close examination of borders, spatial dynamics, and characters' behavior elucidate the rationale behind the socioeconomic structures that the film depicts, who benefits from them, and what their interests are. Focusing on such aspects, this section shows that the different borders that appear in the film control the movement of people and money. By doing so, these borders contribute to creating and preserving several conditions that benefit global financial firms and pose cosmopolitan challenges: the generalization of debt, the casualization of labor, workers' acquiescence, the protection of the financial sector, and the criminalization of the poor.

    In Time offers a cosmopolitan perspective on economic globalization by emphasizing the central role and abusive power of finance in current global structures. In her work on global cities, Saskia Sassen associates new border formations in cities with the neoliberal interests of global corporations (2013b, 68). Sassen notes that, since the current global system began to develop in the 1980s, borders have become increasingly "transversal and impenetrable" (68–9). She identifies cities as one of the main places where these new borders sprout (69). The transversality of borders is evident in *In Time*, as borders are not only physical barriers: they are surveillance systems and borders related to wealth, time, and appearance also control movement into, out of, and through areas. *In Time* also provides a more detailed portrait of the scenario that Sassen describes. While Sassen refers to financial firms, along with multinational corporations, as one of the main bordering agents in cities, she does not explicitly connect the interests and operations of financial firms with specific kinds of urban borders and their impact on workers' lives. This is precisely what *In Time* does. Writing on contemporary borders and their socioeconomic context, Sandro Mezzadra and Brett Neilson argue that borders and labor are multiplying and connect these processes to the progressive financialization of the economy since the 1970s (2013, 81–5). Building on this work, my close analysis of *In Time* shows how some of the conditions that the multiplication of borders produces meet the interests of global finance.

Urban Differentiation and Transnational Connections

In *In Time,* the contrast between wealthy and poor areas is evident in the radically different urban, architectural, and design models that configure each area. On the one hand, the streets in zone 12 (Dayton) feature brick walls covered in washed-out paint, dull concrete blocks, low buildings, barbwire, fences, and bare open spaces in the vicinity of factories. In Dayton, Will (Justin Timberlake) and his mother (Olivia Wilde) share a modest apartment with just a few pieces of basic furniture, no decoration or paintings, and almost-empty closets and food drawers. In general, the mise-en-scène delineates a space characterized by time-worn, run-down buildings and scarce resources. Yet, as Will puts it, "Dayton is not the only zone that could use a few extra years." Towards the end of the film, a television channel shows people from zones 11 (Circadia), 12 (Dayton) and 14 (Livingston) massively crossing borders between areas, reminding viewers that Dayton is not the only poor area. New Greenwich (zone 4) has a completely different appearance: modern high-rise buildings, upscale luxury hotels, glass façades, avenues, casinos, mansions, and private beaches signal the concentration of wealth in the area. Even though the ornate, ostentatious mansions and casinos contrast with the functional, polished offices, they show the same reality: that the elite has all the resources that they need and want. The film also points towards the uncontestable power of New Greenwich's financial corporations and institutions by including several long shots in which the façades of the police headquarters, the Weis Timelenders building, or other banks' skyscrapers fill all the frame.

The vast dimensions of these buildings—that exceed the limits of the frame—give the socioeconomic actors that operate from them an imposing appearance.

Even though *In Time* focuses on one city, the film employs visual and narrative strategies to clarify that the urban environment in the film reflects global dynamics. More specifically, *In Time* highlights the centrality of transnational webs of financial interests and the role of borders in the mapping of such interests in urban spaces. Despite the differences and borders between zones, *In Time* features a highly connected world. After Will kidnaps Sylvia (Amanda Seyfried), her father—banker Philippe Weis (Vincent Kartheiser)—talks to other overseas leaders, trying to reassure them that no ransom money/time will be paid for the kidnapping of his daughter. In turn, they show their fear that the problem might spread to other parts of the world and that the system might collapse. Throughout the conversation, an electronic world map covering an entire wall in Philippe's office appears onscreen. The map indicates that Philippe is calling from California and his counterparts are in Europe (probably Germany or Poland) and in central Russia. In addition, the screen—like the one in Carlyle's office in *Elysium*—offers a live feed on markets. Similarly, the timekeepers' headquarters are equipped with computers and large screens that display live time-flow and per capita time on maps and charts. As Philippe talks to timekeeper/policeman Raymond Leon (Cillian Murphy) later on, the screen always appears in the background, either directly or reflected in the window glass (Figure 1.2). The constant presence of the world map highlights Philippe and Raymond's role in the international economic system: they represent the interests of global finance and Philippe responds directly to it. In fact, after Sylvia and Will steal a million years from Philippe, the screen in the banker's office starts flashing and beeping with calls from all over the world. In this sense, *In Time* resembles movies such as *Captain America: The Winter Soldier* and *Elysium*, which also feature politicians and corporate managers from different countries or of different

FIGURE 1.2 Even when characters talk about personal and local matters, the shadow of transnational financial interests looms large in *In Time* (Niccol 2011).

ethnicities having video or even hologram conferences, pointing to the interconnected interests of global money.

The previous examples from *In Time* show two contemporary socioeconomic
dynamics: first, the elites are becoming increasingly 'dephysicalized' and exert
extraterritorial power (Bauman 19). Second, the 'needs' of global finance structure the rest of society. The government is simply absent in the film and the
only presumably public institution (the timekeepers) is at the service of global
markets. The transfer of public sovereignty to private hands is evident in the last
scene, in which a modified version of the Los Angeles City Hall serves as the setting for a bank ("*In Time* Filming Locations"). The film then suggests that those
who hold economic power also hold institutional and legal power. In this way, *In
Time* constructs a world that resonates with the work of several scholars on globalization and borders, suggesting that the concentration of power in global corporate hands hinders sovereignty (Bauman 19; Wendy Brown 23; Sassen 2013b,
68; Mezzadra and Neilson 2013, 85). Reflecting such a reality, *In Time* presents
what could be called 'virtual financial governance.'

Networked Borders: Monitoring Bodies, Money, Time, and Identities

Zygmunt Bauman links "the pressure to pull down the last remaining barriers to
the free movement of money and money-making commodities and information"
with "the pressure to dig new moats and erect new walls" (93). Similarly, *In Time*
presents a society in which money moves mostly in one direction while simultaneously employing a range of visual cues to underline the centrality of physical
borders in its fictional world. Apart from highlighting the appearance of highway checkpoints through close-ups, the camera also emphasizes the presence of
fences and other kinds of barriers, often filming characters and action sequences
through them (Figure 1.3). Fences and barriers seem to appear accidentally, as in

FIGURE 1.3   By framing the protagonist through window security bars, *In Time* (Niccol
2011) draws attention to borders from the very beginning of the film.

the opening scene in which we see Will waking up in his room after he introduces viewers, through voice-over narration, to the film's novum (time as currency). A few seconds after he tells us about his precarious situation, the camera frames Will through security bars as he looks out of the window. In this way, the film foregrounds the pervasiveness of barriers in characters' lives and hints at a potential interrelationship between the socioeconomic system and the role of borders in the film. Fences also feature prominently in several scenes. For example, when Sylvia and Will leave a hotel room to escape from the police or when the Dayton gang forces a few workers to line up against a fence to pressure them into saying whatever they may know about the whereabouts of the runaways. By regularly including barriers, fences, and checkpoints in the frame, the film reinforces characters' entrapment and marginality and invites viewers to look for other kinds of borders. The superhero film *Jupiter's Moon* (Mundruczó 2017), which clearly establishes parallels with Europe's migrant crisis after 2014/15, also employs a similar strategy as it opens with an extreme close shot of a hen behind bars, filming it from the outside of a cage, and then cuts to a close shot of Aryan (Zsombor Jéger), the protagonist Syrian refugee, lying against the same cage that the film introduced seconds ago. The connection between the entrapment of the hen and the refugee is emphasized by the distinctive yellow color of the bars against the dark background and reinforced by the clucking of the hens which continues throughout the opening scene as the following shots feature other people traveling on the same truck. In this way, *Jupiter's Moon*—like *In Time*, *Elysium*, and other sf films—relies on bars and fence analogies to invite viewers to read this film as a border narrative.

Besides *In Time*'s emphasis on physical borders, the film depicts a larger network of borders that order and other bodies according to wealth, time, and appearances. Screening technologies supplement these systems of differentiation. One of the main kinds of borders in the film revolves around time/money and economic status. Raymond says that when a person brings time/money to the 'wrong' place (Dayton), "what matters is what happened to their time." In the film, authorities (only represented by the timekeepers) are interested first and foremost in ordering time/money. As in *Elysium*, an effective way to do this is through embodied borders. *In Time* is built on the premise that people have been genetically modified to be born with time/money counters in one of their forearms. The film brings attention to the small scale of borders by opening with an extreme close-up of Will's skin. The camera slowly zooms out of Will's skin, revealing a time counter on his forearm and hinting at the central role of embodied time/money in bordering processes. After this, embodied money borders appear several times. In order to get a taxi to go from Dayton to New Greenwich, Will has to show the taxi driver his forearm, that is, his money. When Will crosses the border checkpoints to other areas, he has to pay with his forearm. The same happens at a casino, where a doorman advises Will to make a 'voluntary' donation of a year before he walks in. Through these examples, *In Time* emphasizes that the border comes down to the level of the body and moves with the person through the city. The body and its time/money spending capacity allow or prevent mobility and access to certain places.

In Time also presents embodied borders as temporal borders. Sandro Mezzadra and Brett Neilson explain that "the compression, elongation, and partitioning of time" work as mechanisms of "control, filtering, and selectivity" that facilitate or hamper mobility (2013, 132). In *In Time*, Will has to pay one year in order to get from Dayton to New Greenwich. As he approaches New Greenwich, the amount of time that he has to pay rises. Such amounts of time are prohibitive for Dayton citizens, which makes it impossible for anyone from Dayton to get to New Greenwich, as they would need to save a whole years' salary when most people barely have 24 hours on their clocks. This evokes the situation of people from African countries who try to migrate to Europe. They often have to make several stops on their way in order to work, save money, and be able to go on with their journey. Similarly, people without the money for an education may have to save it for it (which takes time) and those who can afford to buy tickets for high-speed trains move (and live) three times faster than those who can only afford to travel by bus. In general, it takes time for people to move both socially and spatially. In contrast, capital moves around almost instantly and those who control it usually move faster than the rest.

In Time literally holds that money orders people in different temporal groups (time zones) with disparate degrees of mobility. In addition, the film's strategy of integrating money and time highlights that money accumulation and dispossession are connected to life length. This is evident in the fact that people pay for everything with their lifetime. The film also draws attention to this situation when Will and Sylvia mug a woman on the highway. Will tells her: "I'd say [give me] 'your money or your life,' but since your money is your life ...." Lack of money actually costs some characters their life. As in the film, running out of money in real life may eventually lead people to run out of time, to die. The quality of life, diet, healthcare, and safety that people can afford are often directly related to their wealth. These factors make people's lives longer or shorter. In this sense, money borders are also temporal borders, allowing some to live longer than others. Both in the film and in real life, money does not only buy physical and social mobility, it also buys time.

The influence of time/money on behavior and social codes also brings bordering practices to the level of the individual. Characters' attitudes towards time evince whether someone is out of place. This is a consequence of the disparate lifestyles that people can afford to have in different areas, which indicate economic status. Will's arrival in New Greenwich provides the most obvious example of such a dynamic in the film. Just as he gets off the car, he starts running. Yet, he soon notices that nobody else is running, looks at his watch, and realizes it is no longer necessary to run: he has plenty of time. Timekeeper Raymond, however, notes that running is "a hard habit to break" and a waitress tells Will that he does things "a little too fast." In this way, pace works as an embodied border in the film, indicating whether someone 'belongs' in a place or not. Such markers help presume the identity of the individual moving through the city in order to assess, as Popescu notes, "the risk [that] it poses to society" (107).

Despite the variety of borders that *In Time* depicts, it is oblivious of a type of embodied border that is deeply connected to wealth and economic status: race. The division between the time zones in the film seems to be deployed along a typically Angeleno East/West line, with New Greenwich loosely identified with the Oceanside affluent communities and Dayton with East LA. Even though Dayton has an undeniable East LA Latino flavor, ethnicity plays an insignificant role in the film. Writing about sf cinema in general, Adilifu Nama identifies a "structured absence of blackness" in sf films, although his examples indicate an absence of racial diversity in general (10). He also notes that when black/non-white characters are part of the story, their appearance rarely works as more than a "token presence" (13). This is the case of *In Time*: it presents a racially mixed society (guests at Philippe's mansion are black, white, and some appear to be Latinos). Yet, these are secondary characters who rarely utter a line: they appear as tokens. In addition, the film does not provide any explicit information about the social or historical reasons of this mix. Even though Will's surname (Salas) suggests that he is of Spanish-speaking descent, *In Time* does not explicitly feature any Latino character. Considering that Los Angeles had a 48.5% Latino population in 2010, according to the United States Census Bureau, the invisibility of Latino ethnicity and culture(s) in the film is striking. In her analysis of borders in global LA, Camila Fojas also pinpoints race as the main feature that conditions where people "belong" or not in non-sf films such as *El Norte, Star Maps* (Arteta 1997), and *Bread and Roses* (Loach 2000) (181). So, while *In Time* denounces segregation and stresses the significance of economic status in practices of differentiation in urban environments, the film overlooks the central role of race in such processes. Philippe Weis' remarks illustrate the film's ambivalent stance towards race. He says: "Of course, some think [that] what we have is unfair: the difference between time zones. [...] But isn't this the next logical step in our evolution? And hasn't evolution always been unfair? It's always been survival of the fittest." By using the term "survival of the fittest," Philippe evokes racial Darwinism and, at the same time, presents a new stage of natural selection: economic segregation. While Philippe's words seem to link race and economic status, he does not refer to race explicitly. In short, discrimination practices in *In Time* leave race aside and revolve around economic position, overlooking the connection between race and borders.

Other recent science fiction films that deal with borders such as *Elysium, Code 46, Total Recall, Upside Down, The Hunger Games* installments, and *Code 8* also present variations of the "structured absence" of racial diversity typical of the genre and commercial cinema in general. An exception to this group of films is *Sleep Dealer*, which imagines a world where Latino migration to the US has ceased. In this future, the US still depends on the labor of Latinos, who work from Mexico through a virtual reality program. As an "infomaquila" manager explains, the United States benefits from having "todo el trabajo sin los traba-jadores [latinos]" ("all the work without the [Latino] workers"). At first sight, *Sleep Dealer* may appear to imagine an overwhelmingly white US. Yet, the film focuses almost exclusively on the Mexican side of the border. The only US inhabitants who have a relevant role in the film are a Latino drone pilot and, to a lesser extent, his parents. In this manner, *Sleep Dealer* subverts the structured whiteness that is common in the sf genre. Adilifu Nama argues that the "struc-tured absence of blackness" or rather, racial diversity, in sf cinema often works towards the affirmation of "racial fantasies" of white dominance and survival in films such as *When Worlds Collide* (Maté 1951), *The Time Machine* (Pal 1960), and *Logan's Run* (15, 17, 27). Yet, in *In Time*—and in the border films mentioned above—the lack of emphasis on racial hierarchies contrasts with the main dis-courses on global finance and economic exploitation, generating an ambivalent discourse on cosmopolitanism.

Finally, another element that plays a central role in the film's system of net-worked borders is technological surveillance, as it allows timekeepers to monitor people's actions and mobility and to make sure that money does not leave the zones where it is supposed to be. Detail shots of different surveillance cam-eras draw attention to the monitoring of citizens' lives in Dayton. Thanks to such cameras, timekeepers manage to match images of Will with his identity. Another means of control is the timekeepers' database and their live time dis-tribution feed. When there is more time in an area than there 'should' be, com-puters automatically set an alarm off at the timekeepers' headquarters and at Philippe's office. In addition, screens in both places display constantly updated data in green and red color indicating the status of each area. These colors and the non-stop time/money flow may remind viewers of stock exchanges, rein-forcing the connection between borders and finance. The surveillance technolo-gies that appear in the film allow Raymond to "keep time," that is, to maintain the time/money order and the economic status quo. These borders look out for undesired kinds of mobility of money and people, supplementing physical and embodied borders. As Zygmunt Bauman (18) and Gerard Delanty (2006, 32) hint, networked borders signal a shift from enclosure based on the dichotomy national/foreign to an organization of space governed by the (im)possibility of moving at free will.

(B)ordering People and Money: Protecting and Feeding the Financial System

So far, my analysis of *In Time* has considered the kinds of borders that the film makes visible and hinted that many of these borders are connected to the finan-cial world. But why is this network of borders in place? What are the logics behind them? Who benefits from them?[5] *In Time* suggests that borders control the mobility of money and people in order to produce the right conditions to increase financial revenue. Of course, the film does not completely separate the interests of financial firms from those of other corporations. Yet, it emphasizes the predominance of finance in the running of the current global system and suggests that borders are at its service. Henry Hamilton (Matt Bomer), a broker, explains to Will that time zones serve the interests of those who live in New Greenwich and help divert time/money from Dayton to New Greenwich. All the main characters from New Greenwich are connected to the financial sector (Henry, Philippe, and Sylvia) or defend its interests (timekeepers). Throughout the film, Sylvia and Will's contestation efforts are directed at banks, channeling viewers' attention towards financial actors. Apart from the visual references to stock markets, characters' time clocks also allude to the financial sector, as they resemble the contactless payment wrist bands, cards, and mobile phone apps that many real banks already offer to their clients.

In Time presents five conditions generated by borders that allow financial extraction to work smoothly: the generalization of debt, the casualization of labor, workers' acquiescence, the protection of finance, and the criminalization of the poor. The different kinds of borders presented in the previous section order people and their money, making sure that people in Dayton are often short of time. Since Dayton citizens live "day to day" and missions (charities) often run out of time, some people have to borrow money from New Greenwich banks in order to stay alive. This situation is quite lucrative for banks, as there is a regular demand for credit and they can charge higher return rates of interest. A bright screen showing a bank's lending rate going up to 37% stands out against a dark background in the scene in which Sylvia and Will consider whether they should give up. In this way, *In Time* hints that the reason why the system is not interested in the flow of money across most areas is that the elites extract a significant amount of capital through debt. Writing about the contrast between speculative finance and speculative fiction, Aimee Bahng argues that financialization often works to render future scenarios knowable, minimizing uncertainty, and "mitigating risks for wealthy elites" (170). In the film, Philippe Weis confirms the centrality of debt to the securing of financial projections when he says that "flooding the wrong zone with a million years [...] could cripple the system." The name of his bank (Weis Timelenders) further emphasizes the importance of debt in the running of the system. At the same time, *In Time* recalls the burden of debt to so-called developing countries and, more recently, also to European countries and the US. The film suggests that the global economic system is more interested in extracting value through financial mechanisms than through consumption or labor, although the film also shows how companies continue to make money through these methods. Some scholars also emphasize the dominant role of finance in today's economy. Christian Marazzi explains that nowadays finance is "pervasive" and "spreads across the entire economic cycle" (81–2). Sandro Mezzadra and Brett Neilson add that finance even permeates "the subsistence economy," that is, it produces revenue from all social groups (2013, 92). It is no coincidence that *In Time* brings both finance and borders to the personal level of the body. As Mezzadra and Neilson argue, people are not excluded but differentially included in the global financial system (159). Borders are then essential to the regulation of hierarchical inclusion.

In Time does not explicitly address the relationship between the interests of financial firms and other corporations. Yet, it makes clear that actors other than financial companies contribute to creating the conditions that lead people to borrow money. Networked borders also play a part in this system, holding Dayton citizens hostage and leaving them no other choice but to accept the conditions that companies offer them. Job and income uncertainty prevent workers' physical and social mobility and generate situations in which workers cannot sustain themselves and their families, thus needing to borrow money. Electronically modifiable prices vary at the will of companies. Firms also modify production quotas and workers' salaries unilaterally. As a result, workers progressively need more time to pay for their living expenses and new conditions force them to work longer hours for less time/money. At the same time, fewer jobs are available. Sassen refers to this kind of working condition as the "casualization of the employment relation" (1998, 145–8). That is, the precarious kind of work available and its temporary character drives workers to accept any kind of job, less security, and lower remuneration. Some people do not manage to survive: Will's mother dies because she presumably does not get any time for her last day of work. Such events indicate that New Greenwich conceives Dayton citizens as a "surplus population," to use Sassen's term (2013a, 199). Sassen explains that financial actors have worked towards a "systemic deepening of advanced capitalism" in which the system no longer values people as workers and consumers (199–200). *In Time* shows that people are useful for the system as long as they finance their own lives and are able to pay the money/time back. This is also clear in *Repo Men*, a film in which those who do not pay the debt for their manufactured organs on time are forced to give them back to the corporation that makes them, sometimes dying. In the systems that *In Time* and *Repo Men* depict, some people are disposable. These scenarios resonate with Peter Sands' interpretation of the cities in *Metropolis, Blade Runner, Brazil,* and *The Matrix* as representations of the "cannibalistic nature of global capitalism" (139). In a similar manner, *In Time* also depicts a cannibalistic economy: precarious work conditions, casual work, rising prices, and debt devour workers. Meanwhile, financial firms keep raising their profits, as they exploit a network of borders built to suit their needs.

The (b)ordering of economic resources leads to the generalization of two attitudes: acquiescence in Dayton and greed in New Greenwich. At the very beginning of the film, Will says: "I don't have time. I don't have time to worry about how it happened. It is what it is." Later on, a dead man lies on the floor as his colleagues walk into the factory and past his body. Only Will and a colleague stop for a second, but their supervisor stares at them and they quickly go into the building. Later, workers waiting in line complain when Will protests about his salary reduction and makes them lose time. These two scenes elucidate the fragmentation of the workforce in the film. In his discussion of *In the Pit* (Rulfo, 2006), a film about the construction of a bridge in Mexico City, Vicente Rodríguez analyzes the attitude of one of the workers (Chaparro) and notes that he does not seem frustrated or outraged: he accepts 'his role' (11). Rodríguez argues that global socioeconomic structures benefit from hampering workers' attempts to improve their quality of life, as their cheap labor is necessary for the system (11). Multilayered borders (transnational, urban, embodied, etc.) are essential in this equation, as they order people according to the money they own and control their mobility, embedding the poor in a set of circumstances that barely leave any time for them to reflect on their situation and to call it into question.

Other recent films such as *Advantageous* (Phang 2015), *Downsizing*, and *Sorry to Bother You* (Riley 2018) also draw attention to the centrality of workers' acquiescence and their acceptance of precarious conditions in the smooth operation of the system. In *Downsizing*, Ngoc Lan Tran attempts to mitigate the suffering of the largely Latino community that surrounds her through her unpaid care but has stopped questioning the system in place after facing repression from the Vietnamese government (which led her to migrate to the US). *Advantageous* presents a context of widespread female under- and unemployment in which its middle-aged Asian American protagonist is given the 'opportunity' of keeping her current position if she undergoes an operation that makes her appearance more "universal" and less "alienating" for potential customers. Coming to grips with an equally dystopian reality, *Sorry to Bother You* revolves around the unionizing efforts of a highly precarious workforce that works for a company that is proud of "selling the cheapest labor in the world" to global clients and benefits from the conditions generated by a nightmarish housing market (which leads people to live in their cars, garages, or in hostel-like corporate facilities). Approaching workers' acquiescence from slightly different angles, these films, together with *In Time*, attest to an increasing preoccupation with global labor markets that often expect people to put up with precarious work conditions.

At the other extreme of *In Time*'s highly compartmentalized society, in New Greenwich, everything people appear to care about is their endless path towards time accumulation. Both Philippe Weis and the broker Henry Hamilton say what seems to be a catchphrase in New Greenwich: "for a few to be immortal, many must die." Such a phrase elucidates that those who belong to the financial sector in the movie seek to increase the amount of time that they own at any cost. This catchphrase also resonates in other recent sf films in which the elongation of some privileged lives comes at the expense of other people's lives. *The Island*, *Daybreakers*, *Transfer*, *Jupiter Ascending*, *Scorch Trials*, and *Self/less* construct narratives in which wealthy people extend their lives thanks to the death (or practical death) of other people or sentient clones, who sometimes live or are from other nations or planets, as in *Transfer*, *Jupiter Ascending*, and *Self/less*. These films, along with *In Time*, show a growing concern with the limits of greed: for a few to enjoy certain privileges, many have to sacrifice their lives.

Another function of networked borders is to protect finance in two senses: they guarantee the safety of those who control capital and reduce the opportunities of people from other areas to make their claims visible, preventing potential risks for financial interests. *In Time* presents what Edward Soja would call a "carceral archipelago" (299). New Greenwich secludes Dayton citizens and voluntarily isolates itself. In this manner, *In Time* depicts a city made up of islands that keep citizens in open-air urban prisons, just like skid rows and gated communities in real LA (Soja 305–6, 312–3). While these areas are very different, their inhabitants live—some willingly, others involuntarily—in confined spaces. Aesthetically, Dayton resembles a prison: workers wear uniforms that are similar to those of convicts, fences and barbwire abound, and gray, washed-out tones predominate. In New Greenwich, most inhabitants are concerned about any possible threat to their safety, are often accompanied by bodyguards, and avoid going to other areas. In addition, timekeepers' cars, which have shooting equipment, are banned from using it in New Greenwich. Saskia Sassen argues that, for global corporations, networked borders (which she calls transversal borders) should protect capital, facilitate its movement, and restrict the mobility of anyone or anything else (2013b, 69). Yet, Sassen also notes that cities are ideal places to make claims visible and question power structures (69–70). Even though acquiescent workers in the film are not likely to draw attention to their situation in public, networked borders further reduce this possibility. They help to keep the system running without being questioned. In this way, *In Time* shows, in a similar way to *Elysium*, that one of the main functions of networked borders is to avoid challenges to the system in place and to ensure the personal safety of those who move capital around.

New Greenwich inhabitants, through their influence on discourses on crime and theft, present Dayton citizens as a threat and conceal the real menace for the largest part of the society: their own abusive practices. Throughout the film, New Greenwich companies, the media, and timekeepers treat Will and Sylvia as criminals. Networked borders in general and embodied borders in particular are essential for this purpose, as they make it easy to identify and label people. That way, authorities can assess the risk that each person poses, depending on where they come from, as Popescu points out in his work on borders (107). Timekeepers assume that Will has stolen the time that he actually received from the broker and that he later won at the casino. The media also report on Will being a murder "suspect" and, later, on Will and Sylvia being "criminals." Bauman denounces that crimes perpetrated by the elites are often ignored and sometimes even go unnoticed (123–4). He asserts that "complicity," "loyalty," and the complexity of some of the legal and financial operations are the most obvious reasons behind their invisibility (123–4). Even though such crimes affect more citizens and on a wider scale than other offenses, Bauman notes that misbehavior at the top is seldom perceived as a threat (123–4). *In Time* reflects such a rationale behind the system, and then lays it bare. Will tells Raymond: "if you guys are looking for stolen time, maybe you should arrest everyone here [at Philippe's mansion]." Will also denounces that there is "mass murder in the ghetto every day." In this manner, the film highlights that acting legally does not imply respecting other people's rights. *In Time* denounces the role of networked borders in framing and criminalizing the poor and points to significant, wide-scale crimes being committed at the top. The criminalization of the poor makes it harder for them to make claims and to challenge the logic of the system.

Challenging Dichotomies and Doing Borderwork

Despite the clear differences between Dayton and New Greenwich, *In Time* does not produce antagonistic images of their dwellers. Early in the film, broker Henry Hamilton decides to give his whole fortune to Will. For Henry, the system does not work anymore. He is 105 years old, has the body of a 25-year-old, and the time/money to enjoy life, but he does not find any incentive to keep on living. In addition, Jaeger (Collins Pennie), one of the timekeepers, questions the orthodox beliefs and decisions of his colleague Raymond throughout the film, empathizing with Dayton citizens. Sylvia also shows that people cannot be as easily classified as networked borders and virtual financial governance do. Being the daughter of the owner of an important bank, she can have everything she wants. Yet, when she meets Will, she realizes that, despite all the money that her family has, they are too fearful to enjoy life. At the same time, she comes to realize how deeply troubling it is to expand their lifetimes at the expense of other people's lives. Sylvia also tells Will: "you must hate me, where I come from;" to which Will responds: "it's nobody's fault what they're born with." This short conversation shows that *In Time* does not demonize any particular group of people. Instead, the film denounces the logic behind the global financial system. Therefore, the image that *In Time* paints is not black and white.

Taking advantage of the maneuvering margin that borders give them, Sylvia and Will challenge the system's status quo and attempt to kickstart a grassroots redefinition of their society. They notice that the uneven distribution of economic resources in the film is directly linked to borders and dispute the idea that an unbalanced distribution of wealth is the natural order. These modern Robin Hoods do not think of their actions as theft crimes. "Think of it as repossession," Will tells a woman. The separation between zones, despite its insidiousness, also allows them to redistribute time more easily. In this sense, they do what Anthony Cooper and Chris Rumford call "borderwork:" borders do not only put limits on their lives, they are also "potential mechanisms of everyday [cosmopolitan] empowerment" (273). *In Time* points towards change as people go out on the streets massively, cross to other areas, and disrupt the normal operation of the system. Meanwhile, timekeepers observe how time markets lose control over other time zones. One of them notes: "it's spreading." Wealth redistribution and the mobility that comes with it become ways of asserting power, claiming rights, and re-appropriating space. In the end, the film hints that citizens at least entertain some hope: they are not indifferent and resigned anymore.

In Time's emphasis on contestation differs from earlier SF classics. David Desser notes that *Metropolis* and the *Star Trek* episode "The Cloud Minders" (Taylor

1969) resort to the figure of a mediator to solve conflicts (89). Another common solution in films like *Fahrenheit 451*, *Zero Population Growth* (Campus 1972), and *Soylent Green* is for the protagonists to leave the dehumanized city (Desser 88–90). Conversely, *In Time* and other recent SF films such as *Upside Down*, *The Hunger Games*, *Elysium*, *Snowpiercer*, and *Sorry to Bother You* offer alternatives that originate at the bottom. These contemporary dystopias present borderwork as a means of alleviating inequalities. Yet, in an article about *In Time* and other recent dystopian films, Mark Fisher wonders whether Will and Sylvia's efforts are "futile or [...] pre-revolutionary" (2012, 31). Certainly, *In Time* and similar films often imagine easy solutions to complex problems, but by developing stark critical portraits of the organization of socioeconomic structures, they give viewers cosmopolitan food for thought. Extrapolating from its social context, *In Time* identifies a specific group of global socioeconomic structures that do not work for most people, explores how they operate and the challenges that they pose, and offers viewers a framework that can help them think about possible ways to address such problems.

In Time presents a world of intense virtual, financial connections and networked borders that order people according to their economic status. The film suggests that these borders contribute to increasing financial revenues through the generalization of debt, the casualization of labor, workers' acquiescence, the protection of financial areas, and the criminalization of the poor. By making these processes visible, *In Time* draws attention to the often-unnoticed role of a socioeconomic sector (finance) that has a deep impact on cosmopolitan questions related to rights, resources, working conditions, welfare, quality of life, and the porosity of borders. At the same time, *In Time* shows the cosmopolitan potential of borderwork as a means of countering the effects of global networks of financial interests. Of course, robbing banks is far from being a realistic solution to the inequalities generated by finance. Yet, the Robin Hood metaphor that *In Time* uses to represent borderwork makes two points clear: first, global finance contributes to the accumulation of disproportionate amounts of wealth by a handful of people. Second, for people to live decently, financial profits need to be controlled. Social awareness of the unchecked power of financial companies is also evident in a recent transnational political initiative that, like *In Time*, has resorted to the Robin Hood metaphor. In 2010, several NGOs launched an international campaign to root for a 0.05% financial transaction tax (FTT) that they called "The Robin Hood Tax" ("The Robin Hood Tax Campaign"). Drawing on their cosmopolitan imaginations, governments would then use the money raised from this tax to fight poverty, climate change, help create jobs, and fund education and health programs both in the tax-collecting countries and abroad. This idea is not new: James Tobin proposed a similar tax on foreign-exchange transactions in the 1970s, but it was not implemented (Felix 57; Buckley 154, 162). While the impact of global finance on people's lives may not have been so evident at the time when Tobin proposed this tax, globalization and telecommunications have brought about systemic changes that now make a tax on global finance necessary

(Buckley 156, 161–2). However, the implementation of this kind of tax has been quite uneven and limited so far, with countries adopting measures at an individual level and thus indirectly creating loopholes.

The ultimate implications of *In Time*'s discourse coincide with the proposals for changes regarding taxation that some scholars have recently made. Ross Buckley notes that financial firms have been the largest beneficiaries of globalization so far and their operations are having a negative impact on poor regions, jobs, and working conditions (166–7). Others have also advocated for similar kinds of (global) taxes on capital that allow no exceptions (Stiglitz 343; Piketty 517–8). While these taxes are more general than the FTT (including also property and business assets), financial transactions are obviously one of their central targets (Stiglitz 348; Piketty 515–8). In all of these cases, the objective of such taxes is to diminish the impact of financial operations/capital accumulation and to use the money raised to curb inequalities (Stiglitz 344–7; Buckley 166–7; Piketty 518). Through the Robin Hood metaphor, *In Time* connects with these debates and points to taxes on financial transactions as a way of doing cosmopolitan borderwork. The film reminds viewers that instead of letting global finance and capital (b)order people, societies need institutions to (b)order finance and capital.

Both *In Time* and *Elysium* engage with a wide variety of concerns that have proliferated in science fiction cinema at the turn of the twenty-first century as a result of the globalization processes and the accompanying financialization and neoliberalization of socioeconomic systems since the 1970s: a general preoccupation with borders, their heterogeneity, superposition, and pervasiveness; economic stratification; precariousness; workers' acquiescence; endless quests for profit and expansion; and extreme profit-making strategies, including the commodification of bodies. Although several other films such as *Code 46*, *Sleep Dealer*, or *Upside Down* also approach these concerns, *Elysium* and *In Time* draw attention to key aspects and phenomena which are often overlooked: the central role of global corporate actors and their means of operation, territorial reconfigurations, the insidiousness of virtual financial governance, and the erosion of public institutions and welfare. The endings of both films seemingly offer viewers a cosmopolitan alternative to the rigidly divided world that they initially present. Yet, they also adopt an ambivalent position towards borders, showing their role in the articulation of global designs at multiple scales, but also perpetuating racial boundaries and proposing patches to the system or simplistic solutions rather than a revision of the function of borders and substantial systemic reform.

Notes

1 Portions of this chapter have been previously published in a different form. A shorter version of the section "*In Time*: Connecting Borders and Global Finance" first appeared in the article "Keeping Workers at a Distance: The Connection Between Borders and Finance in Andrew Niccol's *In Time*" in the journal *Geopolitics*, vol 21, no. 1, 2016, pp. 195–214, https://www.tandfonline.com/doi/full/10.1080/14650045 .2015.1132704. Portions of the article "Dystopias Go Global: The Transnational

Reorganization of Territories and Societies in *Elysium*" in the journal *ELOPE: English Language Overseas Perspectives and Enquiries*, vol 15, no. 1, 2018, pp. 111–25, https://doi.org/10.4312/elope.15.1.111-125 have been brought up to date and included, in a revised form, as part of the section "*Elysium*: Incorporating Markets, Bordering Benefits" in this chapter.

2 See, among others, Appiah (163, 169), Beck (2006, 83–4), Papastergiadis (36–77), and Mezzadra and Neilson (2013, 202–35, 245).

3 For more information on reterritorialization and rebordering practices, see Sassen (2008, 2014), Popescu, and Mezzadra and Neilson (2013). On the networking, personalization, and mobility of borders see Walters, Popescu, and Amilhat-Szary and Giraut. The work of Amoore, Popescu, and Potzch analyzes the growing use of biometrics.

4 For further information on the economic annexation of territories in the historical and present development of capitalism, see Quijano and Wallerstein, Mignolo (2000), and Dickens and Ormrod. On the expansionist logics of neoliberalism and the proliferation of special economic zones (SEZs), see Ong and Mezzadra and Neilson (2013). See also Strauss on extraterritorial concessions and Sassen (2014, 80–116) on foreign land acquisitions. On the automation and privatization of violent force, see Singer, McFate, and Varin.

5 Gabriel Popescu argues that asking this kind of questions contributes to understanding the contexts in which borders evolve (22, 152). David Harvey has also noted the importance of asking similar questions when attempting to develop a cosmopolitan perspective through the analysis of neoliberal globalization (2009, 57–8).

2

GREENING APOCALYPSE

Eco-Conscious Disaster and the Biopolitics of Climate Change

Following the release of *The Day After Tomorrow* (Emmerich) in 2004, several films have used the extrapolative power of science fiction to deal with one of the most pressing global issues: climate change. Since climate change is a group of threats that do not respect national boundaries, affect all countries (to varying degrees), and are sometimes produced by actors hundreds or thousands of miles away from the places that suffer the worst consequences, cosmopolitanism offers a particularly suitable perspective to approach these phenomena. Sf films about climate change go from the desert landscapes of *Young Ones* (Paltrow 2014), the deadly cold of *Snowpiercer* (Bong 2013), and the waste in *Wall-E* (Stanton 2008) to the more spectacular catastrophic events of *2012* (Emmerich 2009) and the galactic searches for resources and habitats in *Avatar* (Cameron 2009) and *Interstellar* (Nolan 2014). Apart from presenting environmental and geographical changes, many of these films suggest that one of the most significant transformations that climate change brings about is the need for large groups of human beings to migrate, find homes far from home, reorganize social structures, survive lethal weather conditions, and even attempt to live in outer space. That is, they point to the biopolitical implications of climate change. These sf films tend to deal with radical environmental transformation through disaster-packed spectacular rides or post-apocalyptic scenarios. In this chapter, I focus on sf disaster films such as *The Day After Tomorrow*, *The Day the Earth Stood Still* (Derrickson 2008), *Godzilla* (Edwards 2014), and *2012* because of their novel combination of the conventions of the sf and disaster film genres to draw attention to ecological concerns in general and the global scope of climate change in particular. *2012*, the film that mounts the largest spectacle in scale in this group, is an example of how spectacle, however mindless it may seem, can also address relevant socio-environmental issues. Using theories on spectacle and biopolitics, I argue that *2012* uses disaster sequences to draw attention to the magnitude, unpredictability, and global scope

DOI: 10.4324/9781003164517-3

of the catastrophic impacts generated by climate change and to explore opposite scenarios of biopolitical privilege and equality through a cosmopolitan lens. The wide range of themes that *2012* touches on also allows me to draw comparisons between it and several other eco-conscious sf films.

Although sf films have dealt with environmental issues at least since the 1950s and recent films share some of their concerns about the environment with twentieth-century sf movies, climate change constitutes an unprecedented challenge in terms of scope and scale. This spate of recent films tends to focus on these time-specific concerns. Following studies on climate change (Frame and Allen, Beck 2009, Giddens, Vanderheiden, Golub and Maréchal, Klein), this chapter relies on the reports published by the Intergovernmental Panel on Climate Change (IPCC), a body that is part of the United Nations and whose main task is to write publicly available reports about climate change for policymakers. Scientists from different parts of the world volunteer to participate in the drafting of IPCC reports drawing on research that is already available. The evidence for human-induced climate change is indisputable. Pointing to a similar temporal framework to that of the acceleration of economic globalization and the rise of neoliberalism from the 1970s to the present, the IPCC 2014 Synthesis Report[1] registers that "about half of the anthropogenic [human-induced] CO_2 emissions between 1750 and 2011 have occurred in the last 40 years," especially from 2000 to 2010 (5). At the same time, the report also reflects that the period from 1983 to 2012 "was likely the warmest thirty-year period of the last 1400 in the Northern Hemisphere" (2) and that the current "atmospheric concentrations of carbon dioxide, methane and nitrous oxide [...] are unprecedented in the last 800,000 years" (4). Despite the frequent equation of 'climate change' and 'global warming,' the term 'climate change' entails a variety of effects that go beyond temperature increase. The IPCC 2014 Synthesis Report mentions environmental impacts such as cold and warm temperature extremes (7), heat waves (8), droughts (8), water scarcity (13), wildfires (7–8), ice-melting, glacier retreat (5), ocean acidification (6), rising sea levels, coastal erosion (7), landslides (15), air pollution (15), heavy precipitation and storms (7, 8, 15), cyclones (8), floods (8), and crop damage (6). In certain scenarios, some crops such as wheat, rice, and maize could disappear regionally or even globally (13). Although the report considers mostly future scenarios, we can already perceive several of these impacts with the current global mean temperature increase of 1.09° C in the period 2011–2020 with respect to 1850–1900 (IPCC 2021, 5). An increase of over 2° C is considered the point at which climate change involves medium to very high risks and begins to pose a serious threat to human life (IPCC 2014, 13).

The changes to our environment are so profound and so clearly forced by human activity (particularly in Western countries) that some scientists are even proposing that humans have provoked the development of a new geological epoch: the Anthropocene. The concept of the Anthropocene was popularized by Paul Crutzen and Eugene Stoermer in 2000 when they argued that human activity was working as "a major geological force" that was (and is) altering ecosystems profoundly (17–18). The Anthropocene constitutes a radical change, as transitions between geological periods do not happen frequently: the previous, post-glacial period—the Holocene—lasted between 10,000 and 12,000 years (Crutzen and Stoermer 17). The concept of the Anthropocene does not only refer to the radical environmental disruption brought about by greenhouse emissions—it also alludes to a whole array of human activities and their impact on the natural functioning of the planet's ecosystems. Accordingly, Crutzen and Stoermer mention events and activities such as population growth, resource consumption (specially water), the burning of fossil fuels, urbanization, land usage, the use of fertilizers in agriculture, species extinction, and the release of "toxic substances in the environment" (17–18). Apart from these, later scientific studies also refer to dam construction, mining, landfills, sediment movement, and the terraforming that cities require (Wilkinson 161–4; Steffen, Crutzen, and McNeill 616–8; Zalasiewicz et al. 836). The idea of the Anthropocene, therefore, suggests that, apart from generating the emissions that produce climate change, humans also perform other activities that unsettle natural forces severely and present environmental challenges for human and non-human life. As Steffen, Crutzen, and McNeill note, the Anthropocene begins in the late eighteenth century with the Industrial Revolution, although they indicate that the impact of human activities has been particularly forceful from the 1950s to the present, a period that they refer to as "the Great Acceleration" (616–8). Since this chapter analyzes the proliferation of environmentally conscious films in the 2000s and 2010s, the term 'climate change' often helps to describe the concerns that these films depict more accurately, although I sometimes use the concept of the Anthropocene to situate questions in a wider framework and refer to broader impacts.

My approach to eco-conscious sf films from a cosmopolitan perspective takes into account the ways in which films draw attention to ecological connections at a transnational level, the kind of knowledge about ecological processes that they offer viewers, and the social and biopolitical dimension of the impacts that they imagine. Regarding the first aspect, Ursula Heise notes the limitations of traditional approaches to the environment based on a local "sense of place" (53–5). Instead, she proposes a shift towards a "sense of planet" that helps to explore transnational "networks of ecological links" while taking local particularities into account (55–6). From a cosmopolitan perspective, understanding the interconnectedness of environmental phenomena is just the beginning. The transnational dimension of climate impacts requires, in addition, extending the range of action and mitigation beyond national borders, both in ethical and pragmatic terms (Beck 2010, 172; Harris 5–6; Skillington 145). Concerning the second element, Ursula Heise suggests that cosmopolitan approaches to the environment should pay attention to the "systemic functioning" of ecology (55). Indeed, only by understanding how the environment works and how climate threats develop can human beings live in sustainable ways that may contribute to the protection of human and non-human lives. To that end, my analysis of disaster in *2012* and other sf films evaluates the kind of ecological knowledge that they offer. In this respect, my analysis may not always draw attention to the connection between disaster and cosmopolitanism. Yet, as Heise suggests, understanding mechanisms (and their mediated representation) contributes to mapping larger connections and so both tasks are essential for the development of a sense of planet (62).

The last aspect of the cosmopolitan approach that this chapter employs reflects the fact that climate change and the Anthropocene are not just about the environment but also about social organization, human and animal well-being, and, ultimately, the right to live (Heise 60–1; Harris 2, 8–11). The focus of this chapter is then not so much on the science of disaster and on whether films get it right or not. Rather, the question is how film stories, their narrative development, and their spectacular scenes draw connections between environmental and social impacts that have cosmopolitan implications. Ulrich Beck's theory of risk society helps to frame this question through its connection of risks and modernity. In the risk society we live in, financial, environmental, and terrorist dangers are not controllable (Beck 2009, 15). These risks do not indicate that the system is malfunctioning. Rather, the dangers of the risk society are a sign of the success of modernity. They are simply side effects that show that the technocapitalist system is working at full speed and fulfilling its purpose (Beck 2009, 8). Beck's link between modernity and risks (climate change) is particularly useful because it also indirectly points to the modern/colonial complex from which cosmopolitan conflicts and possibilities often emerge. As Walter Mignolo notes, coloniality is "the darker side of modernity" (2011, 2). That is, modernity has a colonial dimension. Climate change is no exception: it is produced by modernity and governed by colonial logics. From a cosmopolitan point of view, the colonial side of climate change has two interconnected dimensions: 1. The ruthless exploitation of nature and Earth's resources by humans. 2. The aggravation of already-existing precarious life conditions by industrial/technological economies that are responsible for most emissions and circumvent environmental agreements through practices such as emissions trading. Meanwhile, societies that barely emit damaging gases often bear the brunt of climate change. Responding to these realities from the perspective of cosmopolitan justice, Paul Harris notes the importance of denouncing and restricting the unequal and abusive access of affluent individuals to the planet's resources (2, 7–9).

Social structures and logics are not just relevant in the production of climate risks and impacts but also in their management. Signaling the more dystopian side of climate change, the IPCC warns that climate impacts worsen current problems such as hunger, forced migration, and violence (16) and generate other kinds of impacts that may affect ecosystems, food production, health, livelihood, and economics (7). Even though climate impacts are virtually global in scope, they are unevenly distributed (Beck 2010, 171; IPCC 11–12). In fact, the 50 countries that generate the least emissions—contributing 1% of the global emissions rate—bear the brunt of 90% of the impacts of climate change (Skillington 145). The IPCC points to the particular vulnerability of people living in "developing countries with low income" (15) and of those who "lack the resources for planned migration" (16). At the same time, those who live in certain highly developed areas or who belong to certain social groups can prepare for climate impacts better or move to areas with lower risks without much trouble. A cosmopolitan approach to the uneven social impacts of climate change requires interrogating the colonial logics that generate asymmetrical exposures to climate risks. Some of the key foundations of colonial logics are based on biopolitical aspects. As Sherryl Vint explains, biopolitics establish which "lives [are] deemed 'worth living'" and which ones are "deemed expendable" (2011, 163). In short, the question at stake regarding the interplay between biopolitics and cosmopolitanism is who suffers the consequences of climate change and why. Although contemporary disaster films have developed visual and narrative strategies to portray climate change, not all of them draw attention to its colonial logics and biopolitics. In this chapter, I attempt to draw attention to this dimension of climate change by looking at some films that call for biopolitical readings such as *2012, The Day After Tomorrow, Wall-E, Snowpiercer,* and *Interstellar.*

Getting the Worst Out of Nature

Climate Change in Science Fiction Cinema

Working on the concept of ecology, Pat Brereton argues that ecological considerations have been present in US cinema at least since the 1950s, particularly in the sf genre. He reads films such as *The Beast from 20,000 Fathoms* (Lourié 1953), *Them!* (Douglas 1954), *The Incredible Shrinking Man* (Arnold 1957)—and, I would add, *The Day the Earth Caught Fire* (Guest 1961)—as films that deal with the challenges that humans have to face when adapting to new environments shaped by the side effects of nuclear power (144–9). Other scholars such as J.P. Telotte (2001, 104), Lincoln Geraghty (52), and Mark Bould (2012, 171–2) coincide in identifying the 1970s as a period in which sf films about environmental degradation proliferated. Bould notes that films such as *No Blade of Grass* (Wilde 1970), *Silent Running* (Trumbull 1972), *Z.P.G.* (Campus 1972), and *Soylent Green* (Fleischer 1973), to name four of the most representative cases, dealt with "overpopulation, resource depletion, pollution, habitat destruction[,] and species extinction" (2012, 171). Apart from the widely discussed *Blade Runner* (Scott 1982), the 1980s and 90s also saw other scattered (and seldom commented on) examples that included environmental degradation as part of their narratives. Some of these are *Mad Max* (Miller 1979) and its sequels (1981, 1985), *Steel Dawn* (Hool 1987), *Moon 44* (Emmerich 1990), *Waterworld* (Costner and Reynolds 1995), *Tank Girl* (Talala, 1995), and *The Arrival* (Twohy 1996). These films also show, especially in the case of *Waterworld* and *The Arrival,* emerging concerns about climate change in the form of rising sea levels and rising temperatures respectively.

Sf films about climate change and environmental degradation began to proliferate at the turn of the century, following a decade of deliberation on climate change at the international level—the first UN Framework Convention on Climate Change was held in 1992—and coinciding with the growth of scientific and social consensus around the role of humans in the generation of harmful emissions and other impacts in the first years of the twenty-first century (Steffen, Crutzen, and McNeill 618). When looking at discourses on the environment in contemporary sf cinema, scholars tend to focus on the same movies: *The Day After Tomorrow,*[2] *Avatar,*[3] and occasionally also *Wall-E*[4] and *Snowpiercer.*[5] Yet, a much wider range of sf films reflect, both in overt and unwitting ways, what Mark Bould calls "the Anthropocene unconscious": the repressed awareness of the fact that humans are living in an age of anthropogenic ecological crisis (2021, 15–17). Although the volume *Green Planets: Ecology and Science Fiction* is predominantly devoted to the exploration of literary narratives, Gerry Canavan's introduction hints at some key ways in which contemporary sf films deal with the current environmental crisis. Canavan notes that recent films such as *Wall-E, Daybreakers* (Spierig 2009), *Avatar,* and the short film *Pumzi* (Kahiu 2009) show concern about capitalism's endless quest for growth, entertain hope for magical societal change, or envision ecotopian Earths without humans (2014a, 12–16). More recently, Neil Archer and Kirk Boyle and Dan Mrozowski have identified, in different articles, a group of films that engage with the current climate crisis by looking at outer space. They coincide in analyzing *The Martian* (Scott 2016), *Interstellar, Gravity* (Cuarón 2013), and *Elysium* (Blomkamp 2013) as representative examples of this group of films. By dealing with space exploration, terraforming, or the construction of orbital habitats, these and other films draw attention to the increasing hostility of Earth's environment, even if their narratives seem to obviate ecological realities in some cases. In this way, Archer, Boyle, and Mrozowski show that contemporary sf films sometimes develop narratives about the current environmental emergency in unexpected places.

An even larger number of early twenty-first century sf films imagine eco-catastrophic scenarios that are often governed by new social structures in contexts of resource scarcity, social unrest, refugee camps, and militarization—all situations that present cosmopolitan challenges. That is the case of the scorching, dry scenarios of *Acquaria* (Moraes 2003), *Hell* (Fehlbaum 2011), *The Rover* (Michôd 2014), *Young Ones, Autómata* (Ibañez 2014), *Mad Max: Fury Road* (Miller 2015), *Pumzi, The Last Survivors* (Hammock 2014), *Crumbs* (Llansó 2015), *Dawn* (Hultgreen 2014), and *The Bad Batch* (Amirpour 2016); the ice ages of *Snowpiercer* and *The Colony* (Renfroe 2013); and the decrepit, polluted landscapes, and rubble aesthetics of *Children of Men* (Cuarón 2006), *The Road* (Hillcoat 2009), the short film *The Rising* (Mattukat 2012), and *Index Zero* (Sportiello 2014). Several films feature rising sea levels, super storms, and general ecological instability, including *The Day After Tomorrow, Japan Sinks* (Higuchi 2006), *The World Sinks Except Japan* (Kawasaki 2006), *2012, Tidal Wave* (Youn 2009), the Neo Seoul scenes in *Cloud Atlas* (The Wachowskis and Tykwer 2012), *NUOC 2030* (Nguyen-Vo

2014), *Credence* (Buonaiuto 2015), *Geostorm* (Devlin 2017), and *Blade Runner 2049* (Villeneuve 2017). Other films like *The Host* (Bong 2006), *The Happening* (Shyamalan 2008), and *Train to Busan* (Yeon 2016) focus on the side effects of toxic substances, while space junk becomes life-threatening in *Gravity*.

Developing slightly different concepts, *The Day the Earth Stood Still* (2008), *Godzilla* (2014), *Kong: Skull Island* (Vogt-Roberts 2017), and *Godzilla: King of the Monsters* (Dougherty 2019) feature powerful natural or alien forces that force humans to reconsider their relationship with nature and their environment. *Annihilation* (Gardland 2018) may not come readily to mind when thinking about the global impacts of climate change. Indeed, the ecological scenario that it presents is the consequence of the arrival of an alien flying object to Earth. Yet, the film imagines, like the previous examples, an increasingly common scenario in science fiction: a situation that potentially entails the end of human hegemony on the planet. In this case, the arrival of the alien object implies that all plant and animal species start to randomly mimic and blend with other species that come into contact with them. The film imagines, for example, trees that adopt the shape of humans or humans whose intestines become a sort of moving serpent. Although the phenomenon is originally limited to a coastal area in the US, this mutation keeps expanding and has the potential of becoming a global phenomenon—although the film's ending does not confirm, nor deny, this possibility. Other films like *Red Planet* (Hoffman 2000), *Wall-E*, *Avatar*, *Cargo* (Engler and Etter 2009), *Pandorum* (Alvart 2009), *Moon* (Jones 2009), *Exaella* (Oudot 2011), *After Earth* (Shyamalan 2013), *Elysium*, *Interstellar*, and *Terra Formars* (Miike 2016) pose questions about alternatives to life on an Earth where life is no longer possible or presents many challenges. They often revolve around the possibility of building life environments outside Earth and the side effects of extracting resources in outer space (and by extension, also on Earth). Even though most of these films present their stories as part of a global scenario, their narratives are often confined to a single location. Only a few of them—*The Day After Tomorrow*, *The World Sinks Except Japan*, *The Day the Earth Stood Still*, *2012*, *Elysium*, *Snowpiercer*, *Godzilla*, and *Geostorm*—make connections between the main location in the film and other places around the world.

Spectacular Disaster, Global Narratives, and Eco-Consciousness

Most of the aforementioned films, except *Elysium* and *Snowpiercer*, are disaster films and participate in a tradition of *science fiction* disaster movies of situating their stories in a global framework. Disaster films, in general, actually tend to focus on specific local sites of destruction. That is the case with disaster classics such as *Airport* (Seaton and Hathaway 1970), *The Poseidon Adventure* (Allen and Neame 1972), *Earthquake* (Robson 1974), and *The Towering Inferno* (Allen and Guillermin 1974) (Keane 16–17; Thompson 12) and even more recent films such as *Twister* (de Bont 1996), *Titanic* (Cameron 1997), *Poseidon* (Petersen 2006),

The Impossible (Bayona 2012), and *San Andreas* (Peyton 2015). Although Kirsten Thompson draws attention to the global scope of 1990s disaster films (12), this global scope is also present in disaster films from previous decades such as *Deluge* (Feist 1933), *When Worlds Collide* (Maté 1951), *The Day the Earth Stood Still* (Wise 1951), *The Day the Earth Caught Fire, Meteor* (Neame 1979) and in 1990s films such as *Independence Day* (Emmerich 1996), *Godzilla* (Emmerich, 1998), *Armageddon* (Bay, 1998), and *Deep Impact* (Leder, 1998). Although post-1990 films feature prominently in this list, it is clear that it is actually sf—rather than the 1990s—that brings a transnational sensibility to the disaster genre.

Many of these sf disaster films include variations on montage sequences that feature several cities from different countries (often through their famous landmarks) being affected by similar events as the ones that take place in the city or area on which the film focuses most of the time. Through this kind of global montage, films imply that the events that they are showing have a global impact. However, seen from a cosmopolitan perspective, the global montage tends to include images of industrial nations only. In addition, the global scope and context of the disasters that these films imagine is often also limited—as in the case of most non-sf disaster films—by their focus on a specific location, often a major city such as London or New York. In the first years of the twenty-first century, films such as *The Day After Tomorrow* and the remake of *The Day the Earth Stood Still* continue to rely on the global montage, while others such as *Godzilla* and *2012* go one step forward and have their stories actually take place in several places around the globe. In this way, sf disaster films seem to be slowly shifting away from global montages and moving towards scripts in which the action, narrative, and spectacle take place in different parts of the world, although US cities continue to be central locations in the narrative.

Apart from drawing on the tradition of planetary awareness in sf disaster movies, twenty-first-century sf movies also exploit the traditional reliance of disaster movies on the spectacular qualities of disaster to address the more recent challenges of anthropogenic environmental degradation. Contemporary sf disaster movies rework a tradition of showing how aliens, monsters, technological miscalculations, floods, quakes, fires, volcano eruptions, tornadoes, and other natural forces destroy cities and civilizations to deal with the harsh socio-environmental impacts and radical transformation that result from human activities. While the effectiveness of framing the Anthropocene through spectacular disasters may be questionable, it is evident that the use of disaster images to deal with anthropogenic environmental degradation is widespread. Apart from sf cinema, scientific studies, the media, and documentaries also rely on the spectacular potential of disaster images to inform and warn about the effects of anthropogenic ecological damage and climate change. Spectacular images of disaster draw people's attention because what they show are (so far) rare occurrences whose magnitude is greater than the norm.

It is indeed no coincidence that it was an sf film that relied heavily on disaster (*The Day After Tomorrow*) that first allowed a number of political and media agents to change the public perception of climate change. As Stephen Rust demonstrates, following the release of the film, the media (e.g. *Newsweek*, *Time*) turned their attention to climate change. Between 1991 and 2007, the number of people in the US who recognized climate change as a real threat more than doubled, rising to 84% by 2007 (Rust 197–8). Rust points out that, although the film did not directly influence audiences in this respect, it generated a discursive impulse that allowed other media to draw attention to climate change (199–200). Since *The Day After Tomorrow* was released, *The Day the Earth Stood Still* (2008), *2012*, *Godzilla* (2014), *Geostorm*, and, to a lesser extent, the B-movie *The World Sinks Except Japan* have linked the spectacles of disaster that they present to their climate change narratives. Even though *2012* is not explicitly about climate change, I pay special attention to it because most of its narrative and spectacle touch directly on the cosmopolitan challenges that environmental disruption presents and because the scale, magnitude, and variety of the spectacle in it are beyond that of any of the aforementioned films. Apart from this, *2012* was a widely popular film in its year of release (2009), ranking fifth in the global box office in a highly competitive year (*Avatar* and films of the *Harry Potter* and *Transformers* franchises were also released) ("2009 Worldwide Grosses").[6] Despite its popularity, many scholars and critics tend to deride the film, particularly because of its over-the-top spectacle (Dargis; Rodríguez Ortega 118; Gomel 118–20; Lebovic 6; Pirro 410). This chapter reads disaster in *2012* and other films closely to show the critical possibilities that disproportionate spectacle offers.

In the cinema and particularly in sf cinema, spectacle plays a more relevant role than is often acknowledged. Building on Tom Gunning's work on the cinema of attractions and concentrating on the evolution of science fiction cinema, Brooks Landon argues that sf "has its roots in spectacle rather than narrative" (xiv). For Landon, sf spectacle represents what he calls an "aesthetics of ambivalence" (xxv, 157).[7] He argues that "the technological accomplishment of the [sf] film sends quite a different message than does its narrative" and encourages other scholars to try and look for connections between the uses of technology and special effects in films in the same way that they often try to organize their arguments around narrative patterns (xxv, 147–8). Brooks Landon shows, from a technological perspective, the centrality and meaningfulness of spectacle in sf films.

Brooks Landon's work, while still highly relevant and unique in the way he points to the critical possibilities of analyzing spectacle in sf cinema, predicts a course of development and growth for visual technologies in 1992 that has not quite come to fulfillment (207). This is evident in Michele Pierson's work on special effects in sf cinema. Pierson and Landon paint a similar landscape regarding computer-generated imagery, virtual reality, simulation, and special effects in general in the 1980s and early 1990s, as they both focus on titles that rely heavily on the new technologies available at their time such as *Tron* (Lisberger 1982), *The Abyss* (Cameron 1989), *Terminator 2: Judgment Day* (Cameron 1991), *Lawnmower Man* (Leonard 1992), *Jurassic Park* (Spielberg 1993), and *Johnny Mnemonic* (Longo

1995) (Landon 145–60, Pierson 93–130). They both identify a tendency to self-reflexively call attention to the novelty of the CGI effects in these films. Yet, Pierson notes a shift towards the seamless integration of CGI effects both in the shot and in the narrative in mid-1990s cinema (131–49). She explains that in *Independence Day*, *The Fifth Element* (Besson 1997), and *Godzilla* (1998), among others, CGI effects no longer have a technological aesthetic. They become part of "complex composite shots" along with more traditional elements such as "models and miniatures" and generate a variety of styles, including B-grade, retro, and camp aesthetics (Pierson 135–47). Consequently, it is not so easy to identify the special effects in the film anymore. Pierson's arguments advance an idea that scholars such as David Bordwell, Keith Johnston, and Mark Bould have emphasized since then: narrative and spectacle intertwine and tend to work in the same direction both throughout the history of cinema in general and particularly in the current blockbuster-dominated era (Bordwell 105–6; Johnston 42, 46–7; Bould 2012, 67–9).

Although the industry has further evolved in the 13 years that separate the release of *Independence Day* and *2012* (e.g. models are hardly ever used nowadays), Michelle Pierson's argument about the integration of effects and other narrative elements in the shot still applies to the sf disaster films analyzed in this chapter. In an interview in the July 2016 issue of the media magazine *Empire*, Roland Emmerich acknowledges that shooting *2012* with a digital camera allowed him to develop some images and ideas that would have been impossible to produce when he made *Independence Day* (Smith 67). Yet, *2012* (like *The Day After Tomorrow*, *The Day the Earth Stood Still*, *Godzilla* [2014], and *Geostorm*) is not about showing the power of CGI. Continuing the course initiated by *Independence Day*, the CGI in these films is seamlessly integrated into the narrative. Although my analysis of *2012* and other films in this chapter emphasizes the prominence of spectacle, I do not do so to claim that the narrative is irrelevant. Rather, I offer a reading of the interrelation of narrative and spectacle in the cosmopolitan, biopolitical, and environmental discourses that the aforementioned films develop.

In Case You Didn't See It Coming: Climate Change Disaster in *2012*

Roland Emmerich's filmography invites us to consider *2012* from an environmental perspective and to situate it in the context of the Anthropocene. From the very beginning of his career, Emmerich's films have shown environmental concerns. His first film, *Noah's Ark Principle* (1984), revolves around a US-European joint venture to operate a space station from which these geopolitical actors try to alter and control Earth's climate. The opening shot of *Moon 44* informs viewers that "by the year 2038, all natural resources on Earth have been depleted." Continuing this eco-conscious trend, the protagonist in *Independence Day* (Jeff Goldblum) is an environmentalist that literally cycles into the office and reminds everyone that they must recycle. Emmerich's remake of *Godzilla* (1998) also includes environmental references. After seeing the first steps of the giant lizard on the rampage in New York, a camera recording a story for television slowly tilts up to show a hole in the middle of the Met Life building, which frames the sky in the background. Bearing in mind that the Kyoto protocol (which sought to stop the enlargement of the ozone layer hole) was signed the year before the release of the film, such a framing of the sky through a hole seems a clear, if isolated, allusion to ozone depletion in the film. Stephen Keane also offers an environmental reading of this film, noting that Godzilla seems to "bring the [bad] weather with him" and sometimes "appears to cofound the storm," even though the film presents this as "accidental disaster" (86–7). More recently, Emmerich has also directed the previously mentioned *The Day After Tomorrow* and produced *Hell*, which projects, through blinding lighting, a future in which Earth temperatures go up 10°C, putting an end to rainfall and ruining all crops. The regular references to environmental issues in Emmerich's filmography, along with the scenes of natural disaster in *2012* and the similarities between the development of its narrative and of climate change, call for a reading of the film through the lens of the Anthropocene.

2012 features a series of earthquakes, volcano eruptions, tsunamis, and side effects such as flying cars and trains, collapsing skyscrapers, sinking freeways and runways, crushed landmarks, and planes about to crash. The film focuses on the attempts of a US American family to survive as they travel from the US to China and then to South Africa. Other main characters include US American scientist Adrian Helmsley (Chiwetel Ejiofor) and White House Chief of Staff Carl Anheuser (Oliver Platt), who adopt different approaches towards the management of the crisis. Although at first sight the series of disasters that unfold through *2012* may not seem connected to climate change or to anthropogenic environmental degradation, the use of spectacle in the film, narrative developments, and some subtle references to ecological deterioration invite to read the film as a reference to the effects of the human exploitation of nature. The beginning of the film includes some subtle but clear references to anthropogenic impact on the environment. For example, people hold signs with messages such as "Stop oil sucking" and "People's planet" in a demonstration that precedes a G8 meeting in Canada. Later on, an earthquake scene in LA situates the action in the film in a context of ecosystemic degradation when a billboard that reads "Heal the Bay" and displays a giant fish skeleton appears as the freeway collapses. Towards the end of the film, a giant wave literally erases a field full of planes, wiping out one of the main emitters of warming gases. This is only a small sample of the references that the film includes. Apart from the connections that these examples establish with anthropogenic environmental degradation, scientific discourses in the film resemble discourses about climate change in real life. For instance, in one of the first scenes in the film, Carl Anheuser mocks Adrian's insistence on the importance and urgency of the information that he wants to provide. In addition, the forecasts that *2012* includes turn out to be too optimistic in most cases. At one point, Adrian exclaims: "I thought we had more time." Through these discursive parallels with climate change and subtle references to ecological damage, *2012* invites viewers to approach the story through the prism of the Anthropocene.

Mirroring Ecological Realities and Envisioning Catastrophes

Recent scientific studies have suggested that there is a connection between human actions, their impact on the environment, and certain unforeseen disasters of the kind that appear in *2012* (earthquakes, volcano eruptions, and tsunamis). In this sense, the film points, by chance, to the unexpected consequences of climate change. In connection with the first major disaster scene of the film (that of the LA earthquake), geophysicist William Ellsworth links earthquakes in areas that are not especially prone to earthquakes to human activity, particularly to water disposal as part of hydraulic fracturing (fracking). He also notes that "earthquakes throughout the world are also recognized to be associated with mining, petroleum and gas production, and geothermal energy extraction" (6). Ellsworth mentions examples in Oklahoma (USA), Konya (India), Wenchuan (China), and Lorca (Spain) as cases in which earthquakes may have been connected to intense resource extraction (6). In the book *Waking the Giant: How a Changing Climate Triggers Earthquakes, Tsunamis, and Volcanoes* (2012), Bill McGuire, one of the authors of the 2011 IPCC Report and former member of the UK Government Natural Hazards Working Group, argues that the impact of human activities in the environment can lead to certain kinds of disaster that involve elements (e.g. the Earth's crust) that so far have not been considered to be connected to climate change, or more generally, the Anthropocene. Thus, the mega-earthquakes, volcano eruptions, and tsunamis that appear in *2012*, despite their magnitude, may not be so detached from potential climate change futures. Their appearance and their order in the narrative development of the film are not arbitrary either. The natural forces in all the major disaster scenes in the film are connected to the movement of the Earth's crust. The film shows a possible—even if exaggerated in proportion—chain of reactions: earthquakes can trigger volcano eruptions and tsunamis. Even though *2012* does not explicitly link these images of disaster to human activity and climate change, it draws attention to the interconnection of natural elements and the unpredictability of environmental impacts in the Anthropocene. In this sense, the film throws light on ecological mechanisms that are, however simplistic, essential to grasp the scope of climate change and contribute to building a cosmopolitan sense of planet.

The film does not only offer opportunities to read environmental disasters from the perspective of scientific predictions—it also makes implicit visual connections to already-perceptible scenarios of climate change. Some of the sequences in *2012* resemble the images of environmental disasters that regularly appear in the news and reflect the kinds of threats that people are beginning to experience as a consequence of climate change. The earthquake scenes, however, are an exception, as they bear little resemblance to widespread images of climate change. Nonetheless, certain parts of the volcano eruption in the film visually resemble some of the amateur video footage of the 2016 Fort McMurray wildfires in Alberta (Canada) that the media disseminated (Decker, Sabovitch, and Edmonson). Both in these real images of people fleeing their homes in their vehicles and in the extreme long shots and long shots first of Jackson (John Cusack) and then of a small airplane flying away from the fire, a cloud of ashes and fire fills the entire screen. As in the case of other increasingly frequent major wildfires in Australia, Brazil, Siberia, Spain, and the US, the conditions that originated the Canada fires were aggravated by anthropogenic climate change: rising temperatures, drought, and land use (McGrath, The Associated Press). In addition, the film also includes drying landscapes. When Jackson and his children visit Yellowstone, they find a very different image of the lake that Jackson had visited before: the trees around it are dying, most of the water has vanished, the shores have receded, and steam comes out of the ground. As the family approaches the lake, the film includes a close-up of a dead deer and the sound of flies hovering around it. This close-up also reveals cracks in the soil and emphasizes the drought that the area is suffering. Similar images of dead donkeys and goats in Somaliland appeared in the media in November 2015 after the country, which is used to enduring droughts, saw their impact rising to catastrophic levels (McCabe). Several of the images of disaster and ecological crisis in *2012* therefore resemble actual images of the impacts of climate change.

2012's disaster scenes also draw connections to climate impacts that involve water and ice. The end of the earthquake sequence in LA visually resembles a different kind of environmental disaster and one of the best-known signs of climate change: the melting of glaciers. After the protagonists take off from the Santa Monica airport and fly past a train that has been sent flying and, moments later, between two towers, the film includes an extreme long shot of the Santa Monica Pier sinking into the ocean. This shot is followed by an even more spectacular shot from a further distance in which not only Santa Monica, but also its neighboring areas appear onscreen (Figure 2.1). In this shot, the ground on which Santa Monica stands has shifted from its original horizontal position to a 30-degree inclined angle, which slowly makes the city sink into the sea,

FIGURE 2.1   The sinking of Santa Monica mirrors the melting of a glacier in *2012* (Emmerich 2009).

mirroring the melting of Antarctic glaciers. Towards the end of the shot, part of the city dislodges from the main piece of ground and drifts off, drawing a visual connection to the chunks of ice that detach from glaciers and have become a symbol of the global average rise in temperatures. Apart from this, the tsunamis in the film also work as a reference to anthropogenic climate disruption. Although audiences may not readily identify tsunamis (both in the film and in real life) with climate change, they may connect the threatening character of water out of control in the film with the floods that have begun to increasingly affect many countries in recent years and the rising sea levels that already threaten the inhabitants of some islands such as Bhola Island in Bangladesh (Braasch) and will likely affect mainland coastal populations in the future. Indeed, Emmerich's earlier film, *The Day After Tomorrow*, overtly presents the waves that flood New York City as a consequence of anthropogenic emissions. Despite the lack of explicit reference to climate change in *2012*, the thematic resemblance of several of the disaster scenes (drought, fire, water out of control) to the aforementioned real anthropogenic disasters sketches a landscape of severe climate disruption.

Staging Climate Change: The Domino Effect and Global Action

In tune with scientific warnings about the effects of climate change, the different major disasters in *2012* are interconnected and part of the film's construction of a cosmopolitan sense of planet. A double graphic match of a ship being flipped over evinces the discourse of global interconnection. The first graphic match takes place between two shots separated by 91 minutes of screen time and the second one between shots in two adjoining scenes. The first instance of this graphic match appears in the first scene in the film when a child is playing with a toy ship in a yard full of puddles in the Naga Deng Copper Mine in India. The moment that becomes part of a graphic match later in the film is when a car driving by the kid flips the toy ship over to one side, giving the impression that the ship has been hit by a wave and is sinking. This mock disaster that opens the film advances what happens later in two contiguous scenes set off the coast of Japan and in Washington DC, respectively. Mimicking the first scene in India, the first giant wave to appear in the film literally flips over the cruise ship in which the father of the main scientist in the film works as a singer. The next scene opens with the President of the United States lying on the floor as it snows. Shortly after, a shot of a wave carrying a US navy ship follows. As the previous shot hints, the wave is headed towards the White House. In the same way as in the cruise ship scene in the sea of Japan and in the Indian copper mine, the wave flips the ship over, crushing the White House and symbolically destroying a key center of contemporary geopolitics. Through this graphic match that creates a sense of continuity between three distant places, *2012* points to the global scope, interconnectedness, and inescapability of disaster in the age of climate change.

    2012 also relies on other visual effects to present its disasters as part of a chain reaction or domino effect of ecological alteration. The domino-like dynamics of environmental disruption are implied in the first disaster scene, in which the beginning of the earthquake in LA emulates the movement of a wave, alluding to the tsunamis that appear later in the film. In a later scene, camera and in-frame movement reinforce the idea of disaster connectivity by emulating the swiveling movement of a fan: just a few seconds before the conspiracy-paranoid Charlie Frost (Woody Harrelson) is about to witness the eruption of the Yellowstone caldera on site, the off-focus mountain in the background begins to quickly spin to the right as the camera pans in the same direction. This effect gives the impression that the landscape is revolving around Charlie and that the mountains will act as a fan, spreading the soon-to-erupt ash and the lava to other places. Indeed, later on, Hawaii becomes an active volcano and pockets of smoke and fire spread through Las Vegas. The swiveling camera and in-frame movement therefore hints that no place is going to be left untouched by the upcoming disaster. In his analysis of *The Day After Tomorrow*, Stephen Keane notes that the film "has an accelerating and accumulative sense of spectacle as it follows the natural enough snowball effect of global environmental failure" (98). While this effect is implied in the narrative of *The Day After Tomorrow*, *2012* amplifies it by including obvious visual references to it. After the main dome of the Vatican collapses, it rolls on the ground, replicating the movement of a snowball. Later on, the aforementioned ships being flipped over by waves carry out a similar circular movement. Following the scene of the cruise ship being hit by the wave, the film introduces the post-earthquake scenario in Washington DC through a shot featuring a spinning wheel in the right corner of the frame, again showing a similar kind of movement. The idea of snowballing disaster is reinforced by the dialogues between those who monitor the disaster crisis. After the Vatican collapses, Carl Anheuser asks: "so, what happens next?" Through these examples, *2012* suggests that the unleashing of certain natural forces produces chain reactions that spread disaster around the world.

Apart from visually pointing to the interconnectedness and domino effect of disaster in the Anthropocene, *2012* emphasizes the global dimension of environmental threats through the organization of its narrative. Like many sf disaster films, *2012* relies on the popular global montage to render a sense of worldwide impact. The film includes the traditional sf news montage, which in this case features earthquakes in South America, the statue of Christ the Redeemer in Rio de Janeiro crumbling, riots in London, people praying in Mecca, and people of different faiths marching on the streets in the US. Yet, the film takes a step further by making its action global. Although this is an aspect that develops gradually throughout the film, the first 17 minutes clearly establish the global scope of the action through a series of short scenes edited together that take place around the world (although only in the Northern Hemisphere). After the first scene, which shows a series of solar flares erupting from the sun, the next 15 minutes show different groups of people preparing (some unknowingly) for the catastrophe to come in nine different locations and contexts, including a copper mine in India where two of the three main scientists in the film discover temperature anomalies, a fundraising event in Washington DC, a G8 Summit in British Columbia (Canada), the expropriation of land by foreign governments in Tibet, a suite in a London Hotel in which an Arab king considers buying tickets on the arks to be built, the replacement of the Mona Lisa painting at the Louvre Museum in Paris, mass suicide in Guatemala following the predictions of the Mayan calendar, a series of scenes in Los Angeles in which the protagonist, Jackson Curtis, and his family are introduced, and two musicians boarding a Japan-bound cruise ship in San Francisco. These opening scenes boldly situate *2012*'s narrative in a context of global impacts and transnational responses. In addition, some of these scenes include easily identifiable markers such as nationality, race, income, and social position which hint at the film's cosmopolitan concern with people's unequal chances at survival.

The global scope of the action in the film is further reinforced by making the main characters move around the globe or placing their friends, colleagues, and relatives in different parts of the world. In their quest for survival, Jackson, his children, his ex-wife, and her new husband travel from their suburban LA home to the Santa Monica airport, then Yellowstone, Las Vegas, Hawaii, China, and finally, the Cape of Good Hope (South Africa). Through their trip, the film shows the impact of different but interrelated kinds of disaster around the world. In most sf disaster films, the main catastrophes often happen wherever the protagonists are—not in global montage sequences. Although this applies to the three major disaster scenes in *2012*, the film makes use of its secondary characters to introduce additional disaster scenes around the globe. After the earthquakes in LA and Las Vegas that affect the protagonists, a later sequence introduces further earthquakes in Japan, Washington DC, and the Vatican. The scene in Japan registers a phone conversation between a singer (George Segal) and his family in Japan, while he is working on the same cruise ship as Adrian's father (Blu Mankuma). The scene in Washington DC focuses on the US president, who decides to stay with the regular people. Even though the film does not feature any familiar character in the Vatican scene, Anheuser says in the previous scene that the Italian Prime Minister also decided to stay home and pray (which justifies the inclusion of this scene). In this way, these earthquakes are connected to the main line of action in the film and the characters involved in it. Similarly, the tsunami in India features Satnam Tsurutani (Jimi Mistry), the scientist who discovered temperature anomalies (and who is a friend of Adrian), and the tsunami scene in Tibet features a monk (Henry O) who is the teacher of the main character in the Tibet scenes: Nima (Osric Chau). Nima is also connected to the protagonists, as he later crosses paths with Jackson and his family and helps them to sneak into the ark. The aforementioned tsunamis in the sea of Japan and Washington DC, the previous earthquakes in these two areas, and the tsunamis in Tibet and India (which are not edited together) all affect secondary characters and potentially build a sense of identification in viewers that could not be achieved by simply including random references to other places around the world in dialogues or in news broadcasts. Additionally, this allows the filmmakers to show how the same kind of disaster impacts different parts of the planet.

What Are the Odds? The Development and Consequences of Climate Change

Apart from emphasizing the global dimension of climate change, *2012* also highlights some other key characteristics: its imminence, the impossibility of predicting all its effects, their unavoidability, the apparently invisible development, accumulation, and escalation of the side effects of environmental disruption in a context of inaction, and the threat they pose to modern, technology-dependent lifestyles. In this section, I explore each of these aspects in detail and compare *2012* with other recent sf films. Regarding the last aspect, *2012* compresses time to emphasize the devastating consequences of the often-imperceptible development of cumulative alterations to ecosystems over time. As Anthony Giddens notes, the effects of climate change "aren't tangible, immediate or visible in the course of day-to-day life" and people therefore tend not to worry about a danger that they cannot clearly perceive (2). Similarly, in his keynote address at the 2016 Conference of the Science Fiction Research Association, Andrew Milner noted that the fact that climate change is slow is also a problem for its narrative representation. He observed that a way of solving this problem is by setting the events in the narrative after the catastrophe. Yet, sf film narratives, using the genre's ability to play with time and space and relying on viewers' willingness to suspend disbelief, may accelerate catastrophic processes to draw attention to the impending (even if slow and hard to notice) impacts that climate change is already producing. The accumulation of the spectacular scenes of destruction in *2012* and their large scale are not just disaster for the sake of it: they point, in a metaphorical way, towards the often-disregarded disruption that climate change will likely cause in life on Earth and in modern developments.

Several disaster scenes in *2012* show ecosystems giving signs of their critical state and the scarce time left to reverse disastrous environmental processes. Before viewers witness the beginning of the cascading series of disasters that develops throughout the film, a dead deer lying on a patch of land affected by drought and steam coming from the ground in Yellowstone hint at the rising temperature of the ground. These occurrences feature as early signs of the volcano eruption that will happen in this area and of the major changes that this ecosystem, according to Jackson, has gone through. In a later scene in Yellowstone, just before lava and ash erupt from the Yellowstone mountains, an extreme long shot shows large bumps of ground swelling as if the planet were about to burst (as the area eventually does). This visual effect underlines the pressure that the planet is subject to. *2012* and the remake of *The Day the Earth Stood Still* also rely on cracking window glass as a metaphor for the fragility of human life and the ecological and technocultural systems that support it (Gómez-Muñoz 137). When one of the arks hits Mount Everest in *2012*, the crash unleashes an avalanche of rocks that hit the main window of the ark's control room as the ark reverses its course and avoids a fatal outcome for the collision. The cracked glass, along with the aforementioned details in Yellowstone, work as metaphors that present a planet in critical condition and on the brink of disaster.

Once the chain reaction of disasters that appear in *2012* has been unleashed, the film introduces several last-minute actions that save the protagonists from the deadly impact of the different disasters, particularly, the tsunami. Although in-the-nick-of-time rescues and flights are common in cinema (see Williams 33–5), *2012* features a remarkable number of situations in which the protagonists narrowly escape from nature's deadly forces. That is the case of the drive through LA during the earthquake, the take-offs from LA, Yellowstone, and Vegas, the scene in an ark in which a gate malfunction is about to flood the vessel and make it sink, and the partial collision of the ark with Mount Everest. This last scene is the one that most clearly represents popular perceptions of climate change at the time that the film was released: it suggests that there will likely be some impacts, but it is possible to mitigate or even reverse this situation. The allusion to climate change in this scene is not only evident in the metaphorical use of the cracking glass mentioned before and the last-minute intervention analyzed below, but also in its visual reference to glaciers, whose melting has become one of the most noticeable effects of climate change. Despite the fact that the ark hits Mount Everest, detail shots of the icy surface of the mountain and of the collision give the impression that the ark crashes into a glacier. After one of the giant waves hits the ark carrying the protagonists, the ark approaches a side of Mount Everest as a computer informs viewers that the ark is only 50 meters, then 40 meters from it. The ark eventually hits the mountain and yet, shortly after that, the computer again informs passengers and viewers that the ark is reversing its course and is first 10 meters away from the mountain and then 20 meters away from it. This scene shows that the impacts of the wave and the mountain have caused some damage to the ark, but it is still operational. The scene also suggests that a certain amount of damage is unavoidable: the ark reverses its course several meters before hitting the side of the mountain and yet it still collides with it. By including this kind of event as the last disaster scene in the film, *2012* suggests that climate change offers little time to react and its consequences are unavoidable. Yet, at the same time, it also suggests that these impacts can be diminished with the right preparation and, literally, with a change of navigational/environmental course.

2012 and Emmerich's previous eco-conscious film, *The Day After Tomorrow*, also come up with concepts that challenge common environmental patterns as a kind of narrative spectacle that draws viewers' attention towards the unexpected effects of climate change. Keith Johnston notes that spectacle extends beyond special effects and may also include star personae, music, set designs, and clothes (47–9). Concepts also can be spectacular, as they draw our attention by presenting unusual ideas or events. A scene at the beginning of *The Day After Tomorrow* illustrates how concepts serve as spectacle when a series of tornadoes rampage LA, including its well-known Hollywood Sign and Capitol Records Building.

In this scene, a reporter says: "yes, a twister in Los Angeles," pointing at the unlikeliness of this event taking place. Emmerich uses a similar technique of conceptual dislocation in *2012*. Even though the LA area is earthquake-prone, the Yellowstone caldera can erupt, and tsunamis in the Pacific can be particularly devastating (as in the 2004 catastrophe), the magnitude of these events highlights the unpredictability of the environment in the film. Apart from the appearance of disasters themselves onscreen, *2012* develops spectacular concepts through dialogues (mostly between scientists and politicians) and screen animations added in post-production to economically point at the difficulty of predicting the nature, scale, scope, location, and development of the disasters that climate change brings about. These dialogues and animations show unexpected side effects and scientific miscalculations, including the propagation of earthquakes around the world, the destabilization of the Pacific plate, the displacement of the Earth's crust by 1,000 miles, the course and speed of giant waves, and the Drakensberg Mountains in South Africa becoming the highest peak in the world instead of Mount Everest. In one of the arks that appear towards the end of the film, scientists brief a politician about the development of the global catastrophe. A scientist explains: "The Earth poles have reversed magnetic fields," to which the politician replies: "So, you're telling me that the North Pole is now somewhere in Wisconsin?" A scientist responds: "Actually, that's the South Pole now," further reinforcing the sense of unpredictability of the transformation of the environment in the film and in the current era of climate change. As characters say these words, the mise-en-scène features animated screens illustrating the radical geographical dislocation that they discuss. The unbelievable character of the concepts and spectacles of disaster in *2012* is therefore not just a strategy to generate awe in the viewer but also to draw attention to the unpredictable and unexpected consequences of climate change.

2012's spectacular concepts and images of destruction capture the threat that climate disruption poses for all kinds of lifestyles, be they urban or rural. Yet, the film particularly emphasizes how environmental threats can shatter the developments of technological and urban modernity. At the G8 meeting at the beginning of the film, the US president could not be clearer about the challenge that the world faces in the film. He says: "The world as we know it will soon come to an end." Of course, by "the world as we know it," he refers to modern ways of life and comforts. The main scientist in *Godzilla* (2014) (played by Bryan Cranston) shares similar concerns, forecasting that the natural forces unleashed by Godzilla are going to "send [them] back to the Stone Age." Such comments also hint at the emergence of a world where cosmopolitan considerations are likely to dwindle in the face of struggles for resources and survival.

2012, as it is usual in disaster cinema, creates havoc through collapsing buildings and landmarks, crumbling roads, explosions, and rubble. Less common is the appearance of vehicles falling from the sky or flying, which in this case indicate the foundering of modernity. This is most evident in the earthquake scene in LA, in which parking lots appear to vomit cars (Figure 2.2), giving the impression that the city

FIGURE 2.2 In *2012* (Emmerich 2009), freeways collapse and parking lots vomit cars, showing the inability of the planet to cope with more cars and the collapse of modernity in the city.

cannot take any more of them. The film also has a truck crash against a gas station, setting it on fire. The destruction in this scene seems to be particularly directed at modern means of transport (cars) and their source of power (oil), which are responsible for many of the emissions that have contributed to climate change and continue to do so. Later, as the protagonists fly away from LA on a small plane, a train flies past them diagonally from the back to the front of the screen in the process of crashing against the ground. The unbelievable trajectory of this train reinforces the emphasis of this sequence on the malfunction of the modern capitalist system and its technical developments. Mark Bould notes that throughout the history of sf, trains have been first an object that inspired awe and later a symbol of "democratising politics" (2012, 63–4). The contrast between these generalized uses of the train in sf and the one in *2012* emphasizes the potential (and ever more likely) collapse of modernity under the impact of climate change. Vehicles out of control also feature in *The Day After Tomorrow*. In this film, tornadoes make cars and buses fall from the sky and wreck airplanes on the tarmac, while the extreme cold makes the machinery of several helicopters fail, making them crash. The appearance of this motif in Emmerich's two most clearly eco-conscious films establishes vehicles out of control as a symbol of the fragility of modernity and of the threat that climate change poses to it. *2012* shows that disruptions to the climate and ecosystems challenge the mobility and fast-paced, have-all-you-want lifestyles associated with modern vehicles. In addition, the film ironically and literally smashes and blows up one of the major sources of the problem: contemporary means of transport that burn fuel and emit exhaust fumes.

The Ambivalence of Disaster in *2012*

Despite the references to the spatiotemporal dynamics that the current planetary ecological crisis is bringing about and to the malfunctioning of modernity, *2012*, unlike other recent sf disaster films, obscures the causes of climate change. This, in turn, undermines the cosmopolitan attempt of the film of making environmental impacts and their transnational dimension visible. The film never links explicitly human action to the disasters that appear in it. It develops an ambivalent position towards climate change by showing its outcomes while misdirecting viewers' attention to another cause of the crisis: an unprecedented solar eruption. The film opens with a scene featuring a range of flares erupting from the sun's surface. The second scene establishes anomalies in the size of these flares as the trigger for the disaster domino that develops throughout the film. A passing reference to the role of the sun is also made later in a video made by conspiracy theorist Charlie Frost. Yet, apart from these three moments, images or references to the activity of the sun are virtually absent in the rest of the film. After the second scene, *2012* focuses on other kinds of information: scientific discourses that are similar in tone and content to those about climate change, images of destruction that bear visual resemblance to actual disasters triggered by climate change, and a set of spatial and temporal processes and dynamics that characterize the development of disasters induced by human activities. In addition, even though audiences are unlikely to be familiar with the scientific theories that suggest that climate change can cause earthquakes, volcano eruptions, and tsunamis, they may still interpret the disasters in *2012* as references to climate change. The aforementioned details encourage them to do so. *2012* also makes clear connections to the Noah's Ark story from different religions, in which God floods the world as punishment for human misbehavior (in Darren Aronofsky's 2014 cinematic version of the story, for their abusive attitude towards nature). In *2012*, the three giant arks that transport the few who are supposed to survive also carry animals from different species and Jackson's son is named Noah. Yet, despite the film's obvious reference to the Noah story, it does not use this as an opportunity to point at humans' reckless attitude towards the environment. In sum, *2012* crafts an ambivalent discourse, both fostering and preventing eco-conscious readings of the film.

After *The Day After Tomorrow* received substantial media attention and originated a heated debate about the plausibility of climate change (Rust 196–200), it is perhaps not odd that *2012* downplayed its references to this threat to life on Earth. Such ambivalence perhaps helped the film reach wider distribution and avoid the reticence that climate change skeptics might have had towards a film that had dealt with climate change more overtly. Indeed, other films like *Interstellar* have deployed similar strategies to circumvent the opposition of climate-change deniers (Archer 12). *2012* relies on political subtlety to make people aware of environmental challenges. The publicity campaign of the film focuses on the idea of the catastrophe being a prediction of the Mayan calendar. Except for the teaser trailer, the three different full trailers of the film open with images and sound referring to this forecast. Although this prediction will become almost irrelevant in the film (being introduced through the news and only used to reflect Jackson's lifestyle and later also in Charlie Frost's home-made video), its prominent use in the publicity campaign shows how the film directs viewers' attention away from more realistic causes of disaster. Yet, the ambivalence of disaster in *2012* has a more problematic side: since the premise of the film is that solar flares unleash the chain of disasters in the film, there is not much that humans can do about it. They only try to adapt to the circumstances, as the premise on which *2012* is built leaves no room to imagine how humans could change the way they run their lives and reduce their impact on the planet. In contrast, both in *Godzilla* (2014) and in *The Day the Earth Stood Still* (2008), humans must face monsters and aliens respectively in an attempt to stop the disasters that they bring about. While in both films human efforts to stop the monsters are in vain (they cannot control them), in *The Day* humans are able to stop the apocalypse by agreeing to change their behavior towards the planet.

Therefore, other eco-conscious sf disaster films are not so ambivalent regarding the impact of human activity on the environment and, by extrapolation, its role in producing climate change. The 2014 remake of *Godzilla* introduces new destructive monsters, the MUTOs (Massive Unidentified Terrestrial Organisms), which come to life as a result of human actions and technologies. In turn, Godzilla features as a representative of nature that aims to restore environmental balance. The film establishes humans as active agents in the unleashing of catastrophic events from the very beginning, which takes us to a mining site of the Universal Western Mining company (a name that features prominently in the film's opening shots) in the Philippines. There, a group of people find the bones of a creature and an egg, which is later identified as one of the MUTOs. In a later scene, a scientist says that the drilling of the mining company woke up a MUTO, which looked for "the nearest source of radiation": a power plant in Japan, where it cocooned and fed on nuclear energy for 15 years. The film covers its awakening and its destructive power as it searches for nuclear nourishment. By linking the MUTO's awakening to intensive mining and nuclear power, the scientist's description shows the unintended, unexpected, and transnational effect of modern technological developments.

The Day After Tomorrow, *The Day the Earth Stood Still* (2008), *Wall-E*, and *Snowpiercer* include even clearer references to the impact of human activities on the planet. In *The Day After Tomorrow*, the US president's speech at the end of the film clearly acknowledges that humans (particularly US inhabitants) cannot "continue consuming the planet's natural resources." The 2008 remake of *The Day the Earth Stood Still* also points at humans' lack of environmental responsibility. Klaatu (Keanu Reeves), the representative of an alien species, warns humans that they must change their attitude towards the planet. Otherwise, aliens will use their technology to annihilate humans in order to ensure that the planet continues to be alive. *Wall-E* shows that humans have had to leave Earth because of their unrestrained consumption, their mindless use of natural resources, and the ecological impact of their behavior (e.g. plants do not grow anymore). In the opening scene, the camera flies through a compact layer of satellites surrounding Earth and later shows a new urban landscape of skyscrapers made of trash. The film does this through long aerial and overhead shots that dissolve into each other, giving a sense of spatial continuity and suggesting that this kind of cityscape has become the norm. A few seconds later, the film introduces close-ups of the robot Wall-E organizing the waste that surrounds it followed by a montage showing an abandoned landscape of "ultrastores," gas stations, giant billboards that clutter the city skyline, and freeways that highlight the hyper-consumerist character of a society run by the monopolist company Buy n Large (BnL). The opening scene of *Snowpiercer* also alludes explicitly to humans' impact on the environment, as a radio broadcast explains the course of implementation of "a revolutionary solution to mankind's warming of the planet," which then of course backfires and puts humans in an even more precarious position. Even though *The Day the Earth Stood Still* and *Godzilla* (like *2012* and other apocalyptic films) do not make explicit references to climate change and/or the Anthropocene, the films mentioned in this paragraph are less ambivalent than *2012* in establishing links between human activities and planetary environmental degradation. Yet, despite pointing at anthropogenic ecological disruption, each of these films is ambivalent towards some other aspect of climate change: *Wall-E*—like *2012*—is ambivalent towards biopolitics, *Godzilla* and *The Day the Earth Stood Still* ignore biopolitics altogether, *The Day After Tomorrow* focuses on the impact of disaster in the US, and, as Gerry Canavan notes, *Snowpiercer*'s ending is open to both hopeless and utopian interpretations of the future of humanity (2014b, 59–60).

Other aspects that reinforce the ambivalence of *2012* are the series of meetings between governments from different countries and their collaboration in the ark construction project, which situate the realm for political action at a transnational level. In this case, the film reflects ambivalent responses to the consequences of disaster rather than towards the causes of climate change. Although the film appears to hint at the importance of cosmopolitan cooperation, the collaboration between governments—in contrast to disaster—is not global: Latin American, African, Middle Eastern countries, plus India, and many other smaller territories do not participate in this project, although the film never explains why. During the G8 meeting, in one of the first scenes in the film, the US president alerts the heads of state of Japan, Canada, Russia, Germany, the United Kingdom, Italy, France, and the US of the impending catastrophe. Later on, the film features a videoconference of the G8 leaders plus China in which Adrian briefs them about the time left before they have to board the arks. A discussion towards the end of the film about the inhumanity of leaving people standing by the gates of the arks reveals that the arks depend on the political elites of the countries that participate in the videoconference and, for some unknown reason, also Spain. By show-ing several nations actively organizing a plan for survival, the film suggests the need for transnational collaboration in order to face the consequences of anthro-pogenic environmental disruption. This contrasts with most sf disaster films, which tend to show the reaction of one government only, typically the US' (as in, for example, *Independence Day*, *Armageddon*, *The Core* [Amiel 2003], *The Day the Earth Stood Still* [2008], *40 Days and Nights* [Geiger 2012], *Godzilla* [2014], and *Interstellar*). Some films mention the occasional collaboration between two governments, for example, Russia and the US in *Meteor* and *Deep Impact* or the US and Mexico in *The Day After Tomorrow*. Bearing these conventions in mind, *2012* stands out from these films in its attempt to present environmental disasters as problems that require the cooperation of different countries. Through this depiction, the film also reflects the cosmopolitan challenges that climate change generates in the realm of geopolitics. Yet, it is only the major economies that join their efforts to ensure their own survival, excluding the rest of the world. In this sense, the collaboration between countries in *2012* resembles the alliances that *Elysium* and *In Time* depict: they serve the interests of the economic and political elites, as the previous chapter shows.

The Biopolitics of Disaster: Sovereign Individuals and Bare Life in *2012*

The previous section hints at the role of politics, wealth, and power in deciding who gets to live and who does not, that is, at the role of biopolitics. Like classical disaster movies (e.g. *The Towering Inferno*), *2012* articulates what Stephen Keane identifies as "the disaster movie game": guessing who is going to survive (38–9). Although chance also plays a part in these narratives, Keane notes that class, race, and gender are the most common markers of survival in disaster cinema, especially since the 1990s (64). Adhering to this generic convention, *2012* also relates survival to clearly identifiable social markers. In addition, by including a large ensemble of different characters and focusing on political decision-makers, the film situates its narrative in the realm of biopolitics. It clearly establishes who is, according to biopolitical logic, supposed to board the ark and who is not. Biopolitics explores the political logics that render certain kinds of lives more valuable than others. Through its focus on such logics, biopolitics offers prime opportunities to address cosmopolitan challenges related to the right to live and to have a decent life. In his work on biopolitics/biopower, Michel Foucault notes that since the eighteenth century "the ancient right to *take* life or *let* live was replaced by a power to *foster* life or *disallow* it to the point of death" [emphasis in original] (138). These operations of power are clearly established in *2012*, as some lives are protected and fostered and others are let perish.

Developing Foucault's work, Giorgio Agamben bases his biopolitical theories on the distinction between the Greek terms *zoē* (politically-excluded "bare life") and *bios* (politically-included, empowered bodies) (134, 140). More specifically, Agamben's work focuses on the Roman concept of the *homo sacer*, which is roughly equivalent to *zoē*. Although *homo sacer* literally means "sacred man," in practice, the term refers to a person who "may be killed and yet not sacrificed" (Agamben 8). Despite the differences between Foucault and Agamben's approaches to biopolitics (see Agamben 140), both authors coincide in their emphasis on the sociopolitical structures that disregard some lives to the extent of allowing their end. In the context of *2012* and the catastrophes that it displays, it is the latter aspect of biopolitics (letting the *homo sacer* die) that becomes particularly relevant, with the film highlighting it through dialogue, mise-en-scène, and disaster spectacle. Apart from analyzing this dimension of *2012*, the last part of this chapter also considers how other films such as *The Day After Tomorrow*, *Wall-E*, *Snowpiercer*, and *Interstellar* present wealth, profession, nationality, and race as major references in the organization of the new social scenarios that climate change produces.

Even though the notion of bare life plays a key role in *2012*, the film also pays attention to the kinds of lives that power fosters. *2012* includes multiple references to billionaires, royalty, and, to a lesser degree, politicians and scientists as the lives that 'deserve' saving. One of the opening scenes in a hotel suite in London features an Arab king who is offered tickets on the ark for the price of one billion euros. When Charlie has a conversation with Jackson in his trailer, the conspiracy theorist mentions that the arks have been built for people like "Bill Gates, Rupert Murdoch, or some Russian billionaire." A Russian billionaire, Yuri Karpov (Zlatko Buric) is indeed introduced minutes later at a boxing event during which he receives a biometrically encrypted message telling him to start a boarding procedure.

As the film advances towards the end, the references to the kinds of lives that are fostered become more obvious, bringing cosmopolitan concerns to the forefront. Right after scientists get off the helicopter that transports them to the site where the arks have been built, a shot showing their faces looking at something invites viewers to pay attention to two close-ups of a corgi dog and the feet of a woman. These two shots are followed by a long point-of-view shot revealing that the woman is Elizabeth II, Queen of the United Kingdom, who is bringing her two well-known dogs with her. Moments later, a conversation between Adrian, Laura Wilson (the US president's daughter [Thandie Newton]), and Anheuser about the selection procedure for those who get to board the ship explicitly points to the reason why some people make it on board and others do not: their money. Again, the film relies on a point-of-view shot to emphasize the kind of passengers entitled to board. In this case, the film shows a line of passengers (who are all white Anglo, except an Arab family) marching into the ship after Adrian literally points at them with his finger in the previous shot. The film also directs viewers' attention towards the identities of these people by staging the scene as if it were a police line-up. After Adrian and Laura show their skepticism at Anheuser's explanations, he admits: "Without billions of dollars from the private sector, this entire operation would've been impossible." As the work of several scholars suggests, biopolitics need to be understood in relation to capital (Vint 2011, 164–5; Cupples, 15, 25–7; Dalby 187, 190; Baker, 115–9). By highlighting the centrality of money in the operation of biopolitics in catastrophic scenarios, *2012* unveils some of the economic logics of biopolitics. Yet, the film only addresses the role of capital in the biopolitical management of disaster, but not in its production.

Through its multiple references to the privileged biopolitical status of the extremely wealthy, *2012* shows that climate change does not affect everyone equally. In addition, the film hints at a *de facto* privatization of state decisions by showing the adaptation of the neoliberal model of public-private partnerships to the realm of catastrophe management.[8] This model is most evident in Anheuser's reference to the billions of dollars that private investors have contributed to the project. Even though states orchestrate the construction of the arks and government representatives are the ones who make the decision to open the gates later, these governments do not build the arks for the benefit of any of their citizens. Representatives do so for themselves and for other wealthy individuals. In relation to this, Brian Baker's work on biopolitics and mobility in *Code 46* is particularly relevant. Baker explains that he uses the term "sovereign bodies" instead of "states" "because the very notion of the state is under erasure in *Code 46*" (116). Instead, entities or actors such as corporations establish regulations, procedures, and emit official documents. 'Sovereign bodies' is also an apt term to describe the working of biopolitics in *2012*. 'Bodies,' though, would carry a slightly different meaning in the scenario that *2012* projects: the term would refer to the individual bodies who protect their personal interests and lives only. In *2012*, it is individuals who are sovereign—sometimes through their capital and other times through their corrupt political power. These sovereign bodies decide which lives are to be saved (their own and those that are essential for their survival) and which ones are not (everyone else's). These privileged bodies ride roughshod over the sovereignty that citizens confer to their governments to defend, in theory, the general interest. Even some people who have paid to get on board, such as Yuri (the Russian billionaire) and his family are prevented from doing so in order to guarantee the safety of those who are already onboard. *2012* then suggests that, in a situation of catastrophe, sovereignty does not reside in the state or in non-governmental entities but in individual bodies.

The almost uncontestable right of billionaires (except Yuri) to protect their own lives and let others die in *2012* contrasts with the role of the millionaire in the 1951 film *When Worlds Collide*. In this film, a scientist stops the attempts of a millionaire to decide who should be onboard the spaceship that will allow some people to survive the apocalyptic catastrophe that is about to hit Earth. The identities of those who will be allowed to travel on the spaceship are established through a raffle, although the millionaire and the scientists have guaranteed spots because they fund and develop the operation, respectively. Eventually, though, the chief scientist forces the millionaire (who is in a wheelchair) to stay on Earth with him in order to save fuel and give those on the spaceship a higher chance of survival. *When Worlds Collide* also presents private actors as essential for the development of the operation, but they are not, as in *2012*, sovereign over everyone else: the millionaire is not allowed to choose who should or should not be on the spaceship. In Foucauldian terms, the figure of the millionaire does not have the power to let die. The contrast between the roles of capital in both films suggests a change in the public perception of the power of money in the current neoliberal context, particularly in situations of exception. The boarding criteria in *When Worlds Collide* are based on a cosmopolitan appreciation of the equal value of human lives. In contrast, *2012* develops an ambivalent cosmopolitan position: on the one hand, it criticizes the unequal, hierarchical, and monetary value of lives and, on the other, it fails to challenge such a system.

2012's focus on the fostering of the lives of sovereign bodies and, as a result, the generalization of the condition of *homo sacer* in the Anthropocene does not mean that the film ignores the biopolitical role of factors such as nationality, race, and profession (the film does not explicitly point at gender, although it clearly focuses on the survival of male characters). The earlier section on disaster in this chapter already showed that the plan to build the arks was orchestrated by economically powerful nations, leaving others to their own fate. In addition, the part of the film that deals with the boarding of the arks provides more information about specific biopolitical markers. When Adrian, showing cosmopolitan concerns, asks why workers (in general) do not get passes, Anheuser replies: "if you want to donate your passes to a couple of Chinese workers, be my guest." The emphasis of Anheuser on the nationality of the workers shows his biopolitical reasoning: in the state of emergency of the film, he sees the Chinese as *homo sacer*. Chinese workers also stand out in the extreme long shots of a mass of people waiting for the arks' gates to open, thanks to the yellow color of their uniforms, which contrasts with the dark color of the outfits of the rest of the people waiting. While the workers who built the ships are markedly Chinese, the captain of the US ark is white and speaks perfect US American English. The physical appearance of the crew in the US ark in general invites to surmise that the nationality of the crew coincides with that of the nations that are responsible for each of the arks. A comparison between the two main scientists in the film confirms this point: Adrian, a black US American scientist, boards the ark, while Satnam and his family are left stranded in India. Although people from all kinds and origins are subject to this biopolitical system, the emphasis on the exclusion of Indian and Chinese people clearly demarcates an additional biopolitical line between citizens from major economies and citizens of developing nations (the first line being that between sovereign bodies and the rest).

Relying on crosscutting and spectacular images of impending disaster, the scene of the death of Satnam Tsurutani is the moment that most overtly visualizes the opposing statuses that biopolitical logics establish. His death is particularly significant as Satnam is, after all, the character who first discovers and shares the signs of environmental alarm. The conversation about the selection procedure is followed by the sight of the second major wave in the film approaching a city in India. A large group of people including Satnam move forward in slow motion carrying bags, suitcases, and other belongings, and thus showing that they have abandoned the area where they live. They stop, look back, and the screen shows, through an extremely long establishing shot, a giant wave forming over an Indian city already in the distance. The next shot cuts to Adrian settling in his sleek room on the ship and noting: "you could fit ten people in here." Shortly after dropping his bag, Adrian gets a phone call from Satnam, who informs him of the unexpected evolution of the mega-tsunami (which was not meant to hit his city so soon) and lets him know that he and his family did not get picked up. By crosscutting between the impending disaster scene in India and the sleek and spacious ship that will keep its passengers safe from the giant waves, the film exposes the distinction between *zoē* (*homo sacer*, bare life) and *bios* (the sovereign bodies who have biopower). The criticism of this system is particularly powerful because it is a familiar and likable, even if secondary, Indian character and his family that get killed after the previous scenes highlight the nationality and economic status of the passengers in the arks. Indeed, Satnam and his family are the only characters who are shown to be literally hit by disaster once the evacuation has already started. Their example additionally shows the interweaving of narrative and spectacle both in the environmental and in the biopolitical discourses that the film develops.

Satnam's death also works as a turning point in the film, articulating two biopolitical options that correspond to what Janet Fiskio calls "the lifeboat" and "the collective" metaphors (14–32). She identifies these two terms as the "dominant narratives" in discourses of global climate change (14). Even though Fiskio does not use biopolitical terms, the metaphor of the lifeboat loosely corresponds to the distinction between *homo sacer* and sovereign bodies mentioned before. In turn, Fiskio describes the collective as a "courageous and generous" attitude in a chaotic environmental context (14). She uses the example of Rebecca Solnit's *A Paradise Built in Hell: The Extraordinary Communities That Arise in Disaster* (2009) to explain that, in the metaphor of the collective, "spontaneous communities form in response to disaster" and "ordinary people come together to care for one another" (22). In other words, the collective could also be described as a cosmopolitan stance in a situation of environmental crisis.

The crosscutting between Adrian's room in the ark and the impending tsunami in India serves as a catalyst for change that introduces the metaphor of the collective in *2012*. The cosmopolitan spirit of the collective resonates in Adrian's address to political leaders from all over the world when he tries to convince them to open the arks' gates and let the people outside board the ark. He asks: "Can we really stand by and watch these people die?" Adrian uses the personal story of the death of his friend Satnam to move people from different nations in the arks and change their minds. In order to do this, Adrian also calls the presumably civilized character of sovereign bodies into question, arguing that if they consider themselves civilized, they should open the gates. The film also underlines Adrian's personal commitment and invites viewers to identify with his cosmopolitan discourse through the frequent use of close-ups that frame him, his cracked voice, his performance (he looks at different directions, seeking empathy), and by alternating between shots of his speech and shots of different leaders considering his argument. In this way, *2012* intertwines disaster, drama, and biopolitical allusions to discredit the metaphor of the lifeboat and endorse the cosmopolitan orientation of the metaphor of the collective. Apart from the opening of the gates to let a large group of people in, the film narrative also reinforces the metaphor of the collective by showing a Tibetan family unselfishly helping the protagonist American family and Yuri's Russian girlfriend to stow away on one of the ships. In these scenes, *2012* praises specific moments in which characters decide to adopt cosmopolitan modes of action.

Steering towards Cosmopolitanism, a While

Stephen Keane argues that "disaster movies are not so much about clinging onto dear life as making your way, out of the rubble, towards a life with renewed perspective" (22–3). Yet, even though *2012* replaces the metaphor of the lifeboat with the new perspective of the cosmopolitan collective, the film is also ambivalent towards the biopolitics of climate change. As noted earlier, *2012* ignores the role of humans (particularly of Western industrialized nations) in unleashing ecological disasters, it grants the US American family a central position in the future that the film hints at, and, in addition, it envisions a new beginning for humanity in South Africa in which South Africans do not appear. After the Tibetan, Russian, and US stowaways are saved from a flooding sector of the ark, the film includes an intertitle that reads: "Day 27 Month 01 Year 0001," showing that a new period has begun for humans. In the second scene in this sequence, the film presents the humans that are going to be part of this new society. The film first includes long and extreme long shots of a racially diverse group of people combined with medium shots of some of the main characters. As the gates open to let people walk on the platforms for the first time since they boarded, the film highlights the presence of the protagonist US American family and the Tibetan family through the casting of the hard light of the sun on their faces in two separate medium shots, followed again by a longer shot of the large group of people walking out on the deck. In this way, *2012* seems to celebrate the survival of different groups of people. The film then includes a series of shots that show the arks en route and reveal South Africa as the destination of the ships. Yet, before the film introduces its final zoom-out shot, the last shots of characters closely focus on the white, heterosexual, middle-class US American family talking about their future home. Therefore, *2012* appears to present a racially diverse future but eventually privileges the white US American family.

The film also develops an ambivalent biopolitical position through its presentation of South Africa as the place where survivors will settle. One of the scientists informs Adrian that the Drakensberg Mountains in KwaZulu-Natal (South Africa) have become the highest point in the world and that the African continent has suffered the least impact from environmental upheaval. On the one hand, the designation of an African country as the place where the survivors on the arks are supposed to live suggests a potential revision of world geopolitics, in which a continent that has traditionally suffered from the abuses of Western nations and companies is now regarded as a haven of hope. On the other hand, the ending does not consider the situation of the people living in South Africa, many of whom could still be alive, as the information provided by the scientist invites to think. *2012* does not include a single image of, not even a comment about, South African survivors. In this way, the film presents South Africa as an empty land ready for the passengers of the ships to occupy and silently reproduces the logics of colonialism. This ending contrasts with that of *The Day After Tomorrow*. In Emmerich's earlier film, climate refugees from the US are allowed into Mexico, but Mexico retains its sovereignty and demands changes in the way that the global economy works (for example, asking the US to condone the debt of all Latin American countries). Even though Mexico demands something in return, this demand is a cosmopolitan one (from which other countries also benefit). The Mexican government in the film pushes for a more egalitarian global economic system and, ultimately, US citizens are allowed to cross the border into Mexico in what is also an exercise of empathy and cosmopolitanism. By overlooking South African citizens altogether, *2012* passes over their sovereignty and undermines the seemingly cosmopolitan discourse of its ending.

The final shot, which zooms out from the ships to show an almost-complete image of Earth from outer space, also evinces the film's ambivalence towards biopolitics and climate change. Similar images of the Blue Planet have often been related to environmentalist discourses (Heise 22–3). Indeed, the last scene of the eco-conscious film *The Day After Tomorrow* also includes a shot of the Blue Planet from outer space. As Ursula Heise explains, this kind of image has been interpreted in varying, almost opposite ways. In the 1960s and 1970s, many environmentalist movements embraced images of the Blue Planet for their depiction of Earth as a singular, precious, common home for different beings (Heise 22). More recently, the image has been criticized, as Heise notes, "for its erasure of political and cultural differences" (24). The appearance of the Blue Planet image at the end of *2012* fits into both discourses. At first sight, the sublime image suggests that humans may have another chance at living on an Earth that now appears to be borderless. Yet, the transition from the close-ups of the US American family to the blue marble image of Earth all but reinforces the discourse that sees such images of the planet as an erasure of diversity, here depicting this family as a projection of the whole of humanity.

The ambivalence of the biopolitics of climate change is not unique to *2012*. Films such as *Wall-E*, *Snowpiercer*, *Interstellar*, and, to some extent, *Elysium* develop similar discourses. *Interstellar* presents a global human extinction scenario: once crops start to fail massively and dust storms become routine, humans must find a way of continuing their lives outside planet Earth. Some of the dialogues at the beginning of the film explicitly refer to biopolitical and cosmopolitan questions: John Brand (Michael Caine) says that authorities realized that "dropping bombs [on starving people] was not a long term solution" and Amelia Brand (Anne Hathaway) mentions that genetic diversity is necessary for the colonization of other planets. Later on, characters also show concerns over humanity in planetary terms. For example, Joe Cooper (Matthew McConaughey) warns that "the people on Earth [...] are gonna die" and later on mentions that the advanced beings who built the outer-space maze chose Murphy (Jessica Chastain) "to save the world." Despite these cosmopolitan concerns, *Interstellar* only shows the impact of Cooper's intergalactic quest for a solution to environmental degradation through the lives of its white US American protagonists. Indeed, *Interstellar*'s visualization of the space station where humanity is supposed to continue living is a celebration of Americana in outer space. The Americanness of the sets (the baseball field, the corn fields, Cooper's farmhouse, and its porch) along with the almost-exclusively white US cast of the space station scenes suggest that the lives of white US citizens are the only lives that viewers should care about. Although *Interstellar* develops a compelling story of the bond between a father and a daughter, it ignores the obvious cosmopolitan and biopolitical questions that climate change and the prospect of life off Earth pose.

In *Wall-E*, an advert for a spaceship at the beginning of the film presents the idea of living in space as an inclusive project in terms of race, gender, and age (the advert's narrator explicitly says "even grandma can join the fun"). The advert also shows that there are several ships and focuses on "the jewel of the BnL fleet," which later turns out to be a ship that seems to carry US Americans only. By mentioning that ships would depart every day (implying that many people would be able to leave), the film papers over the fact that everyone living on Earth most likely did not fit on the spaceships. In addition, by focusing on one of the ships only, *Wall-E* does not draw attention to the biopolitical logics that likely governed this turning point for humanity. Although the film barely develops human characters, the narrative implies, via their American accent, that *Wall-E* deals—in a similar way to *Interstellar*—with a US spaceship. Therefore, despite criticizing the avid consumerism of the passengers and portraying a racially diverse spaceship, *Wall-E*, in practice, takes for granted the biopolitical supremacy of US citizens. In contrast, *Snowpiercer* develops the opposite discourse. As Gerry Canavan notes, the last shot of the film features the presumably only survivors of the freezing eco-apocalypse: "an Asian woman and a young black child, dressed as Inuits, [who] stare out into a non-white, and presumably non-Western, future" in which both characters will have to start from scratch (2014b, 59). In general, the biopolitical imaginations of *2012*, *Interstellar*, *Wall-E*, and *Snowpiercer* work in an either/or manner, privileging US American nationality and/or whiteness or doing away with it, as in the case of *Snowpiercer*. This apparent reciprocal exclusiveness of racial categories contrasts with the both/and character that Ulrich Beck ascribes to cosmopolitanism (2006, 4–5). That is, from a cosmopolitan perspective, cinematic discourses on the Anthropocene should be able to imagine futures in which both whites and other races and both US Americans and people from other countries belong. In other words, excluding a biopolitically privileged group does not offer viewers a more cosmopolitan perspective.

To conclude, this chapter has shown how over-the-top, seemingly meaningless spectacle can develop a detailed portrayal of the socio-environmental dynamics and impacts of climate change. Through the speculative character of its special effects, matches on action, camera movement, and the globalization of its action, *2012* highlights, like few other films, the planetary scope of climate change and the connectivity of its impacts, not only conceptually (as in most sf films) but also narratively. The spectacular character of many of the scenes in *2012* also contributes to signaling the critical condition of ecosystems, exposing the almost-invisible intensification of climate change, and pointing at some of its key characteristics such as the unpredictability and unavoidability of its effects, its imminence, and the threat it poses for human lives worldwide, even for people living in Western countries. Although *2012* provides an elaborate picture of climate change dynamics, it also overlooks a central element of climate change: its anthropogenic origin. *2012* develops an ambivalent position towards climate change: it offers a cosmopolitan perspective by emphasizing the transnational dimension of its impacts and fails to point explicitly at the responsibility of humans over its production.

Similarly, Ulrich Beck refers to climate change as "pure ambivalence" (2010, 175). He explains that climate change unleashes catastrophes in which hierarchies make specific groups and regions more vulnerable, but he also notes that such situations of crisis provide an opportunity for cosmopolitan organization (175–6). The larger and stronger the impacts, the more people are likely to be affected by them, making transnational collaboration and actions on a global scale a necessity. This chapter has shown that *2012* also presents climate change as an opportunity for cosmopolitics and adds a further dimension to Beck's argument, suggesting that ambivalence is also inherent to attempts at organizing and depicting cosmopolitan responses. This additional layer of ambivalence towards environmental dislocation stems from the film's simultaneous denunciation and reproduction of the biopolitical logics of disaster crises. Through the metaphors of the neoliberal lifeboat and the cosmopolitan collective, the film exposes the system that allows the extremely wealthy, the royalty, and top government representatives of major economies to exercise ungranted power in order to protect their own lives and let everyone else (even highly-qualified, non-Western people) die. By endorsing the metaphor of the cosmopolitan collective, *2012* celebrates racial diversity, the inclusion and value of people of all nationalities, professions, and incomes, and the restructuring of global geopolitics. Yet, at the same time, it reinforces the supremacy of white US Americans (as also happens in *Interstellar* and *Wall-E*) and disregards South Africa's sovereignty.

Even though *2012* presents the ideal of the cosmopolitan collective as an effective response to large-scale disaster, Frédéric Neyrat points out that an emphasis on the management and biopolitics of catastrophe obscures the more urgent and more necessary task of distinguishing between disaster as "misfortune" and as "injustice" (261). That is, to differentiate between those catastrophes that are 'natural' and those that are 'forced.' Although Neyrat does not situate these ideas within the framework of cosmopolitanism, his argument suggests that addressing the threats that climate change poses from a cosmopolitan perspective involves identifying who and what generates the conditions that unleash or aggravate natural disasters. This, in turn, makes it possible to identify responsibilities and prevent the operation of the biopolitics of catastrophe in the first place (Neyrat 261–2). *2012*'s lack of attention to the role of human activities in forcing climate change gives the impression that the disasters it portrays are natural, even though the film's mise-en-scène often suggests the opposite. This presentation of disaster as misfortune rather than injustice therefore contributes to the film's cosmopolitan ambivalence. Even sf films that link disaster to human activities (e.g. *The Day After Tomorrow, Godzilla, Wall-E,* and *The Day the Earth Stood Still* [2008]) fail to identify specific actors and activities—other than humans or neoliberalism in general. Nor do they emphasize the connection between specific actors or activities and the environmental degradation and life-threatening hazards that they produce. Despite their powerful visualization of climate change catastrophes, sf disaster films are still missing a crucial element that should be part of their cosmopolitan imaginations: the concept of disaster as anthropogenic injustice.

Notes

1 The next IPCC Synthesis Report is due for release in late 2022/early 2023.
2 For studies on *The Day After Tomorrow,* see Cubitt, Branston, Reusswig and Leiserowitz, von Burg, Crespo and Pereira, Ivakhiv, Rust, and Svodoba.
3 On *Avatar,* see Adamson, Bergthaller, Ivakhiv, Collins, Morton, Anglin, and Reber.
4 On *Wall-E,* see Anderson, Whitley, and Reber.
5 On *Snowpiercer,* see Canavan 2014b, Bordun, Freedman, and Haupts.
6 *The Day After Tomorrow, The Day the Earth Stood Still,* and *Godzilla* respectively ranked sixth, twenty-fifth, and fourteenth in the global box office in their year of release ("2004 Worldwide Grosses," "2008 Worldwide Grosses," "2014 Worldwide Grosses").
7 My use of the term 'cosmopolitan ambivalence' in this book does not derive from Landon's concept of "an aesthetics of ambivalence" (xxv, 157). The cosmopolitan ambivalence of eco-conscious sf films is addressed in the last part of this chapter.
8 Saskia Sassen, among others, has described similar systemic trends concerning the relationship between state and markets since the 1980s. She mentions, for instance, the privatization of state authorities and public functions and the privileging of the market (2006, 186).

3

LOVE FOR THE ALIEN SAME

Interplanetary Romance and Kinship as Harbingers of Ambivalent Cosmopolitanism

One of the main ways in which early twenty-first century sf cinema is structuring its discourses around globalization is through transnational love. While romantic relationships have enjoyed regular attention in sf throughout its history, a number of recent sf films, starting with *The Fifth Element* (Besson) in 1997, have reshaped the use of romantic relationships in the genre to address cosmopolitan concerns. This does not mean that the films mentioned in this chapter are necessarily cosmopolitan or offer visions of an ideal world whose inhabitants live in harmony with others, appreciate difference, and have reasonable access to economic resources and decent healthcare. Rather, these films, echoing some recent work on cosmopolitanism in the social sciences (Mezzadra and Nielson 2013; Woodward and Skrbiš; Stacey 2015a, 2015b), explore cosmopolitanism through personal struggles, occasional collaboration and alliances, moments of empathy and bonding, and the ambivalence of cosmopolitanism itself. In order to develop this argument, I start this chapter with a brief account of the conceptual and narrative use of romantic relationships and kinship in the sf genre, introduce romantic relationships between humans and aliens as a metaphor for transnational love, and offer a close reading of two radically different films in terms of aesthetics. I first focus on *The Host* (Niccol 2013), a commercial Hollywood production based on the novel of the same title by Stephenie Meyer (2008), and then examine *Codependent Lesbian Space Alien Seeks Same* (Olnek 2011), a zero-budget film which echoes the style of B-movies such as *Plan 9 from Outer Space* (Wood 1959) and seems to draw from the campy aliens with bald heads and robotic speech from *Saturday Night Live* (1977–9) and the movie *Coneheads* (Barron 1993). Despite their very different aesthetics, I argue that these two films develop a similar ambivalent position towards cosmopolitanism. They do so by presenting the formation of transnational couples as a harbinger of cosmopolitan attitudes in

DOI: 10.4324/9781003164517-4

their societies and, at the same time, reinforcing social dichotomies by casting only white American actors as the members of the transnational couple.

While sexuality, romance, intimacy, reproduction, and gender may not have traditionally occupied a central position in discourses of globalization and cosmopolitan challenges—when compared, for instance to economics and politics—(Padilla et al. x), they are a central dimension in the daily lives of many people influenced by and shaping global processes. In a context of increasingly mobile labor, one member of a couple may have to go to another country to work and live for a period of time while the other stays home. Partners may meet for the first time while they are abroad, online, or across the border a few miles from their home and then try to continue their relationship at a distance or relocate together at some point. People from different countries and/or cultures may attempt to start a new life together in one of their countries or in a different country altogether. Sometimes, people are forcefully driven into migration (because of their sexual orientation or the unequal statuses of sexes in their countries, or because of economic reasons, political dissidence, or religious beliefs). Regardless of the different reasons that drive people into transnational relationships, these couples usually have to deal with borders, visa regimes, and social conventions that challenge their relationship.

Clashing human rights frameworks and legislation paradoxically also offer opportunities for certain kinds of individuals to fulfill their intimate needs or their reproductive desires. Queer people sometimes flee the hostile environments in which they live and attempt to start anew in places where their lives are not endangered and their sexual rights are recognized. The protection of LGBTQ rights in some countries may produce a transnational domino effect of rights recognition (for instance, in the case of homosexual marriage), but it may also generate counter-reactions in others (the current escalation of violence towards homosexuals in certain regions of the world, for instance, in Russia). Some couples (often from the Global North) may resort to the cheap (and typically female) labor of the Global South in order to care for their children or elderly. Paradoxically, these women often have to leave their own children behind at home in order to care for the relatives of others. Infertile couples sometimes decide to circumvent the legislation of their country and rent the bodies of surrogate mothers so that they gestate children with the genetic material of the paying couple or individual. Others may adopt a child who has lost their family on the other side of the world. Yet, as comprehensive as this list may seem, it is impossible to fit all the different configurations of global love, sexualities, gender, and kinship in a series of categories. This is evident, for instance, in Ken Plummer's listing of over 60 different instances of modern sexual worlds (43). Transnational intimate interactions and reproductive hopes do not automatically derive from global suprastructures. Rather, individual desires and local understandings of race, class, ethnicity, gender, and sexuality rework systemic influences (Padilla et al. xii–xiv; Beck and Beck-Gernsheim 30–1).

The fact that engaging in transnational relationships and marriages, looking for sexual freedom abroad, conceiving transnational babies, and adopting children from other nations is becoming more and more common (Beck and Beck-Gernsheim 32) may suggest at first sight that transnational kinship promotes cosmopolitanism. Yet, as Ulrich Beck and Elizabeth Beck-Gernsheim note, the proliferation of transnational couples and world families does not necessarily mean that more and more people are opening their minds towards difference. As they note, world families also produce counter-reactions from people who defend more 'traditional' relationships (245). In addition, some transnational/transcultural families can embrace their mobility privileges and be blind to other cosmopolitan causes. More generally, the formation of transnational families and their daily lives are not necessarily cosmopolitan. That is the case, for instance, of children who are born to Indian surrogate mothers and raised by wealthy European families and whose origins, as Beck and Beck-Gernsheim point out, bear "the inequalities of the world" (247). Similarly, John McLeod notes that transcultural adoptions take place in an "uneven terrain" of glocal interactions (9). Still, even though transnational love and families may not embody or cultivate cosmopolitan attitudes, from a narrative point of view and in the past and present contexts of reticence towards miscegenation and of laws forbidding intermarriage in many parts of the world, the narrative celebration of transnational family ties constitutes a cosmopolitan practice of opening up life possibilities and choices.

The purpose of this chapter is not just to identify a group of early twenty-first century sf films that present transnational couples as harbingers of cosmopolitanism. Rather, following Ian Woodward and Zlatko Skrbiš, this chapter approaches cosmopolitanism as "a sensibility that people sometimes draw upon and other times ignore" (132). Through the desire for and the intimate engagement with national/cultural/racial/religious difference, individuals may negotiate their own and their society's cosmopolitan conflicts and struggles. In this sense, the development of cosmopolitan sensibilities is not limited to the sphere of the transnational couple or family. Their experiences can contribute to building cosmopolitan trust, openness, and alliances (and resistance towards them) in their communities and societies as well. To investigate the interplay of cosmopolitanism and love is therefore to consider how desire, intimacy, affection, sex, and care mediate individual and collective approaches to human rights, openness towards difference, conviviality, mobility, and mutually beneficial interpersonal relationships and cultural exchanges.

Although contemporary sf films offer opportunities to explore many of the aforementioned issues related to kinship to a greater or lesser extent, they pay particular attention to transnational/interplanetary romance. This chapter focuses on these discourses, paying special attention to the figure of the alien. I concentrate on human–alien romances for two reasons: (1) discourses on cosmopolitan love have proliferated in heterosexual human–alien romances since the turn of the twenty-first century (especially in young adult films such as Andrew Niccol's

The Host). (2) The human-alien love story at the center of *Codependent Lesbian Space Alien Seeks Same* provides a unique opportunity to bring non-normative sexualities into the analysis of transnational sf film and into discourses on cosmopolitanism. Although the work of Wendy Pearson (1999, 2008, 2009) and Alexis Lothian (2018) has opened opportunities for rich analyses of queerness in sf—particularly in sf literature—and Mark Bould has offered an overview of some of the most significant concerns in queer sf film (2002, 2012), sf film scholarship and sf cinema itself appear to elude looking at non-normative sexualities in general and their transnational dimension in particular. As Andrew Butler notes, full-blown homosexual characters are "almost nonexistent" in sf cinema (2009, 389). Putting the cosmopolitan methodology of border as a method into practice, this chapter challenges the almost complete lack of cosmopolitan discourses about LGTBQ rights in sf film. In a piece on sexuality in sf, Sherryl Vint argues that it is necessary to interrogate the genre's "lack of engagement with sexual politics" and the "masquerading" of dominant sexual practices as natural (2009, 403). In addition, Vint highlights the importance of writing about texts that look beyond sexual normativity (2009, 403). In order to counter the general absence of narratives about LGBTQ issues in sf film, the chapter devotes its last section to a peculiar example which is an exception rather than the norm. *Codependent Lesbian Space Alien Seeks Same* is not part of a larger group of sf films that share similar thematic concerns—as the main case studies of this book are. The film is an unlikely example whose aesthetics and zero budget set it drastically apart from the young adult blockbusters in which cosmopolitan romances are proliferating. Through the analysis of *Codependent Lesbian*, the chapter attempts to question the common exclusion of queer discourses in sf film, particularly in the current context of cosmopolitanization of the genre. Although sf films about queer and heterosexual relationships share many of their narrative strategies and visual techniques, I will analyze them separately. This will allow me to make queer narratives more visible and to simultaneously point to the scarcity of sf films of this kind.

Mapping Transnational Same-Species Romance and Kinship in Science Fiction

Apart from their predominant theme of transnational/interplanetary romances, sf films sometimes feature transnational forms of kinship, although they often do so in passing. *Sleep Dealer* and *Moon* are two of the few examples that offer a glimpse into the affection-deprived daily lives of families who have to live apart in order to accommodate themselves to the global/transplanetary economy. With the exception of the human who cares for the baby of a dead alien in *Enemy Mine* (Peterson 1985) and the CEO, astronaut, and robot who raise a Mars-born human teenager in *The Space Between Us* (Chelsom 2017), sf cinema has not been particularly creative at addressing transnational adoption, either. There is, however, a growing—if still modest—number of sf films that explore questions around transnational surrogate motherhood. *Transfer* (Lukačevic 2010) imagines a world where (wealthy, white, Western) individuals may rent or, in practice, buy other bodies (of younger, black, African people) hoping to improve their economic position. The film introduces an accidental/unexpected pregnancy in this context and points both at fears of miscegenation (Vint 2016, 104) and to the question of who retains the right to decide in care markets. In addition, the animation film *Mars Needs Moms* (Wells 2011) presents a planet where machines give birth to children and robots take care of them. Yet, this society needs the surrogate consciousness of a mother from Earth in order to program the robots that are supposed to raise the children. Most of the action then revolves around the attempts of an earthling child to rescue his mother from the Martians and their exploitative technology. However, in spite of this seemingly cosmopolitan/human rights discourse, the film couples its critique of surrogate motherhood with a reactionary defense of the nuclear family and traditional gender roles. *Mars Needs Moms* emphasizes the division between technocratic females who do not embrace motherhood and uncivilized males who raise the machine-incubated children as a community. Through this division, the film ultimately presents non-normative families as the source of all social ills. Apart from *Transfer* and *Mars Needs Moms*, the short films *Silver Sling* (Gorjestani 2010) and *Refuge* (Chun 2013)—both part of the *Futurestates* series (2010–14)—also point to the disadvantaged economic circumstances of women who are expected to be surrogate mothers and the pressures they are subjected to. Despite the critical potential of these films, their emphasis on neoliberalism and economic exploitation sometimes prevents them from considering issues related to love. In contrast, interplanetary romances usually develop narratives that are more focused on exploring the possibilities and conflicts that emerge around cosmopolitan love.

The almost-boundless imagination of science fiction has allowed the genre to develop multiple kinds of films in which romantic relationships play a strong part. For the sake of clarity, I first focus on films in which both members of the couple are human and then on films in which one of the members is an alien and the other is human. Regarding human relationships, three of the main strands of science fiction cinema that have shown interest in romantic relationships have traditionally framed their narratives within the scope of the nation. These are time-travel films, films about cyborgs and artificial intelligences, and dystopias that revolve around the bleakness of authoritarian regimes.

Many of the twenty-first century sf films that feature transnational couples do so by presenting a more up-to-date spin on systemic dystopias that feature forbidden romantic relationships.[1] Films such as *Code 46* (Winterbottom 2003), *Africa Paradis* (Amoussou 2006), the Neo-Seoul couple in *Cloud Atlas* (The Wachowskis and Tykwer 2012), and *Looper* (Johnson 2012) relate the social rules that oppress transnational couples to the pressures of economic systems. In most cases, the protagonist couples, whose members tend to be of different origins, need to fight to stay by the side of their loved ones as they often face prejudice or are subject to certain rules set by markets and big economic players that hamper their relationship. *Africa Paradis* presents a world where relationships between black Africans and white Europeans are taboo. *Code 46* and the Neo-Seoul story in *Cloud Atlas* establish biological or genetic difference (which coincides with national and ethnic difference in both films) as an obstacle to relationships. *Looper's* time-travel narrative is driven by Joe's (Bruce Willis) love for his Chinese wife (Xu Qing), his inability to cope with her loss, and the barriers that those who control time-travel markets set on their way. Leaving authoritarian dystopias aside, the cosmopolitan point of view of the alien in *PK* (Hirani 2014) questions national, religious, and ethnic borders, which eventually allow a Hindi woman and a Pakistani man to rebuild their relationship after it was previously destroyed by prejudice. A single transnational/transracial couple surviving the apocalypse is the only hope for the perpetuation of the human species in *Snowpiercer* (Bong 2013) and *Second Origin* (Porta and Luna 2015) and so is the miraculously conceived son of a black undocumented migrant in *Children of Men* (Cuarón 2006). Despite the efforts of some of these movies to capture transnational realities and include non-white characters, these films evince the all-too-common failure of the genre to articulate the intersectionality of identity and to address other elements that are significant from a cosmopolitan point of view (e.g., sexuality). Sometimes, they add religion or class to the equation, as *PK* or *Code 46* respectively do. Yet, in all of these examples, the story revolves around a heterosexual couple and it rarely problematizes gender conventions.

In contrast, when twenty-first century sf films do include LGTBQ characters, they often continue to feature couples whose members belong to the same nation or frame them in a context in which these relationships develop at a local/national level. Since the recent and ongoing struggle for LGBTQ rights has developed within the framework of the nation-state, it is no wonder that films typically frame their narratives in national terms. For example, *V for Vendetta* (McTeigue 2005) registers the persecution of homosexual individuals after the rise to power of the fascist Norsefire party in the UK, focusing on an autobiographic letter written on a piece of toilet paper by a woman imprisoned for being lesbian. Adopting a similarly national lens, the short film *Closets* (Eyre-Morgan 2015) relies on time travel to reflect upon shifting attitudes towards homosexuality in the UK in the 1960s and in the present. In addition, the individual and intimate character of questions concerning sexuality and sex change often make their transnational dimension less visible in films. *Teknolust* (Leeson 2002), *Zerophilia* (Curland 2005), *Horror in the Wind* (Mitchell 2008), *Were the World Mine* (Gustafson 2008), *Splice* (Natali 2009), *Open* (Yuzna 2010), *Cloud Atlas*, and *Girl Lost* (Keining 2015) deal with a range of questions around identity and body transformation, including fluid gender identities and sexualities, (viral) sex changes, individuals who change sex after every sexual intercourse, trans and intersex intimacy, and the replication of body features in a couple. Similarly, *Predestination* (Spierig 2014) relies on a time-travel narrative to reflect on the intersex experience of the protagonist at different times. While these films challenge and exploit bodily and temporal borders, they tend to frame their narratives about sexual matters exclusively in national contexts.[2]

Another challenge for the study of cosmopolitan sexualities in sf cinema is that films that feature homosexual characters and relationships such as *Deadly Skies* (Irvin 2005), *Kaboom* (Araki 2010), *Space Station 76* (Plotnick 2014), *Credence* (Buonaiuto 2015), and the post-apocalyptic short *Goodbye Blue Sky* (Zuck 2017) barely use the speculative character of the genre to reflect on sexuality. The same happens with the brief inclusion of gay or lesbian characters (often as tokens) in the dance scene at the beginning of *Matrix Reloaded* (The Wachowskis 2003), *Okja* (Bong 2017), *Annihilation* (Garland 2018), and recent franchise films such as *Star Trek: Beyond* (Lin 2016), *Independence Day: Resurgence* (Emmerich 2016), *Star Wars: Rogue One* (Edwards 2017), *Power Rangers* (Israelite 2017), and *Alien: Covenant* (Scott 2017). As Wendy Pearson notes, this kind of portrait may provide cognitive estrangement to viewers who are not used to LGBTQ visibility but does not offer a path to think about queerness (1999). In this context of national narratives, ruminations on the specificities of individual bodies, and lack of speculative engagement, the short film *Beholder* (Ganatra 2011) constitutes a notable exception that invites a transnational reading. This short film presents a society (Red Estates) where homosexuality is forbidden and genetically deleted during pregnancies. A formerly-lesbian woman pregnant with a homosexual child manages to escape this society with the help of an empathic nurse who is part of a resistance that has established an alternative social model beyond the borders of Red Estates. While the previous examples show a growing visibility of LGBTQ realities in science fiction, the general obliviousness towards their transnational dimension and the superficiality of many of these characters show that (cosmo)queer discourses still have a long way to go in sf cinema, particularly when aliens are not part of the story.

Aliens and the Articulation of Cosmopolitan Discourses

Given the limited interest of human-centered sf narratives in the exploration of the transnational dimension of romance, I now turn to alien figures as a potential vehicle for the exploration of sexual and love matters from a cosmopolitan perspective. The exploration of the relationship between self and other, national and foreign, inside and outside is often built into the premises and concepts of films that feature alien characters. In addition, cinema, since its early days, has regularly drawn on alien–human romances as a means of addressing other concerns (fears of communist infiltration, rising female autonomy, miscegenation, racial relations, migration). Early examples of human–alien relationships in film would be, for instance, *When the Man in the Moon Seeks a Wife* (Stow 1908) or *Aelita* (Protazánov 1924) (Johnston 63; Csicsery-Ronay 2007, 16).[3] Although the alien offers multiple readings, these creatures are often presented and read as a reference to the other in terms of race and nationality, two markers that often intersect and are particularly relevant from a cosmopolitan point of view.

Csicsery-Ronay argues that films tend to present biological difference between human and alien species as "analogous to terrestrial racial difference" (2002, 228). Similarly, Christine Cornea identifies films such as those in the *Planet of the Apes* original franchise (Schaffner 1968; Post 1970; Taylor 1971; Thompson 1972, 1973) and *Enemy Mine* as a "conspicuous allegory" of race relations in the US (182). Regarding aliens' foreignness, Charles Ramírez Berg claims that alien others often stand for Latin American immigrants in sf films (404-5). He relies on figures to support this point: he notes that of all "unauthorized immigrants" to the US in the first decade of the twenty-first century, 80% were Latin American and 60%, Mexican (423). This leads him to read the presence of an other in sf film (and not just aliens, but also cyborgs) as a reference to Latin Americans. Even though Ramírez Berg points in the right direction, at times, his reading may be somewhat over-generalizing. In this chapter, I read aliens in general as a metaphor for the foreigner and then see what particular readings each film favors. For example, the aliens in *Avatar* (Cameron 2009) can be read as Native Americans, those in *I Am Number Four* (Caruso 2011) as a reference to refugees in general, and the ones living Down Below in *Upside Down* as Latin Americans.

Although each particular film encourages viewers to read aliens in different ways, Andrew Butler, in his analysis of *District 9* (Blomkamp 2009), notes that reading abject aliens as "allegorical representations of Black or Coloured South Africans" can easily slip into (probably unintentional) racism (2015, 104). Butler further locates the genesis of such potentially racist associations in the habit of presenting the alien in contrast to a social template configured by whiteness, heterosexuality, maleness, and the middle class (108). In this chapter, I analyze race and nationality in alien narratives by attempting to exercise "a looser sense of engagement" with their representation (Butler 110). That is, I try to avoid equating abject aliens with specific racial groups. Instead, I focus on the racial hierarchies that films reproduce. Whatever the labels that may be attached to the depiction of aliens in a film, the self/other structure of human–alien and even alien–alien relationships offers opportunities to examine transnational scenarios of love, affection, and sexual freedom from a cosmopolitan perspective.

By approaching the alien as a foreigner, this chapter suggests that the figure of the alien allows sf films to articulate cosmopolitan discourses. Drawing on the work of Celestino Deleyto (2017), I have argued elsewhere that aliens and their representation in films can be read as performers of cosmopolitanism (Gómez-Muñoz 128-9). In this earlier piece, I note that films may rely on the figure of the alien to channel discourses of openness, collaboration, negotiation, understanding, and even individual and societal transformation. Sometimes, films also link aliens to the discovery of alternative ways of being and living. Of course, films may also rely on the alien to articulate different discourses that display wariness towards alien others or vilify them. Yet, in the first two decades of the twenty-first century cosmopolitan (or seemingly cosmopolitan) uses of the alien tend to be more common than fearful and hateful approaches to visitors or migrants from outer space. Aliens can also embody the self-reflexive character of critical cosmopolitanism. In the introduction to *Alien Imaginations*, Ulrike Küchler, Silja Maehl, and Graeme Stout point at a key dimension of the alien: this figure brings a variety of often-unknown strangers closer to us and, at the same time, offers an opportunity to "look at ourselves as if from the outside" (2). Through the figure of the alien, films sometimes invite viewers to reflect on their own selves, habits, viewpoints, and the social systems they belong to. Films may lead viewers to reconsider their own ways of being through the perspective of extraterrestrials, but also through the radical alterity or even the surprising familiarity of the stranger. Human–alien interactions have the power to alter the way characters and viewers perceive reality and to modify relation dynamics between different people or social actors. In general, the alien has the potential to widen our outlooks and the range of life possibilities available to us.

Considering these observations, *The Host*, *Codependent Lesbian*, and other films that revolve around human–alien romances constitute valuable case studies of cosmopolitanism in contemporary sf cinema, as they tend to feature remarkably vocal aliens and humans. Sf films do not frequently offer viewers opportunities to consider how aliens see humans. Aliens are often destructive beings who do not utter a word (e.g., *The War of the Worlds* [Haskin 1953]), peaceful beings who can only communicate with humans through rudimentary or limited means (e.g., *E.T.* [Spielberg 1982]), or creatures who do not want to reveal their intentions and their perspective on humans (e.g., *They Live*). In addition, sometimes aliens speak with humans, as in *District 9*, but "cannot speak for themselves" (Butler 2015, 96). In contrast, in films such as *The Day the Earth Stood Still* (Wise 1951, Derrickson 2008), *Stranger from Venus* (Balaban 1954), the *Star Trek* movies, *Enemy Mine*, *Cocoon* (Howard 1985), *Avatar*, the *Transformers* franchise (Bay 2007, 2009, 2011, 2014, 2017), *Arrival* (Villeneuve 2016), and most of the human–alien romances mentioned in this chapter, aliens have an intelligible voice or are able to communicate with humans effectively. The ability of aliens to express themselves offers characters and viewers clear opportunities to reflect on alien perspectives. However, this does not mean that films that feature speechless aliens do not offer opportunities for fruitful cosmopolitan analysis.

Finally, vocal aliens may not necessarily draw attention to cosmopolitan concerns. Human–alien communication may indeed facilitate the erasure of diversity. While listening to aliens may expose viewers to a different point of view, aliens typically speak the same language as humans and films magically breach linguistic and cultural barriers. This is not only the case of English-language films. *G.O.R.A.* (Sorak 2004) features Turkish-speaking aliens and points to the unlikeliness of aliens and humans speaking the same language when a character mockingly notes that everyone speaks Turkish in the alien facility. In this way, the film recognizes the paradox that, in order to establish a dialogue between two cultures in a film, sometimes the most practical thing to do is to homogenize language.

From Enemies to Friends: Alien–Human Romances

While sf films about romance between two human characters barely paid attention to social formations beyond the scope of the nation before the turn of the twenty-first century, this is different in the case of alien films. In some cases, these films address transnational concerns, such as the fear of Soviet communist influence. In *I Married a Monster from Outer Space* (Fowler 1958)—and to a lesser extent, in *Invasion of the Body Snatchers* (Siegel 1956)—the protagonist finds out that her/his partner's body has been occupied by aliens who attempt to take over the US/Earth. In tune with other 1950s sf invasion films, this concept serves as a metaphor for the fear of communist infiltration—although such narratives can also be read as references to concerns about conformity and sameness in 1950s US American society. More positive portrayals of romantic human–alien couples also encourage readings of the alien as a foreign person. *Teenagers from Outer Space* (Graeff 1959) shows how an alien teen deserts his fellow alien invaders when they attempt to colonize Earth and falls in love with the human girl, stopping the alien (communist) invasion in the process. Similarly, *Invasion of the Star Creatures* (Ve Sota 1962), *Moon Pilot* (Neilson 1962), and *Unearthly Stranger* (Krish 1963) feature aliens with suspicious or evil intentions who eventually fall in love with humans, leaving their harmful schemes aside in the process. Yet, despite these exceptionally positive portrayals at the turn of the 1960s, the image of the alien remained a negative one in general terms until the late 1970s and the early 1980s, particularly in better-known films such as *The Thing from Another World* (Nyby and Hawks 1951) or *The War of the Worlds* (1953).

Coinciding with and following the release of *Close Encounters of the Third Kind* (Spielberg 1977) and *E.T.* (1982), sympathetic images of aliens who fall in love with humans by chance began to proliferate in the late 1970s and 1980s. This can be appreciated in films such as *The Man Who Fell to Earth* (Roeg 1976), *Superman* (Donner 1978) and its sequels, *Cocoon* (Howard 1985), *Starman* (Carpenter 1984), *Cocoon: The Return* (Petrie 1988), *Earth Girls Are Easy* (Temple 1988), and *My Stepmother Is an Alien* (Benjamin 1988). Even though both humans and aliens in these films attempt, with varying degrees of predisposition and willingness, to open their minds to the culture of the other, their narratives typically end with the departure of the alien (as in *Cocoon*, *Cocoon: The Return*, *Starman*, and *Earth Girls Are Easy*). As Charles Ramírez Berg notes, "the Sympathetic Alien movies allow us to have it both ways. We can appreciate the aliens, and even learn from them, but in the end the status quo is maintained by sending them home—for their own good" (412). Even in those stories in which aliens stay, they do not bring about much change. The aliens in *The Man Who Fell to Earth* and *My Stepmother Is an Alien* are indeed the only aliens that end up living among humans on Earth, and so their cultural impact is minimal.

More recent films have continued to develop the trend of positive intimate relationships between aliens and humans. *Coneheads, The Fifth Element, What Planet Are You From?* (Nichols 2000), *G.O.R.A.*, *Avatar, I Am Number 4, Upside*

Down, *The Host* (2013), *Patema Inverted* (Yoshiura 2013), and, to a lesser extent, *Thor* (Branagh 2011), *John Carter* (Stanton 2012), *Guardians of the Galaxy*, and *GOTG: Vol. 2* (Gunn 2014, 2017), *Jupiter Ascending*, *The Space Between Us*, and the newest installments of the *Star Trek* franchise (Abrams 2009, 2013; Lin 2016) celebrate the formation of couples whose members are from different planets. In a similar way to 1980s films, both members of the couple typically develop an attitude of openness and understanding towards the other, establishing a relationship in which both members (and sometimes also those around them) learn from each other. But, unlike 1980s films, aliens often stay on Earth or the society that hosts them, challenging social norms and borders, and instilling their environments with cosmopolitan sensibilities that range from conviviality to questioning economic exploitation. Of course, not all contemporary films present human–alien intimate encounters as an opportunity to develop cosmopolitan sensibilities: *Species* (Donaldson 1995), *The Astronaut's Wife* (Ravich 1999), *Under the Skin* (Glazer 2013), and *The Fifth Wave* (Blakeson 2016), to give a few examples, depict aliens who pair up with humans for self-serving reasons, often with fatal consequences. Yet, the growing corpus of films about human–alien conviviality is developing consistent cosmopolitan discourses that deserve closer inspection.

Several of these films such as *I Am Number Four*, *Upside Down*, *The Host* (2013), *Patema Inverted*, and *The Space Between Us* are also part of a wider category of speculative/fantastic films that feature romances between humans and supernatural beings such as zombies, vampires, witches, or wizards. Apart from having couples formed by members of different species (even if they often look alike), what links these films together is that the members of their protagonist couples tend to be teenagers or young adults. That is the case of the *Twilight* franchise (Hardwicke 2008; Weitz 2009; Slade 2010; Condon 2011, 2012), *Vampires Suck* (Friedberg and Seltzer 2010), the zombie film *Warm Bodies* (Levine 2013), and the witchcraft films *Beautiful Creatures* (LaGravenese 2013) and *Ruby Red* (Fuchsteiner 2013). These films reinforce the hypothesis that the film industry has been massively producing narratives of understanding and bonding between seemingly incompatible social groups that are cast in a position of privilege and of liminality, respectively, thus articulating cosmopolitan concerns. As these movies tend to be primarily commercial and, in many cases, are adapted from novels, their production probably depends on projections of economic returns. However, the success of these narratives also suggests that there is an audience of young (and perhaps not so young) viewers and readers who are fond of stories with cosmopolitan overtones. As part of the two aforementioned trends (human–alien romances and young adult romances), *The Host* (2013) constitutes a key site to explore the articulation of cosmopolitan discourses on love and kinship in mainstream productions. Apart from this, the use of framing towards the end of the film provides opportunities to draw parallels with other recent sf romances and points at some formal strategies that several of these films rely on.

Although these films include intimate relationships between beings from two different planets or species, most of them paradoxically feature white anthropomorphic aliens/zombies/vampires and white humans. While films that emphasize racial difference (such as *Avatar* or *Guardians of the Galaxy*) may seem to offer more opportunities for critical analysis, the pervasiveness of relationships between white humans and white aliens makes the films that feature such couples significant objects of study. Moreover, as Richard Dyer points out, whiteness should not be analyzed only in those texts that explicitly situate it in contrast to non-whiteness (1997, 13). Dyer notes that whiteness is present in all texts, whether other races appear as well or not (13). Indeed, he argues that it is important to analyze race in films or texts that only feature white characters in order to see whiteness itself as a race and to expose its privileged, universal status (13). While romances between white humans and white aliens have been the norm throughout the history of sf cinema (from *Aelita* to *I Married a Monster from Outer Space* to *Cocoon*), the proliferation of such stories in recent years makes the analysis of whiteness in them particularly necessary. In addition, the cosmopolitan awareness that many contemporary sf films display makes their whiteness all the more striking. For these reasons, the analyses of *The Host* and *Codependent Lesbian* in this chapter pay substantial attention to the whiteness of these two films.

Despite the abundance of films presenting aliens or supernatural others through a cosmopolitan point of view, queer aliens are surprisingly absent from both mainstream and independent sf narratives. The very few examples of twenty-first century sf movies featuring overtly queer aliens include the Chinese underground film *Star Appeal* (Cui 2004), the highly successful Turkish film *G.O.R.A.*, the zero-budget US film *Codependent Lesbian*, and the low-budget, animation, US film *Strange Frame: Love and Sax* (Hajim 2012). The remarkably scarce examples of queer aliens in recent sf cinema are all the more surprising, considering that earlier films featuring queer aliens comparatively received more support from the movie industry. For instance, 20th Century Fox was involved in the making of *The Rocky Horror Picture Show* (Sharman 1975) and *Enemy Mine* and Dino De Laurentiis produced *Barbarella* (Vadim 1968). The liminality of twenty-first century queer alien films within the movie industry and the scant number of recent productions evince the structural level of cosmopolitan ambivalence within sf as a genre: the genre's megatext presents transnational relationships as harbingers of cosmopolitanism, but only as long as these relationships conform to heterosexual patterns. Indeed, *G.O.R.A.* (the only major production of the four contemporary examples) paints a clichéd image of queerness and presents its homosexual couple as evil plotters. In general terms, sf producers and filmmakers show a general lack of willingness or perhaps—although less likely—imagination when it comes to reflecting on the transnational dimension of LGBTQ experiences.

Although there are not many examples of alien movies overtly engaging with LGBTQ themes, let alone their transnational dimension, in general, the few films that have been made offer a powerful platform to investigate cosmopolitan concerns related to sexuality. Commenting on the sf genre in general, Patricia Melzer notes that "many of the aliens and/or female cyborgs having sex with humans do not rethink desire; they merely channel it into familiar paths through newly configured bodies" (398). Indeed, that is the case in most of the heterosexual alien–human romances mentioned before (e.g., *The Host*, *I Am Number Four*). Although queer alien relationships also mirror normative human sexualities, they tend to offer more chances to imagine alternative modes of desire, love, and kinship. When compared to sf films focusing on queer relationships between humans, films about queer aliens also offer more critical opportunities from a cosmopolitan point of view. In contrast to the national framework of queer sf films that only feature humans, queer alien films pay attention to foreigners (beings from other planets) who, through their mobility, create frameworks for the exploration of potentially different sociocultural and biological systems. That is, human visits to other planets or alien visits to Earth allow characters to be exposed to different affective and sexual cultures, different understandings of kinship, and different modes of reproduction. Queer alien films tend to pit normative heterosexual sexuality (or futuristic versions of it—such as the pill-induced orgasm at the beginning of *Barbarella*) against alternative sexual options and systems that are often presented through camp aesthetics (see Bould 2012, 103–16). Such alternatives go from the wide range of desires and sexual practices that planet Lythion offers to the human Barbarella in her different encounters with a number of locals and even a machine, to the all-male, black, gay, and imperial civilization in *Gayniggers from Outer Space* (Lindberg 1992), the bisexual options that Dr. Frank N. Furter (Tim Curry) opens up for the human couple in *The Rocky Horror Picture Show*, the exclusively female transvestite society in *Vegas in Space* (Ford 1991), or the hermaphrodite alien species in *Enemy Mine*. By featuring characters from different planets and who typically have varying conceptions of gender, desire, sexual possibilities, practices, and norms, sf films do not only expose constructions of gender and sexuality (Pearson 2009, 31), but also shed light on transnational asymmetries with regard to sexual practices and the legal and social systems that regulate them. In this way, queer alien films generally offer a more intersectional approach to sexuality and cosmopolitanism (and potentially also to other elements such as class or race) than other sf films.

The Host: Ambivalent Openness

In spite of the flatness of some of its dialogues and its sometimes clichéd representation of young adult romantic love, *The Host* offers a nuanced insight into processes of cosmopolitan negotiation. In contrast to other films such as *I Am Number Four*, *Upside Down*, and *The Space Between Us*, which feature star-crossed lovers who strive to be together from the very beginning, *The Host* explores the process of personal change with regard to the alien other that both characters in the interplanetary couple experience. Even though the film sometimes deals with character development in a superficial way (e.g., leaving some changes in attitude unexplained), its focus on characters' processes of deliberation and transformation lays a pathway to reflect on cosmopolitan struggles. *The Host* invites viewers to explore the development of cosmopolitan sensibilities through Melanie and Wanderer's (Saoirse Ronan) negotiation of their hybrid body, their symbolic adoption of the name Wanda, the cosmopolitan struggles that are part of the romance between Wanda and Ian (Jake Abel), and, to a lesser extent, of the relationship between Wanda and the rest of the human community. In contrast to other films such as *Avatar*, which show the perspective of the settler (Loza 57), *The Host* offers an insight into the minds of both the alien guest and the human host. Indeed, in Spain, the film was retitled as *La Huésped* (*The Guest*). In general terms, the development of the narrative and the use of filmic techniques in *The Host* show three main aspects of cosmopolitanism. First, that its openness does not appear or develop with ease (Stacey 2015a). The film presents cosmopolitan openness as part of a process of hybrid interactions and struggles. Second, it presents cosmopolitanism as a non-universal attitude and a way of acting that is not necessarily constant, as Ian Woodward and Zlatko Skrbiš note (312). Finally, cosmopolitanism in *The Host*, as in many contemporary sf films, is ambivalent: it both displays openness and perpetuates the privileges of the Anglo, white West and the discrimination of the rest. My analysis of *The Host* first considers the film's exploration of reluctant and intermittent cosmopolitanisms and then adds whiteness to the equation. From a more formal point of view, I also pay special attention to the film's use of framing and camera movement to configure spaces and convey ideas about cosmopolitanism.

In the world of *The Host*, aliens have taken over most human bodies on Earth. They accomplish what we only begin to witness in the 1956 film *Invasion of the Body Snatchers*. Yet, instead of playing on fears of foreign infiltration or exposing the unsettling character of social pressures to conform, *The Host* recycles the body-snatcher theme to explore and eventually celebrate interplanetary hybridization. The film focuses on Melanie, whose body has been taken over by an alien called Wanderer. Apart from the presence of the alien, the protagonist's name (Wanderer) also encourages viewers to interpret the film as a story of interaction between nationals and foreigners from the very beginning. Melanie's mind offers resistance to leaving her body and she and Wanderer engage in a constant conversation (and often arguments) about what to do with their lives. Melanie convinces Wanderer to escape the facility where other aliens are trying to make Melanie leave her body and they go back to Melanie's home inside a mountain in the middle of the desert. There, Wanderer/Melanie is met with hostility, as her boyfriend, Jared (Max Irons) and the rest of the community see her as a potentially dangerous alien. Meanwhile, another man from the group (Ian) and Wanderer get to know each other and fall in love. The film revolves around the conflict created by this situation and eventually shows how Wanderer and Melanie find a solution that allows them to live in separate bodies and have a relationship with the humans they love.

Cosmopolitanism Is Not Inbred: From Struggle to Openness

Even though *The Host* appears to celebrate the development of cosmopolitan sensibilities, the film presents cosmopolitanism as a non-automatic, lopsided, and intermittent process. This is evident from the very beginning of the film. The first sequence presents a future Earth which has seemingly advanced towards cosmopolitan world-building. A narrator tells viewers: "the Earth is at peace, there is no hunger, there is no violence, the environment is healed. Honesty, courtesy, and kindness are practiced by all." As he utters these words, the film opens with an extreme long shot of Earth in which we can also appreciate the reflection of the colors of the rainbow approach Earth and dissolve into it, suggesting that the film may deal with sexual diversity and queerness, a path which is not taken. This first shot is followed by a montage of different zoom-outs and dissolves of a woman and the Eiffel Tower in the background, a man in a convenience store in India, a couple with the Empire State in the background, and a child on a plain that seems to be somewhere in Africa. The film therefore situates the story in a global context of apparent diversity. Through the dissolves, it also points to the interconnectivity between humans and aliens and suggests that they have been affected by similar (but still unknown) circumstances. Yet, the transition between this opening sequence and the next scene is marked by a completely different discourse, as the narrator informs viewers that "the few humans who have survived are on the run." The contrast between the opening scene and the rest of the plot presents streamlined accounts of cosmopolitanism as biased and misleading. Indeed, the society that aliens envision is not so peaceful and open to diversity: aliens chase humans and attempt to occupy their bodies without their consent. In this way, the film encourages viewers to focus on the role of struggles in cosmopolitan negotiations.

As the transition between the opening sequence and the first scene suggests, *The Host* does not present characters, whether human or alien, as if they had an inbred cosmopolitan sensibility from the beginning. Indeed, the film shows Wanderer's relationship with Ian as part of a larger process of getting to know the other and their culture and society. Apart from the entrenched positions that both aliens and humans hold in the film, they also appear to have a different attitude towards personal and intimate relations. Like Aelita (Yuliya Solntseva) in the film of the same name (Protazánov 1924), Wanderer learns about human sexuality almost by accident and gets carried away by this experience later. The Seeker (Diane Kruger), a sort of police officer, warns Wanderer that "humans have strong physical drives," thus suggesting that their alien species have a different social and/or biological conception of affection, desire, and love. Since Wanderer is a guest in Melanie's body, she has access (sometimes willingly, other times unexpectedly) to Melanie's memories. The film presents this interaction as central to the development of a cosmopolitan sensibility in both characters at the beginning. Accessing Melanie's memories is also part of Wanderer's task of facilitating information about humans. In this respect, an activity that is theoretically aimed at neutralizing difference through the location of human resistance has the unintended effect of fueling feelings of cosmopolitan empathy.

Repeated cutting between images that illustrate Wanderer's recollection of Melanie's memories and close point-of-view shots of Wanderer's eyes emphasize Wanderer's interest in what she is seeing. This effect is increased by the proximity of the camera to Wanderer's wide-open eyes and the out-of-focus, depthless background, especially when Wanderer witnesses some of the first romantic moments between Jared and Melanie, which suggest that Wanderer is interested in and empathizes with the experiences that she is witnessing. Although the film also includes close-ups of Wanderer's face and eyes when Melanie attempts to interfere in Wanderer's speech and actions, the proximity of the camera to Wanderer's eyes when she visualizes the scenes of the time that Melanie spent with Jared and Melanie's silence in these particular moments are remarkable, as they highlight that it is Wanderer herself that is interested in what she is seeing. In this way, the film invites viewers to interpret romantic love (and specifically the acquaintance with the romantic feelings of the other) as a particularly powerful driver of cosmopolitanism. Through this initial interaction with the other, *The Host* also suggests that cosmopolitan love is part of a more general scheme of social dialogue with strangers/others. Indeed, it is unlikely that Wanda would have developed a romantic interest in Ian without the previous knowledge of human relations that Melanie's memories and thoughts provide.

Characters do not develop a cosmopolitan sensibility as smoothly as Wanderer's introduction to human love and sexuality suggests. Melanie's influence on Wanderer (and vice versa) is not always direct. Even though Wanderer can access Melanie's memories, they regularly have to negotiate what they want to do. Indeed, in the beginning, both characters withhold information from each other often, as each of them has a different agenda (Melanie wants to return to her family and boyfriend and Wanderer wants to seek the assistance of an alien doctor). An obvious moment when the film shows that cosmopolitanism is not inbred is after Wanderer and Melanie escape the government facility in which they were being held and drive through the desert. They start to argue whether to go to Fort Worth, where the alien facility is, or to the deep desert where Melanie's relatives live. As the argument builds up, Wanderer brakes suddenly and the car turns around a couple of times, showing their competing intentions. Eventually, the car ends up spinning in the air. The sense of confrontation is intensified by the use of the shot/reverse shot technique to show the car spinning from two opposite points of view and by the sudden and loud sounds of the car braking and accelerating, making their initial inability to understand each other even more evident. In this sense, *The Host* reflects what Jackie Stacey calls "uneasy cosmopolitanism" (2015b, 171). Stacey explains that this kind of cosmopolitanism "cautions against the easy optimism of a cosmopolitanism that places prejudice and aversion elsewhere, reluctant to recognize those things in ourselves" (171). As the aforementioned scene shows, *The Host* does not present cosmopolitanism as a gift that some people have and others do not: it recognizes the personal struggles that develop around cosmopolitan possibilities and it does not present cosmopolitanism as inherent to transnational couples.

Although this "uneasy cosmopolitanism" continues almost up to the end of the film, it slowly turns into a less perceptible resistance towards the other. The visual and aural staging of differences and disagreement between Melanie and Wanderer gradually fades away and the film increasingly reflects dissent between both characters only verbally. For instance, when Wanderer first kisses Ian, Melanie grunts: "You're not even from the same planet." Yet, Melanie utters these words as the film frames both characters through close-ups, privileging Wanderer's desires. In addition, the kiss takes place as a balanced, soft melody engulfs a series of flickering notes that had dominated the scene's non-diegetic score up to that moment. In this way, the scene reflects that Wanderer and Ian's emotions are finally surfacing. Wanderer and Melanie still disagree but the scene does not emphasize the struggle between both through the use of visual and aural techniques, as in the car scene.

Carving Out Mental Spaces for Openness

Along with the toning down of differences and struggles between Melanie and Wanderer, *The Host* emphasizes the creation of spaces of trust in the minds of some characters as soon as a group of humans led by Jeb (William Hurt) find Wanderer in the desert. Following the ambivalent logics of cosmopolitanism, humans (particularly Jeb, Jared, Ian, and Jamie [Chandler Canterbury]) only begin to trust Wanderer because she is in Melanie's body. Their cosmopolitanism is at first based on their desire to recover Melanie. The most startling change of attitude towards Wanderer is that of Ian. Soon after she arrives at the cave, Ian—who did not previously know Melanie—attempts to strangle her, along with two other young men. Despite this initial behavior, Ian soon regrets his reaction to Wanderer's arrival in the community when he realizes that Wanderer jumped between Jared and Ian's brother to stop their fighting. As he begins to think that Wanderer may not be as dangerous as he first thought, he begins to pay attention to how she behaves and he gradually begins to desire the alien. He clears some prejudices from his mind in order to consider what Wanda may have to say, show, and teach him. Similarly, Wanderer also gives Ian an opportunity despite his attempt at killing her. Nikos Papastergiadis notes that there is often little emphasis on the role of "the void" in the development of cosmopolitan "engagement with the other" (136–7). He explains that the void consists on the "emptying of the self" of preconceptions in order to give way to something new (153). Although Papastergiadis primarily uses the notion of the void to analyze artistic processes, the development of the relationship between Ian and Wanda in *The Host* suggests that the void can be a relevant element in the development of cosmopolitan sensibilities in general.

The Host stages the opening of a void in Ian's and (to a lesser extent) Wanderer's minds through editing techniques that show an increasing degree of connection in the looks between them despite the spatial distance between their bodies. As Mark Cooper argues, film narratives often revolve around the articulation and resolution of "a spatial problem" (149). Cooper also observes that films regularly rely on looks, particularly "longing looks," to negotiate spatial divisions and explore ways to overcome them (150–1, 156). *The Host* uses the longing looks of Ian and Wanderer to present the division between humans and aliens as a (spatial) problem and to frame cosmopolitan love as its solution. The looks between both characters hint at their desire to trust each other despite their troubled acquaintance and the environment of interspecies hostility that surrounds them. The film highlights the division between the two of them by including Ian in scenes in which he is not present at first or does not talk, such as the first scene in which they help others to rotate a wheel or that in which Melanie tells others about her planet in the kitchen. These scenes hint at Wanderer and Ian's wish to break their separation through a series of eyeline matches that show both characters looking at each other. For instance, when Wanderer is telling everyone about her planet in the kitchen, Ian is also sitting at the table, but at the other end of it, and even though he does not utter a word, the film includes shots of Wanderer and him looking at each other. This scene also includes shots of other characters who do not talk and look at Wanderer, yet their gazes are never met by the alien's gaze. In this way, the film implies that Ian and Wanderer have created a void in their minds that facilitates their interaction with the other.

Apart from the looks between Wanderer and Ian, the film suggests the carving of a potentially cosmopolitan void in the consciousness of both characters through the framing of interactions between the two of them and the visual reformulation of specific spaces. This is particularly evident when Ian shares a bottle of water with Wanderer while they are harvesting. After Maggie (Frances Fisher), a character who is quite vocal about her suspicion of the alien, goes around the wheat field giving bottles to everyone but Wanderer, the film includes a three-quarter shot of Ian reaching out his bottle to Wanderer (Figure 3.1). This

FIGURE 3.1   Ian and Wanderer develop a mental void that offers room for cosmopolitan understanding in *The Host* (Niccol 2013).

shot is then followed by a medium shot of Ian's head, suggesting that this is a personal decision. Finally, the next shot cuts to a medium close-up of the bottle that highlights the significance of this gesture. Indeed, by sharing this bottle with Wanderer, Ian confirms that he is creating a mental void that will facilitate his understanding of the alien other and, eventually, the development of a romantic relationship between him and Wanderer. While this happens, Melanie tries to persuade Wanderer to ignore Ian. Yet, a medium shot of Wanderer smiling at him as she returns the bottle confirms that she has also opened up a space in her mind for considering the human other in a different light.

The act of cutting wheat in this scene further reinforces the idea that both characters are getting rid of some of their and their societies' prejudices. In spatial terms, the development of the story suggests that by cutting wheat, Wanderer and Ian metaphorically remove obstacles in the way of cosmopolitan openness and love. When Wanderer lets Ian know that she has decided to leave Melanie's body and Earth, both characters stand together in the middle of the former wheat field (now empty) kissing and embracing. In retrospect then, the act of cutting wheat in the harvesting scene is also a way of making room for the coming together of the couple. A similar restaging of the relationship between both characters appears at the end of the harvesting scene when characters have to change the position of the mirrors that let light into the cave for a second time. The first time that humans have to change the position of the mirrors, Wanderer and Ian move different wheels and their bodies are framed separately, although they are looking at each other. The second time, Ian and Wanderer no longer appear in different frames and now collaborate to move the same wheel. In this way, *The Host* revisits some of the spaces in which the couple shows its first signs of openness to underline the development of their relationship. In contrast to other films in which desire is established automatically or magically, *The Host* highlights the process of learning and developing a new consciousness that the void opens up. For instance, in *Avatar*, Neytiri decides to trust Jake because the flying seeds of the Sacred Tree magically mark him as a reliable subject. In this sense, *The Host* emphasizes the importance of creating mental spaces of cosmopolitan trust.

The relevance of such mental spaces is also highlighted in other recent sf films that do not feature romantic human–alien relationships, but nonetheless engage with cosmopolitan imaginaries. *Arrival* explores the first steps towards communication between humans and an alien species with a radically different and at first unintelligible language. Both aliens and humans are wary of each other at the beginning, especially humans. For example, the latter wear protective suits and bring a bird in a cage with them when they board the alien vessel/ship to be alerted in case of potential intoxication. Yet, it is only after the two lead spokespersons take their helmets off that humans start making progress in understanding the alien language. This does not mean that aliens are more distrustful than humans. After the concerns of some countries lead to attacks directed at the alien ships in some of their landing sites, aliens decide to place their vessels at a greater distance from Earth's soil. Yet, they still show their

predisposition towards communication by sending a small alien shuttle that carries Dr. Banks (Amy Adams) to the main alien vessel so that she can keep studying their language. This time the transparent screen that used to divide aliens
and humans inside the ship has vanished. Both the attitudes of Dr. Banks and
the aliens highlight the relevance of crafting mental spaces of trust that facilitate
communication and understanding with the other. The alien language that Dr.
Banks is supposed to decode reinforces this idea, as it is non-linear and unlike
any other human language. It is a language that has the potential of changing how people perceive time. As the deciphering and translation process led
by Dr. Banks shows, this change in perspective is not automatic: it requires
gradual openness. Apart from collaboration between countries (e.g., the US and
Pakistan) and extensive professional knowledge of languages and other cultures
(mainly that of Dr. Banks), understanding the alien language requires openness towards radically different possibilities. It depends on the configuration of
a mental void that is ready to assimilate alternative perspectives (e.g., realizing
that "weapon" may actually mean "tool"). At the same time, the aliens do not
offer this tool to understand reality through a new light as a disinterested gift.
The film makes clear that aliens offer knowledge of their language because they
will need the help of humanity in 3,000 years. *Arrival* therefore does not present
a cosmopolitanism based on boundless openness but rather on gradual opening,
trust, negotiation, and collaboration.

The opening of a cosmopolitan void is less obvious but even more radical in
Annihilation. This film registers the gradual, if mostly silent, process by which
Lena (Natalie Portman) realizes that the alien pathogen that has arrived on Earth
and makes different species physically blend with each other does not necessarily
have an agenda and that this process is not necessarily negative. Shocking and
disruptive as this biological process seems (for both characters and viewers), Lena
presents it as something which is not destroying but simply "changing everything." Although the ending of the film suggests that it is actually a new, hybrid
version of Lena that holds these views, her message of radical acceptance of otherness remains unchanged. Indeed, both she and her husband Kane (Oscar Isaac)
are uncertain that they still are the same person they were before entering the
area affected by the alien pathogen and yet they hug each other, suggesting that
it does not really matter whether they still are their previous selves. The mutation
of the mise-en-scène in this last scene actually suggests that they have changed,
as the camera gently tracks to the left as a door slides in the opposite direction,
reframing both characters through blue-tinted glass walls as they embrace each
other. As *Arrival* and *Annihilation* show, *The Host* is not the only film to draw
attention to the void and to present openness towards the other as a process
which may also include contradictory ways of acting and, initially, even negative
feelings towards the other.

Returning to *The Host*, as the story progresses and characters negotiate interspecies conflicts, the film begins to suggest that Wanderer and Ian's feelings
could extend to other places and invites viewers to see cosmopolitan openness

as a spreading awareness. The film does this mainly through the framing of open spaces, specifically through the distance of the camera and its movement. Celestino Deleyto argues that the space in a film, or rather the way a space is filmed, can be a powerful means of conveying ideas about cosmopolitanism (2017, 100–1). In this sense, the presentation of spaces in *The Host* goes beyond the resolution of the spatial problem that the initial division of Wanderer and Ian poses and articulates a more general discourse on cosmopolitanism. The camera often redirects viewers' attention, shifting its focus on characters towards a focus on vast open spaces and the horizon. In the first private encounter between Wanderer and Ian outside the cave, they enter the frame from the left, giving prominence to the landscape. During the rest of the scene, their conversation is sometimes shown through long shots that highlight the space behind them and capture the horizon. The open space behind them is prominent even in closer shots, thanks to the widescreen ratio that the film uses. When they go back to the cave, the camera tilts, leaving them for a second and directing viewers' attention to the vast landscape again. Through the framing of this open space, the film suggests that the couple's emerging cosmopolitan sensibilities may spread to other parts of their society. The development of a cosmopolitan sensibility is even clearer in the second to last scene, in which the camera zooms out from a close-up of the alien–human couple to an extreme long shot of the group of people who resist the authoritarian alien government. The camera then simultaneously tilts up and pans to the right and stops to focus on the hole at the top of the cave. The light fades as the narrator says "if one of them can find a way to live with one of us, I wonder." This panning shot takes viewers from the interspecies couple and the small group of humans inside the cave to the outside, encouraging viewers to see the formation of alien–human couples as something that could also happen in other places. The film therefore forges a connection between the openness and intimacy of the transnational couple and the world outside.

Although *The Host* appears to be about to end after the panning shot inside the cave, the film actually continues beyond this point and offers viewers an additional scene set a few months later in which we can see the protagonist couples driving into the city and being stopped by what at first sight appear to be seekers (alien police officers). Unlike the additional scene at the end of the original version of *Invasion of the Body Snatchers*—which softens the unsettling tone of the film (Grant 2010, 14)—this final scene does not change the reading of *The Host*, but reinforces the cosmopolitan message that it develops and broadens its scope. As someone who is supposed to be a seeker checks whether the occupants of the car are human or alien, the conversation between him and Wanda (Emily Browning) reveals that other aliens are also living in human communities. The last two shots of the film follow shortly after the film makes viewers aware of this new situation. The previous-to-last shot frames the interspecies couple from a medium close-up distance. In this shot, both Wanda and Ian look at each other with a smirk on their faces and then Wanda gazes up to the sky. This shot is followed by an extreme long shot of the LA skyline, which moves up vertically, as if it were a tracking shot, and ends up framing the stars in the sky. The vertical camera movement from the couple to the distant planets and stars in the sky establishes a connection between them and suggests that the cosmopolitanism and love that fuel Ian and Wanderer's relationship may be spreading to other places. This scene then amplifies the message of the previous one by confirming the cosmopolitan possibilities that the panning shot towards the hole at the top of the cave hinted at and pointing towards a wider, galactic scope. The credits further enhance this discourse by including a song with the chorus "welcome to the new age" as the credits flash by against a background of planets and stars in outer space. The last scene in *The Host* then confirms that the use of open spaces throughout the film advances the potential development and spread of a cosmopolitan consciousness.

The last scenes in other twenty-first century romantic alien films employ similar techniques to present cosmopolitan love as a spreading awareness. In *Warm Bodies*, a crane shot gets closer to the embracing human–zombie couple from the back and flies over them to show the walls around the city in the background as they collapse. This camera movement suggests that the cosmopolitanism of the couple is about to extend to the rest of society. In like manner, *Upside Down* presents the expansive force of cosmopolitan love through a shot that, after framing the interspecies couple from a medium-close distance, tracks back to reveal a different urban landscape that suggests that the inequalities that separate two different worlds have faded. The last scene of *What Planet Are You From?* features an interspecies couple discussing whether to live on Earth or on the alien planet. After a medium shot of the couple with their baby from the back of the car, the camera zooms out a bit and slightly tilts up to show their car moving forward on the road towards a horizon that features a mountain range and the sky. Although *I Am Number 4* does not frame the couple together immediately before pointing to an open space or the horizon, in the last shot, the camera—which follows a pickup truck from the back—tilts up to frame the sky on the horizon. In all of these movies, viewers go from seeing close-ups of the faces of the transnational couple together to extreme long shots, literally transporting cosmopolitan love to a broader spatial framework and projecting it towards other parts of the planet and even the galaxy on the horizon.

Cosmopolitan Whiteness

Despite the emphasis of *The Host* on cosmopolitan dialogue and openness, the discourse that the film develops is not as innocent as its optimistic tone of harmony between civilizations suggests. The contrasting discourses that *The Host* develops regarding openness and difference can be captured in a question that Jackie Stacey poses. She asks: "What if the projection of world citizenship is a blended panhumanity that violently erases difference instead of recognizing it?" (2015a, 35). This is precisely the paradox that *The Host* presents viewers with. The film only shows the openness of white people towards white aliens. With the exception of a healer, a doctor, and a few seekers (all secondary characters), *The Host* revolves around relations and negotiations between white characters. In addition, although the aliens in the film are supposedly quite different from humans, the film barely points at their actual differences, except for casual references to the emotional detachment of the aliens, their generalized trust in everyone, and their hyper-efficient economic system and healthcare—differences which the film does not consider as points of struggle and negotiation. Therefore, *The Host*, despite its attempt to present openness to alien difference, celebrates openness to sameness rather than otherness. In this sense, the film uses Wanderer and Ian's relationship to develop what Néstor García Canclini calls "tranquilizing hybridization" (126): a celebration of hybridity which in the end perpetuates the system of racial and cultural hierarchies that actually hamper hybrid cross-pollination.

In his book *White*, Richard Dyer notes that Western discourses present whiteness as "unmarked, unspecific, [and] universal" (45). *The Host* manages to articulate cosmopolitanism through the overwhelming whiteness of its cast thanks to the unmarked character of whiteness in Western culture. As Dyer points out, whites do not define themselves in terms of race (1988, 735; 1997, 9). Given its lack of specificity, whiteness can be anything: it can represent the self, the other, or something in-between. This is what allows *The Host* to put across a message that seems to celebrate diversity and hybridity despite the white uniformity of its cast. Indeed, Dyer also describes whiteness as "a colourless multi-colouredness" (1988, 735). Building on Dyer's work, Dale Hudson has developed a similar argument: he identifies the operation of what he calls "multicultural whiteness" in the vampire films *Vamp* (Wenk 1986), *Vampire's Kiss* (Bierman 1989), and *Carmilla* (Beaumont 1990) (129). In these films, multicultural whiteness is evident in the fact that, first, non-white vampires are present in the narrative in order to reaffirm the hegemonic role of white characters and, second, these vampires can only be accepted as rightful citizens by performing an idealized notion of US whiteness based on material consumption, property acquisition, and reproduction (Hudson 132–3, 146). In more general terms, Hudson argues that "multicultural whiteness negotiates contradictions between an overstated racially blind inclusiveness of multiculturalism and an understated racial exclusiveness of whiteness" (130). Seen against this light, *The Host* also deploys a "multicultural whiteness," yet a more overt version of it than the one in the vampire films that Hudson analyzes. The film evokes a conceptual, elusive alienness that functions without including substantial cultural differences, non-whiteness, or other visual signs/markers of otherness. In this way, *The Host* constructs a post-racial vision of difference in which race seems misleadingly irrelevant. The exploitation of the universal and multicultural character of whiteness in *The Host* eventually dynamites its cosmopolitan narrative: the film builds an ambivalent discourse that simultaneously questions and reinforces supremacy.

The case of *The Host* is far from isolated. Miller and Van Riper point out that 1980s and 1990s narratives of miscegenation in sf tend to highlight differences between species—for instance, through the alien "glowing ball of energy" in *Cocoon* (23). Yet, films from that period (with the exception of *Earth Girls Are Easy*) typically feature interspecies romances between two white, anthropomorphic beings. While naive differences may set aliens apart from humans to a certain extent in the 1980s and 1990s, the presence of these generally banal differences is even more diffuse, if present at all, in early twenty-first century films. *The Fifth Element, Codependent Lesbian Space Alien Seeks Same*, and *Warm Bodies* make subtle references to the physical difference or awkwardness of the alien/ zombie member of the couple. However, *I Am Number 4, John Carter, Upside Down*, and *The Host* barely call attention to it. Except for the Na'vi in *Avatar*, the pink and green anthropomorphic aliens in *Guardians of the Galaxy* (Dey's family and Gamora), and perhaps also the winged half human/half dog hybrid in *Jupiter Ascending*, twenty-first-century aliens indeed look more human and whiter than ever and the visual and conceptual difference between humans and aliens has become less and less perceptible.

The fact that films like *The Host* are not interested in racial difference at all suggests the presence of a deceiving cosmopolitanism in which one race is privileged over the rest. Yet, the depiction of racial difference is not less tricky. Csicsery-Ronay notes that "while *Star Trek* attempts to figure tolerance by displacing racial difference onto alien-human difference, it reproduces the very confusion that inspires confusion about race among real humans, conflating cultural difference with putative natural difference" (2002, 229). The openness to a difference that is actually sameness in *The Host* is then paradoxical. On the one hand, it serves as a vehicle for the exploration of cosmopolitan sensibilities. As Miller and Van Riper suggest, films that have aliens pass as humans (e.g., *Starman* and *What Planet Are You From?*) may "make social inroads in places where more identifiable Others would be turned away" (21). As problematic as multicultural whiteness is, this is particularly accurate in contexts in which it is common to dehumanize the other. The non-menacing character of Wanderer and most of the aliens in the film may question popular narratives of wariness and hatred towards the foreign other. On the other hand, the white masking of difference and race that the film employs to make its cosmopolitanism more palatable to audiences relies on the racist assumption that whites are more human (and more easily acceptable) than anyone else (Dyer 1997, 2). In general terms, *The Host* both replicates and challenges the logics that prevent people from being open to otherness. The film celebrates processes of cosmopolitan negotiation and hybridization while simultaneously rendering them meaningless.

Cosmoqueer Utopianism in *Codependent Lesbian Space Alien Seeks Same*

Like *The Host, Codependent Lesbian Space Alien Seeks Same* celebrates cosmopolitan openness through multicultural whiteness. All the main and secondary characters, both humans and aliens, are white US Americans. Yet, in contrast to *The*

Host, *Codependent Lesbian* presents an alien civilization with a different sexual culture, offering opportunities to consider how the film articulates openness and lack thereof towards both foreign and sexual otherness. In this respect, the film is also a clear example of ambivalent cosmopolitanism: on the one hand, it is only able to picture a white world and, on the other, it imagines a queer alien civilization in sexual, reproductive, and performative terms. By putting two different sexual worlds into dialogue, the film explores how living in societies that offer alternative sexual and/or affective options can be beneficial for individuals. In other instances, *Codependent Lesbian* also exploits the idea of aliens as foreign and sexual others to celebrate the positive impact of interspecies/transnational bonding in the personal fulfillment of the characters. The cosmopolitan discourse of the film focuses on the opening of life possibilities that cosmoqueer sexualities offer rather than on the celebration of emerging bonds across racial/national/religious divides. As in *The Host*, the film's cosmopolitanism also stems from an accidental situation: some aliens have no choice but to travel to Earth because their "strong feelings" are threatening their planet's ecosystem. Their interaction with humans is part of a farcical plan to get their hearts broken so that they stop having the emotions that damage the environment and can return to their planet. In spite of this, *Codependent Lesbian* does not immerse characters in conflicts between cultures. Rather, the film focuses on their experience when navigating an alien culture, the contrast between sexual conventions in both planets, and the new perspectives and unexpected connections that emerge from human–alien interactions.

Interplanetary Camp: Celebrating Aesthetic, Sexual, and Alien Otherness

Codependent Lesbian infuses its narrative with cosmopolitanism by approaching queerness as a utopian exercise. More specifically, the film's camp aesthetics and performance and its ability to conceptualize an alternative social system (especially in terms of sex and affection) are particularly effective means of exploring queerness through a cosmopolitan lens. The cosmoqueer vision that *Codependent Lesbian* offers echoes José Muñoz's call for queer utopian futures. Muñoz argues that queerness is something not yet realized: it is future-oriented (28). At the core of Muñoz's notion of queer futurism is the distinction between "the here and now" of normative kinship, sexuality, and reproduction and "the then and there" of still-non-existent queer possibilities (1, 10, 28–9). Muñoz reclaims the utopian potential of picturing and aspiring to a different time and place against the presentism of heteronormative supremacy and a homosexual agenda solely based on marriage, human rights, and serving in the military (26, 29, 32). In a similar vein, *Codependent Lesbian*'s celebration of sexual, aesthetic, and alien otherness is an exercise in utopian queerness. Although Muñoz's line of argument does not seem particularly concerned with the transnational or the cosmopolitan, he notes that "the here [...] requires the challenge of a there that can be regional or global" (29). In this sense, *Codependent Lesbian* offers an opportunity to critically emphasize the role of the transnational in the utopian process of imagining a queer there: an alternative place that is non-normative.

Since digital filmmaking and other technological advances have generally made it easier to make science fiction films on a tight budget (Pratt 56–7), it is particularly surprising that *Codependent Lesbian* still relies on shoestring special effects and designs. Yet, at the same time, the film turns its zero budget into an advantage, drawing connections to the camp roots of 1950s queer cinema and using camp's awkwardness to build a discourse on transnational/intergalactic otherness. Given the generalized absence of queerness from sf cinema and of cosmopolitan queerness in particular, it is no wonder that *Codependent Lesbian* relies on camp as a vehicle for its queer cosmopolitanism. In his work on camp as a queer mode of film production, Matthew Tinkcom explains that "within the lacunae of [mainstream, capitalist] modes of production, camp filmmakers find the opportunities to press the cinematic commodity into a new form of service that expresses their presence within the domain of production" (28-9). In the present filmmaking context, non-normative cosmopolitan sexualities (especially lesbian sexualities) are largely absent. Big-budget productions rarely feature homosexual characters and, when they do, they tend to appear as male tokens (e.g., *Star Trek: Beyond*). More modest productions sometimes give LGBTQ characters a more central position but barely explore sexual questions (e.g., *Kaboom*) and when they do explore these questions, they do so in national terms (e.g., *V for Vendetta*). *Codependent Lesbian* includes references to other films that situate it as part of a tradition of marginal camp films. The typography of the film's title—which appears a minute into the film—recalls that of 1950s sf B-movies such as *Queen of Outer Space* (Bernds 1958), while its basic settings and props and its black and white cinematography recall those in Ed Wood's sf cult film *Plan 9 from Outer Space*. Just as Ed Wood, Kenneth Anger, Jack Smith, Andy Warhol, and John Waters resorted to camp in the 1950s to "*answer* Hollywood from the margin" (Mennel 36–41), *Codependent Lesbian* relies on camp to resist the heteronormativity of contemporary sf cinema and articulate queer cosmopolitan sexualities.

The reliance of *Codependent Lesbian* on camp is essential for the imagination of a then and there and for the sexual cosmopolitanism of the film. As Muñoz notes, "the queer utopian [...] is drawn to tastes, ideologies, and aesthetics that can only seem odd, strange, or indeed queer" (26). As Muñoz's words hint, camp is indeed an optimal means of expressing queerness. In addition, the strangeness of camp also makes it a potential vehicle for discourses on cosmopolitanism. In general, camp celebrates the breakthrough of the unusual, the uncommon, and the unconceivable in individual behaviors and social relationships. From the perspective of cosmopolitanism, in *Codependent Lesbian*, camp becomes a useful tool to emphasize otherness and to draw viewers closer to it through humor. *Codependent Lesbian* primarily draws on awkward performances (in terms of body movements, dancing styles, ways of speaking, and social interactions) and costumes and sets made from cheap, simple materials to convey a humorous and enjoyable bizarreness. For instance, aliens wear tracksuits and vampire-like, triangle-shaped collars around their necks and the spaceship model is made out of two takeaway food trays and a set of lights. Although many of these details may appear banal at first sight, they infuse scenes with an air of lightness that invites viewers to enjoy not only the story but also its surfaces. Camp provides pleasurable excess because it pushes beyond the usual and the norm. From an aesthetic point of view, it displays resourcefulness by finding new, unexpected uses for everyday objects. Camp adopts a carefree attitude towards its non-normative performance and aesthetics: it celebrates or applauds otherness by putting awkwardness on display for audiences to enjoy. In this sense, *Codependent Lesbian*'s camp channels both queer and foreign otherness.

Of course, camp, in and of itself, is not automatically linked to the foreign other. *Codependent Lesbian* includes a series of cues that present the aliens in the film as foreigners. Apart from the fact that the aliens travel from another planet, they speak an unrecognizable, invented language that would sound foreign to any viewer (although they speak English when they are in New York). In a similar way to the horror classic *Nosferatu* (Murnau 1922), *Codependent Lesbian* also figures the female aliens' sexual and national otherness through the bald heads of the monstrous/alien other. Aliens also convey their otherness through their monotonous way of speaking and awkward performances. Indeed, the aliens regularly show uncommon behavior in social contexts (e.g., by "giving a scarf a ride" in a laundromat) and one of them in particular, Barr (Cynthia Kaplan), shows her concern about the difficulty of navigating a foreign culture. In this sense, some viewers may find parallels between the aliens in *Codependent Lesbian* and the Coneheads, an alien family which appeared in several *Saturday Night Live* sketches between 1977 and 1979 and in the 1993 movie titled after them. The robotic way of speaking of the aliens in *Codependent Lesbian* and the aforementioned vampire-like collars they wear seem to draw directly from these earlier aliens. In a similar way, the Coneheads also have awkward habits. They sleep in a standing position, eat "mass quantities of consummables," and have sex by rubbing their heads against each other and placing "sensory rings" on them. *SNL* and the 1993 film also foreground the foreignness of the Coneheads in more explicit ways. They struggle to understand some common human practices and tell people in the US that they come from France. To underline that they have recently moved to the US, the 1993 film also shows how the alien family is investigated by a pair of ruthless immigration officers. While most humans they encounter wonder about their odd behavior, few seem to question it. More importantly, the humorous nature of the situations in which the aliens are often involved generates sympathy in viewers. *Codependent Lesbian* taps into these already-existing cosmopolitan imaginaries and strategies and gives them a queer dimension.

Despite the multiple elements that invite viewers to see the aliens as foreigners, the use of camp and the aforementioned cues present an otherness that lacks specificity: an otherness that does not engage with the culturally specific situations of queer migrants who do not conform to socially sanctioned affective and sexual behaviors in their home societies. As Karl Schoonover and Rosalind Galt note, Eve Kosofsky Sedgwick's distinction between minoritizing and universalizing discourses is central to transnational queer cinema (69). Universalizing discourses argue for the need to spread practices or attitudes that promote the freedom and well-being of queer individuals. These models, however, tend to be devised by economically powerful geopolitical actors (Schoonover and Galt 15). Minoritizing discourses, in contrast, see queerness as the product of geographical or cultural specificities, thus showing skepticism towards transnational connections in the realm of sexuality (76). Drawing on Sedgwick, Schoonover and Galt note that neither of these categories is preferable to the other. They explain:

> The universalism that hopes to create equality and repeal homophobic laws can often work in practice as a form of neo-imperialism that alienates non-Western governments so that queer people in those countries become more vulnerable to state-sanctioned attack. At the same time, the minoritizing discourse that rejects universal identities can end up demanding a very particularized identity that forecloses on the imaginative and literal spaces available for queers.
>
> *(77)*

While the racial homogeneity of *Codependent Lesbian* may seem to offer a universalizing discourse at first sight, the film does not present queerness as a Western project, as I argue later.

Even though *Codependent Lesbian* does not focus on the culturally specific struggles that queer individuals may face in a given society, the film does point to a key area of concern from the point of view of queer cosmopolitanism: the persecution of those who do not conform to sexual and gender roles and the opportunity that living in a different country may offer for the expression of their identities and desires. Although the three lesbian aliens that the story follows are not sent to Earth because of their sexual orientation, their situation recalls that of people who are almost forcefully driven into migration because their feelings towards the same sex are deemed incompatible with the culture or society where they live. *Codependent Lesbian* presents the strong feelings of some of the alien characters as a danger to their planet's ozone layer, that is, to their environment. This echoes real-life situations in which societies perceive non-normative sexualities as a threat to their social or religious systems and to their economic hegemony. By contrasting regulations and feelings, *Codependent Lesbian* brings to the surface the queer dimension of sexual oppression that sf dystopias about forbidden love such as *Nineteen Eighty-Four*, *THX 1138*, *The Adjustment Bureau*, or *Equals* often erase.

At first sight, *Codependent Lesbian* may appear to establish a parallel with the persecution of non-normative sexualities and gender roles in non-Western societies. Yet, its lack of references to a specific group of people resists that kind of reading and invites us to see the alien misuse of environmental science as a more general reference to sexually repressive societies. As Wendy Pearson explains, Western societies also have traditionally conceived homosexuality and migration as threats to their economic hegemony. She notes that a decrease in the birth rate of (white) babies and an increase in the number of (non-white) migrants endanger the idea of ever-growing white economic power (2009, 302). In addition, the government of Zots conceives the aliens' trip to Earth as a means for certain aliens to get their hearts broken by careless humans so that they stop having strong sexual desires and romantic feelings. This premise recalls the belief that homosexual people can cease to desire the same sex through conversion therapy, a practice that is current and legal in both Western and non-Western societies. In this way, by not including characteristics that invite to link the aliens to a specific nation, race, region, or religion (although actors are clearly white and US American) and by including references to globally widespread practices that restrict sexual freedom, the film keeps its dystopian side open enough to be interpreted as a reference to any society that sees homosexuality as a threat to national or religious structures.

Even though all the aliens in the film are white and they share several behavior patterns (e.g., repeating words), the film presents three female aliens with different attitudes towards sexuality who get involved in different kinds of relationships. In this way, *Codependent Lesbian* does not reduce the alien other to a single image. The first alien that the film introduces on Earth is Zylar (Jackie Monahan). Subtitles present her as a "sexually generous" character. Indeed, Zylar behaves just as she would on her planet: she has multiple intimate encounters with other people but she does not make a big emotional investment in any of these relationships. She just wants to have a good time on Earth. Given her self-confidence and her ability to read other cultures, she is the character who best navigates the dating scene in New York. In contrast, Barr, the codependent alien after which the film is titled, has difficulty getting used to dating conventions in New York. For instance, she scatters "over 2,000 one-line love letters," which obviously do not get her any closer to having a date with a human. Given her initial lack of success in accomplishing the plans of her government, she gives up on earthlings and begins to be romantically interested in Zylar. After experiencing freedom from alien regulations (which forbid "big feelings" and "sentimentalism"), Barr imagines herself living her life on Earth with Zylar and never returning home. However, when Zylar shows her completely opposite view of romance/sexuality, Barr changes her mind and wants to return home, where it is easier for her to fit in, even at the cost of not being allowed to develop strong feelings there.

Although the film's title seems to present Barr as the main character, Zoinx (Susan Ziegler) is the alien that gets most of the narrative attention, as she gets involved in a relationship with the human Jane (Lisa Haas). In addition, her sexuality is the most undefined. As she travels to Earth, subtitles present her disposition as "uncertain." Although Zoinx is perhaps the clumsiest of the three aliens, she is lucky to bump into Jane, a nerdy lesbian presumably without any romantic experience and very open to Zoinx's weirdness. Both develop a stable relationship in which they find an opportunity to share moments and feelings that they had not experienced before. The completely different attitude of these aliens towards sexuality and relationships helps build a non-monolithic image of the foreigners, which is essential from a cosmopolitan point of view. As Plummer notes, "cosmopolitanism needs a globalization that creates diversification and heterogeneity rather than pushing for homogeneity and essentialist categories" (93). In this sense, *Codependent Lesbian* offers a peek into the varied and deeply personal forms that the cosmopolitan dimension of sexuality may adopt.

A central element of *Codependent Lesbian*'s cosmopolitan discourse on sexuality is its ability to imagine alternative alien sexual and affective practices. The clearest example is the aliens' sexual/intimate practice of touching their noses. Zoinx and Jane's first intimate encounter consists of Zoinx touching Jane's nose and then Zoinx leading Jane's hand towards her hose (Figure 3.2). For both characters, this is a new experience: Zoinx has never touched noses "so quickly" and Jane has "never done that at all." By including a camp depiction of alien sex or affection that looks ridiculous (at least by Western standards), the film engages in the practice of cosmoqueer utopianism: it depicts a sexual practice beyond usual or normative patterns, beyond cultural conventions. Camp also occupies a central place in the other key queer intimate moment in the film. During the shower scene that features Jane and Zoinx, both characters adopt a position that the film presents as awkward (Figure 3.3). Although the fact that two persons appear together under the shower should not, in theory, appear strange, the film

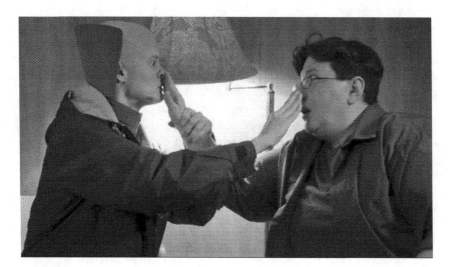

FIGURE 3.2 By having characters touch each other's noses, *Codependent Lesbian Space Alien Seeks Same* (Olnek 2011) queers affection and sex.

FIGURE 3.3 Compositional imbalance and pleasurable awkwardness in *Codependent Lesbian Space Alien Seeks Same* (Olnek 2011).

presents it as such. Jane's body appears to be trapped in an uncomfortable position by Zoinx's leaning figure, as Jane retreats into the very corner of the shower to let Zoinx wash her head properly. In addition, the fact that Zoinx always has to wear her alien collar and the compositional imbalance of the shot increase the oddity and campiness of the moment. Yet, despite the bizarre appearance of the shot, Jane's face shows her pleasure and Zoinx's expression denotes a self-contained feeling of satisfaction. In this way, the film reframes an everyday activity as odd and simultaneously presents it as a utopian moment. This weirding or queering of the characters' sexualities has cosmopolitan implications. In his work on cosmopolitan sexualities, Plummer notes that when people move, "a transforming world of sexualities moves with them" (67). As both scenes suggest, these experiences do not only open new pathways of sexual fulfillment for Jane and Zoinx: both characters see their daily lives transformed through the presence of a foreign otherness that offers previously unknown possibilities to them.

In tune with Muñoz's vision of utopian queerness, *Codependent Lesbian* also uses camp to imagine a cosmopolitan queerness that transcends sexuality. The film relies on this broader sense of queerness to explore the notion of cosmopolitan openness. Examining Andy Warhol's *Still Life (Flowers)* (ca. 1956), Muñoz asserts that "utopia exists in the quotidian" (9). *Codependent Lesbian* also finds utopian possibilities in the quotidian, often through camp moments. Whenever Zoinx laughs out loud at the movies while nobody else does, when she dances in her own way at a bar where she gets stares from the crowd, or when she hands Jane an empty love card that she has just bought from her, she is performing a queer then and there: she is, as Muñoz would say, "taking ecstasy:"

behaving beyond normativity and following her desires (185–7). Although Jane expresses herself in a much more reserved and standard way in these situations, these experiences are for both of them what Muñoz calls "moments of queer relational bliss" (25). Indeed, during her stroll with Zoinx along Coney Island's boardwalk, Jane fondly recalls some of these moments. They are important for her because Zoinx embodies a quality that she admires and does not have: she expresses her emotions freely.

Both sexual and quotidian queerness help articulate attitudes of openness in both characters. Indeed, the embracing of otherness appears as one of the foundations of their relationship. When Zoinx laughs at a disproportionately loud level at the movies, Jane discreetly looks at her with a smirk on her face. Similarly, Jane does not question Zoinx's looks: when Zoinx reveals that she is an alien, Jane acknowledges that she "did wonder about the gills." With these words, Jane suggests that Zoinx's conspicuous otherness is not an obstacle to their relationship. Jane also shows her sensibility towards difference (and sexual consent) when she asks Zoinx if she should wash under her collar when they are in the shower. Yet, Zoinx also shows her cosmopolitan side: she seems particularly interested in learning about US/Earth sexual cultures. As Zylar says, Zoinx never misses the TV program "Studz," which seems to revolve around heterosexual dating. Through these moments of openness, the film envisions everyday moments of utopian queerness in which characters find opportunities to learn about and connect with the other.

Imagining and Doing Otherwise: Queer Resourcefulness and Cosmopolitan Horizons

Codependent Lesbian also practices queer utopianism by having Jane and Zoinx creatively adapt objects or circumstances so that they meet the needs of their transcultural and transplanetary relationship. More specifically, the film resorts to props such as a self-customized mug and portable folding chairs in order to show both their flexibility and their ability to shape their realities into a then and there that suits them. The mug is a present that Jane gets for Zoinx. Since Zoinx is a name that does not exist on Earth, Jane buys a mug with the name "Zoey" on it, covers half of the name with what appears to be Tipp-Ex, and writes the letters "inx" over the erased part. This small detail evinces Jane's resourcefulness: she imagines alternatives and remakes circumstances in order to be able to express her feelings towards Zoinx. Jane's ability to make do also works as a broader metafictional reference to the nature and status of the film: both Jane and the film reconfigure the resources available to them to create objects, moments, and spaces of cosmoutopian queerness.

The short scene in which the folding chairs appear revisits the famous Queensboro Bridge scene in *Manhattan* (Allen 1979) to offer a different perspective on the space by the riverside. For Sam Girgus, the original scene in *Manhattan* hints—through the fog that engulfs the city in the distance and the disruption of the symmetry of the bridge by the structures on the left—at the "ultimate failure" of the relationship between Mary (Diane Keaton) and Isaac (Woody Allen) (70–1). The almost identical framing and lighting in *Codependent Lesbian* in conjunction with the addition of the alienating sound of traffic and new props such as a line of garbage bags and an "END" sign elicit a similar reading of the scene at first sight. Yet, there are two substantial differences: the substitution of a couple of portable folding chairs for the bench in *Manhattan* and the subject matter of the characters' conversation. In contrast to the fixity and rigidity of the bench, the folding chairs are portable and flexible. They can adapt to circumstances and they are mobile (like the characters who carry them, as the film's ending confirms). The folding chairs suggest that if this environment does not suit Zoinx and Jane, they are ready to move to another place where they may find comfort. Indeed, they are sitting in front of the Queensboro Bridge but not talking about the view, like Mary and Isaac do. Jane is fantasizing about going to the beach in the summer with Zoinx even though the latter "would have to watch out for the syringes." Jane's comment about the syringes suggests that her utopian summer may not be perfect but is nevertheless more appealing than the here and now of the Queensboro bridge. Like the fine-tuning of the mug, the folding chairs and the restaging of *Manhattan*'s scene highlight the importance of imagining and doing otherwise.

Jane also shows that she dares to imagine and do otherwise when she gets into the spaceship that is supposed to get the lesbian aliens back to Zots. Like Isaac at the end of *Manhattan*, Jane arrives at the last minute before Zoinx leaves and yet, unlike in Woody Allen's film, the two members of the couple do not part ways. This scene is not only the most utopian moment in the film, but also when camp peaks. Apart from featuring a spaceship model that is made from two takeaway food trays and apart from presenting aliens in the same camp manner as through the rest of the narrative, the film includes several details that reinforce the campi-ness of the mise-en-scène: Barr, the pilot, wears a set of headphones made from two plastic bowls joined with some duct tape and the interior of the spaceship consists of plain metal-like wallpaper, rivets, a pair of pipes, and a few light bulbs inside what seem to be cardboard boxes wrapped in foil paper (Figure 3.4). The convergence of such a large number of rudimentary, camp details in this scene invites viewers to see the whole situation (like the mug and the chairs previously) as a product of make-do and queer resourcefulness.

Through its campy mise-en-scène and its dialogues, this scene articulates a tension between social norms and cosmoutopian possibilities. At first, Zylar adopts a realistic position warning Jane that "no-one is worth leaving your gal-axy for." In addition, Zylar notes that Jane will be "rejected," "a freak," and "an oddity" in Zots. Zylar's comments point at the unforeseeable character of Jane's intentions: she does not fit into the here and now of Zots, where no human has lived before. The use of remarkably hard lighting in the second half of the scene also underscores the risk that Jane is taking. Zylar's comments and the use of hard lighting suggest that geographical distance and differences between

FIGURE 3.4   Camp all over: *Codependent Lesbian* (Olnek 2011) emphasizes its own and its characters' resourcefulness.

species and cultures are paramount obstacles to interplanetary relationships. Yet, just as the aesthetics of this scene look deliberately precarious and improvised, Jane and Zoinx make do with their circumstances. Despite the spontaneous character and unpredictable outcome of this situation, they hang onto their ticket to ecstasy: to the possibility of sharing more time together. They look beyond their respective social environments and follow their utopian desires. In visual terms, the campiness of the scene also pushes beyond the usual and the norm. It introduces viewers to a visual there: an old-fashioned oddity in the current context of widespread CGI and expensive special effects. At the same time, the camp mise-en-scène and performances make this a deeply enjoyable moment. In this sense, the film crafts a powerful moment of utopian queerness. As Muñoz explains, "queerness as utopian formation is a formation based on an economy of desire and desiring. This desire is always directed at that thing that is not yet here, objects and moments that burn with anticipation and promise" (26). By getting into the spaceship, Jane steps into what is not yet here: she is about to be the first human to travel to a different planet for love. The spontaneity of Jane and Zoinx's last-minute decision to stay together indeed suggests that their actions are driven by the anticipatory power of their utopian desires. Yet, the film offers a version of queer utopia that is slightly different from Muñoz's, emphasizing the transnational dimension that often remains in the background in *Cruising Utopia*. In *Codependent Lesbian*, the alternative place that characters envision emerges from queer desire, but its development depends on cosmopolitanism. Jane and Zoinx's image of a utopian there depends on cosmopolitan openness rather than on queer possibilities, even though most of the film focuses on imagining and celebrating non-normative ways of feeling and desiring.

As in many sf films about transnational love, the last scene in *Codependent Lesbian* establishes a visual relationship between the love of the protagonists and vast spaces such as Earth and outer space. Yet, in contrast to most of these films, the camera in *Codependent Lesbian* never leaves the couple. One of the last shots begins by featuring Jane and Zoinx against an image of Earth that occupies most of the background. As the shot advances, the camera dollies in and zooms out simultaneously to keep framing Jane and Zoinx from a medium distance and to make Earth become smaller in the background. This visual effect keeps the focus on the interspecies couple while it shows viewers how the couple's cosmopolitan love ventures into outer space. Yet, this shot does not suggest that the couple's love spreads cosmopolitanism across Earth or through the universe. In contrast to the endings of *What Planet Are You From?*, *The Host*, *I Am Number Four*, *Upside Down*, and *Warm Bodies*, the camera in *Codependent Lesbian* does not move away from the characters to frame a wider, more open space. Jane and Zoinx always remain inside the frame. In his book on cosmopolitan sexualities, Plummer argues that cosmopolitanism should emerge from "little-grounded utopian processes of hope" rather than from grand schemes (189). This is precisely what *Codependent Lesbian* does: it keeps viewers focused on the small actions of Zoinx and Jane while celebrating cosmopolitanism by linking them to the cosmopolitan symbol of the blue marble. Indeed, when Jane and Zoinx simultaneously touch their noses, the image of the globe frames their sign of affection from the background.

The shift from black and white to color in the shot in which Zoinx and Jane touch each other's noses with Earth in the background reinforces the utopianism of the ending. As characters get closer to the cosmoqueer there that they desire, their reality gets literally brighter. The last shot of the film celebrates the queer ecstasy of the couple by recreating one of the key moments of intercultural queer affection in the film, as both women touch each other's nose. Yet, as Muñoz points out, "if queerness is to have any value whatsoever, it must be viewed as being visible only in the horizon" (11). Although the last shot appears to suggest that Jane and Zoinx are now living in a cosmoqueer utopia, both women look upwards, towards something beyond the frame: something unknown which is never shown and remains in the horizon. The presence of both women in the lower part of the frame, giving prominence to the starry sky above them, emphasizes the presence of the horizon in the shot. In this sense, the last scene of the film projects a cosmopolitanism that is based on the free expression of queer personal feelings that are always yet to come.

Both the strength and the weakness of *Codependent Lesbian*'s cosmopolitan queerness lie in its lack of cultural specificity. Even though the film revolves around the experiences of characters played by white US actors, camp makes the whiteness of the aliens weird and different. Yet, their otherness is abstract enough to discourage racist readings that link the aliens to a specific group of people.

In this sense, the film practices and favors the "looser sense of engagement" with alien representation that Andrew Butler calls for (2015, 110). Although this implies that the film fails to represent non-Western people and their sexualities, its last scene contributes to toning down its seemingly universalistic/ Westernizing discourse. To begin with, by having Jane move to Zots, the film indicates that New York and the Western world are not necessarily the natural or logical homes of cosmopolitan sexualities. This narrative move is quite significant. As Schoonover and Galt note, more realistic transnational queer films tend to present the West as the place that best accommodates queer individuals (59, 76). Although *Codependent Lesbian*'s protagonists are markedly US American, the location of the last shots of the film in outer space suggests that the queer utopian space that the film projects on the horizon does not belong to a particular nation or planet. Another problematic issue that Schoonover and Galt find in films that deal with transnational queerness is that their universalism is sometimes based on discrediting localisms (50–3, 60). *Codependent Lesbian* also resists this universalistic tendency by having Jane wear alien clothes in the last scene, suggesting that she finds herself at home in the aliens' local culture.

Despite its general lack of cultural specificity, the film points at the constructedness and lack of rigor of discourses that aim to subdue non-normative sexualities. As Zylar informs Zoinx, the science that indicated that big feelings damaged their planet's ozone layer was far from accurate. Instead, the cause of the depletion of the ozone layer is the reflection of the sun on the aliens' bald heads. By drawing once again on camp humor, the film both exposes the ridiculousness of the situation and infuses the moment with an air of lightness. This presents the scientific and political discourse that leads Barr, Zoinx, and Zylar to leave their planet as a mistake in perception. Thus, *Codependent Lesbian*, on the one hand, locates the source of sexual and affective oppression in unfounded beliefs and prejudice rather than in specific cultures, nations, religions, or regions. On the other hand, the little information that the film provides about the change of situation on planet Zots deceivingly suggests that societies that exert a rigid control over their citizens' affective and sexual lives may change overnight. By doing this, the film overlooks the struggles that people who cannot love freely go through in order to gain gradual recognition for their rights. This magic turn at the end obscures the importance of activism, protest, education, and visibility in raising awareness of LGBTQ experiences and rights. Therefore, in spite of its powerful cosmoqueer utopianism, *Codependent Lesbian* cannot help but give in to the cosmopolitan ambivalence that characterizes contemporary sf cinema at certain points.

Coming from two different ends of the production spectrum of contemporary sf cinema, *The Host* and *Codependent Lesbian* exemplify that the formation of transnational couples as harbingers of cosmopolitan attitudes in their social contexts is a recurrent motif in the genre at the turn of the twenty-first century. In these films, aliens are not just accepted or welcome in small communities as in some 1970s and 1980s films, but they often gradually transform the environments that host them. These two films, like other contemporary examples, also highlight the intermittent and sometimes reluctant character of cosmopolitan attitudes and the importance of carving out mental spaces of trust and openness in processes of cosmopolitanization. The opening of life possibilities for the main characters does not only depend on the transformation of the self. Both films draw attention to the reformulation of social conventions and spatial practices and the modification of spaces themselves. Yet, *The Host* and *Codependent Lesbian*, along with other films such as *Warm Bodies* and *What Planet Are You From?*, also emphasize that cosmopolitan challenges are not over as soon as solidarity, trust and openness begin to emerge. As José Muñoz notes, queer utopias are always yet to come. In a similar way, the framing of open spaces in some of the films mentioned in this chapter suggests that cosmopolitanism is only visible on the horizon: cosmopolitanism is also always yet to come. To conclude, *Codependent Lesbian*, despite its own contradictions, constitutes an act of resistance towards the ambivalent production trends and discourses that permeate contemporary science fiction cinema, a cinema that despite its seeming investment in cosmopolitan ideals, tends to look the other way when it comes to LGBTQ stories and racial diversity. From a theoretical point of view, contemporary science fiction cinema also has a lot to learn from *The Host* and films with similar cosmopolitan narratives like those of *Arrival*, *Annihilation*, or *Upside Down*. Just as aliens sometimes question social structures and conventions and their interaction with humans leads to the transformation of spaces and perspectives, the genre could certainly profit from questioning its conventions more often. In this sense, exploring other racial and sexual realities can contribute to transforming its spaces and imaginaries in productive ways.

Notes

1 This category includes films that frame their love stories within the scope of the nation such as *THX 1138* (Lucas 1971), *Nineteen Eighty-Four* (1984), *Brazil* (Gilliam 1985), *The Adjustment Bureau* (Nolfi 2011), *The Giver* (Noyce 2014), *Equals* (Doremus 2015), *Identicals* (Pummell 2015), and *The Lobster* (Lathimos 2015). Some systemic dystopias such as *Liquid Sky* (Tsukerman 1982), *Born in Flames* (Borden 1983), and *V for Vendetta* (McTeigue 2005) also consider issues related to non-normative sexualities.

2 In this sense, the previous examples follow the pattern of earlier films such as *Caught Looking* (Giannaris 1991) and *Dandy Dust* (Scheirl 1998), which explore the possibilities that virtual reality offers to accommodate queer bodies and desires and to establish personal connections.

3 Csicsery-Ronay refers to Alexey Tolstoy's novel *Aelita* (1923), but his reference to this novel as an early example of human-alien "partnering" also applies to the film (2007, 16).

4

THE COSMOPOLITAN POTENTIAL OF CONNECTIONS ACROSS TIME AND SPACE

Cosmopolitanism is primarily about a sense of shared humanity or, more generally, a sense of shared sentience with other beings. As Anthony Kwame Appiah notes, cosmopolitanism looks for connections beyond ancestry and shared cultural conventions (135). This chapter looks at a variety of films that draw connections across time and/or space, often bringing human beings from different backgrounds and parts of the world together as part of transnational networks. The films in the first two chapters of this book deal with more general types of connections—the transnational influence of powerful economic actors, the networking of borders, and the domino effect of environmental impacts. This chapter focuses on connections of a more personal or individual type, but not based on affection or intimacy, like those related to kinship and love in Chapter 3. Many of the connections that these films draw potentially involve all human and sentient beings. In addition, unlike in the previous chapters, the films mentioned in this one do not belong to a more or less homogeneous trend: most of them establish connections through disparate strategies. They rely on a wide range of premises, concepts, and narrative forms. These films may develop transnational and cross-temporal narratives in a single location and time, like *The Man from Earth* (Schenkman 2007). Sometimes, this kind of film narrative unveils world-shaking knowledge, as in *I Origins* (Cahill 2014). Other films like *Project Almanac* (Isrealite 2015) show how a change in the past has transnational implications in the present and the future. In other cases, they may link characters across centuries and continents, like *Cloud Atlas* (The Wachowskis and Tykwer, 2012) does. From a formal point of view, the films included in this chapter may not appear to share much. At the same time, all of them revolve around individual human connections of some kind or another.

The chapter begins with a brief overview of the main ways in which contemporary sf cinema imagines connections between individuals across different

DOI: 10.4324/9781003164517-5

times and/or spaces from a cosmopolitan perspective. It then offers a close analysis of *Cloud Atlas*, a film based on David Mitchell's 2004 novel of the same title. The film stands out because of its ability to combine spatial and temporal dimensions and present a wide range of identities and cosmopolitan challenges as part of a planetary network of humans. My analysis of *Cloud Atlas* is divided into two parts: the first examines the film's emphasis on economic coloniality as a historical continuum and its relationship with other kinds of colonial difference. The second focuses on cosmopolitan connections and the cosmopolitan potential of small actions that have a seemingly personal or local scope. In general, *Cloud Atlas* celebrates cosmopolitan impulses by drawing attention to a multiplicity of transnational connections between humans and to the transgression of a range of colonial borders (in the broader sense of the term) through time.

The term 'connectivity' often brings to mind the development of the network society. Early interest in network theory was related to the cybernetic theories of the 1940s and 1950s, the development of chaos and complexity theories in the 1980s and 1990s (Shaviro 10), and the internet and cyberculture boom of the 1990s (Bukatman; Castells; Shaviro x). Yet, networks are not only related to cybernetics and they are not an exclusive feature of telecommunication-centered societies. Manuel Castells defines a network as "a set of interconnected nodes" (500) and Robert Holton notes that networks are "forms of multicentered social organization distinct from two other major organizational types, namely markets and hierarchies" (2008, 4). Holton, in addition, distinguishes between interpersonal, institutional, and electronic (telecommunication) networks (2007, vii; 2008, 2–3). Although people, goods, ideas, traditions, and other cultural artifacts have always moved along transnational routes and have formed networks, technical innovations and telecommunications have enabled a proliferation of nodes and an intensification of the connections between them at the turn of the twenty-first century. Contemporary interpersonal and institutional networks often rely heavily on technical developments. In the 2010 prologue to *The Rise of the Network Society* (1996), Manuel Castells points at two key elements in the development of the network society after 1996: (1) wireless connectivity and the spread of the internet and (2) the rise in urbanization and the growth of metropolitan regions (xxv–xxvi, xxxii–xxxv). These two elements enable "perpetual communication" (Castellls xxx) and faster and more intensive mobilities, respectively. Both are key elements in the globalization of networks (Holton 2008, 6). At first sight, this kind of development may appear to suggest that the space of flows (virtual spaces, instant financial and informational flows, temporal compression) is reinforcing its dominance over the space of places (everyday interpersonal relations, customs, and work). Yet, in contrast to Castell's early theorization of the network society—which emphasized the increasing separation between these two kinds of spaces (459), more recent studies remark on the entanglement between both spaces (Holton 2008, 27–8; Castells xxxvi, xxxix; Deleyto and Azcona 107). Science fiction offers a prime platform to explore these social developments. A substantial number of contemporary sf films construct virtual, magical, and cross-temporal connectivities on transnational scales and speculate on the ways in which places shape connectivities and vice versa.

Despite the technological advances that enable the growth of transnational networks, their development is not necessarily positive or even neutral. Transnational networks facilitate the expansion of large corporations and the consolidation of neoliberal systems. They allow finance and capital to operate freely and to be permanently in search of more convenient and favorable legislations. Logistical networks lower the prices of products, but also raise CO_2 emissions and help dump the waste of the wealthiest societies in deprived places. The mobility that these socioeconomic systems foster also increases the chances of pathogens spreading at previously unseen speeds and geographical scales. Networks also contribute to spreading bigoted outlooks. Terrorists draw inspiration from international networks of influence and so do populisms and religious lobbies (Plummer 78-9). Conversely, Robert Holton sees networks as "major sites of intercultural engagement" and as mechanisms that allow people to resist and reshape some of the aforementioned processes (2008, 133). In other words, electronic, interpersonal, and institutional connections allow actors to organize into networks that enable them to advance cosmopolitan causes. Such actors range from migrants, refugees, "professionals exchanging knowledge," and aid workers (Holton 2008, 3, 8) to any kind of person working for a transnational organization, journalists, activists, and even social media users.

Cosmopolitan connections and collaborations do not just depend on networks but also on spaces, objects, and situations that enable connections at a smaller scale. Gavin Kendall, Zlatko Skrbiš, and Ian Woodward have coined the term "cosmoscape" to refer to "spaces, practices, objects and images which afford and construct networks within which cosmopolitan engagements become possible" (154). Although this definition appears to suggest that cosmoscapes always form networks, Kendall, Skrbiš, and Woodward clarify that such engagements happen in "particular sites and situations" which do not guarantee cosmopolitan practices (9). Following the same line of thought, these sites and situations may sometimes also nurture more modest cosmopolitan encounters and collaborations. That is, they may just enable a connection of two or three points or persons in space or time—an idea that sf films seem particularly keen on exploring.

Although my focus on networks and connections so far has been mostly on space, networks also connect points across time. From a linear perspective of time, a series of actions across the past and the present shape the future. For instance, certain infrastructures and interpersonal relationships may allow networks to develop across time. In addition, ideas develop as they travel not only in space but also in time. Human evolution and actions across deep (geological) time determine the kind of environment that future generations will have to deal with. All these elements raise cosmopolitan concerns which seem to require future planning. Yet, as Willian Brown notes, different times and their corresponding spaces do not relate in a linear way. Drawing on chaos and butterfly-effect theories, he notes that a given event is "the result of so many simultaneous and intertwined phenomena that we cannot find a true, linear cause" (105). Thus, time is "interconnected and interdependent" but not causally linear (Brown 101). The non-linear character of events is even more evident in what Gilles Deleuze and Felix Guattari call "reverse causalities" (431 in Shaviro 245). Reverse causalities draw attention to the fact that projected futures may shape the present itself. Similarly, the present may also modify the past, for instance, by manipulating historical accounts. While a linear perspective of time may suggest that cosmopolitan futures can be planned, non-linear causalities show the limitations of such expectations.

Regarding spatial connections in sf cinema, most films focus on different ways of combating or challenging neoliberal or politically extreme uses of electronic or magical transnational networks. Some films such as *Jumper* (Liman 2008) and *Now You See Me* (Leterrier 2013) present ordinary people with the ability to be highly mobile and flow across space by teleporting (annihilating time in the process). At the beginning of *Jumper*, David (Hayden Christensen) describes his daily routine from the top of a pyramid: coffee in Paris, surfing in the Maldives, a nap at the Kilimanjaro, flirting in Rio, attending the NBA basketball final— all before lunch. David, as an ordinary young man from a disadvantaged family background, challenges the predominantly elite and corporate uses of the space of flows. *Jumper* and *Now You See Me* show the concern of corporations, governments, and even fellow citizens when ordinary people manage to move as quickly as finance, money, and information. Similarly, the mystic superheroes in *Dr. Strange* (Derrickson 2016) jump between New York, Kathmandu, Hong Kong, and London through magical teleportation holes as they fight another group of mystics who defend the interests of an abstract, ever-expanding, alien entity (neoliberalism), which plans to swallow Earth. *Sleep Dealer* exposes the dark side of connectivity and how it contributes to the advancement of neoliberal interests by reshaping migrant mobilities, tightening borders, virtualizing physical labor, and adapting Central and North American geopolitics to the interests of US corporations. These films emphasize the transnational dimension of the dystopian view of the space of flows that was already present in *The Matrix* (The Wachowskis 1999).

Offering a slightly different perspective, *X-Men: Apocalypse* (Singer 2016) shows the demi-God En Sabah Nur (Oscar Isaac) taking control of Cerebro, an electronic network that allows Charles Xavier (James McAvoy) to connect with all mutants. Yet, En Sabah Nur uses Cerebro's network technology to broadcast messages to all humans and mutants around the world and let them know that he will destroy the world because humans worship false Gods. *X-Men: Apocalypse* thus employs Cerebro as a metaphor for the fundamentalist misuse of religions to fuel terrorism through the internet. Several films about viruses and epidemics also establish transnational connections. *Outbreak* (Petersen 1995), *Contagion* (Soderbergh 2011), *Resident Evil: Retribution* (Anderson 2012), and *World War Z* (Forster 2013), to name a few, show viruses spreading across national boundaries. In these films, however, viruses often depend on the physical mobility of virus carriers rather than on virtual or magical connections. In general, epidemic films tend to present more scientifically accurate depictions of networks, although such depictions often also serve as metaphors for other more superstitious concerns related to guilt, control, and borders (Echeverría 140).

Films that make connections across time often depend on the inclusion of foreign spaces in their stories in order to explore transnational connections and address cosmopolitan concerns. Otherwise, films often focus on local environments. Time-travel and time-loop films such as the *Back to the Future* franchise (Zemeckis 1985, 1989, 1990), *Groundhog Day* (Ramis 1993), *The Butterfly Effect* (Bress and Gruber 2004), *Déjà Vu* (Scott 2006), *Timecrimes* (Vigalondo 2007), *The Time Traveler's Wife* (Schwentke 2009), or *About Time* (Curtin 2013) typically focus on small communities or local events. Other well-known time-travel films such as *La Jetée* (Marker 1962), *12 Monkeys* (Gilliam 1995), *The Terminator* (Cameron 1984), and *Terminator 2: Judgment Day* (Cameron 1991) ground their narratives in global contexts (the Third World War, a virus that has spread across the globe, a machine-dominated world) but often fail to establish clear connections between local places across national boundaries.

More recently, a few time-travel films have begun to point at the transnational implications of the butterfly effect: an action somewhere may trigger a seemingly unrelated action or event on the other side of the world. In *Looper* (Johnson 2012), Joe is sent back in time from his happy life in China to be terminated by his past self, who lives in the US. The film revolves around the paradox that, in his attempt to modify the past to prevent being sent back in time in the future, old Joe forces Joe to shoot himself, thereby erasing the future in which both Joes (as the same future Joe) are happy in China. Yet, Joe's decision makes sense because by sacrificing himself he prevents the child who will control the most important crime organizations in the future from becoming that person. In *Project Almanac*, a group of high school teens in the US develop rudimentary time-travel technology through which they alter apparently minor details in their past and future. Yet, such minor modifications lead, among other things, to the crash of an airplane flying between London and Madrid. Similarly, *X-Men: Days of Future Past* (Singer 2014) features a group of mutants changing the course of history by time-traveling from near-future China to the US in 1973 and then by plane to a peace summit in Paris about the Vietnam war that same year. Their time trip to change the course of history successfully alters the future in China: at the end of the film, mutants are no longer threatened and they do not need to travel to the past anymore.

Mobility across time and space has even larger geographical implications in *Arrival* (Villeneuve 2016) and *Tenet* (Nolan 2020). Apart from connecting multiple world locations, the protagonists in both films need to find a way to prevent uncosmopolitan scenarios from happening at a planetary scale. In order to do so, protagonists do not only need to work across national borders, but also understand how the past, the present, and the future interweave. As a man (Martin Donovan) tells *Tenet*'s protagonist (John David Washington) at the beginning of the film, his "duty transcends national interest" and everyone's survival is at stake. Indeed, the future superrich aim at destroying everyone in the past in order to prevent rivers from running dry and oceans and temperatures from rising. Both setting in motion and stopping this process requires traveling to different parts of the world and points in time. Following a chronological order, *Tenet* first takes viewers through Kyiv (Ukraine), Mumbai, London, Oslo, the Amalfi coast in Italy, and Tallin (Estonia), forging one link at a time, and pointing at the transnational interconnectedness of the actions of elites (represented by a Russian man, an Indian woman, and a British woman). At the same time, during the last hour of screen time, the film explores the notion of time inversion by revisiting previous scenes in Tallin and Oslo and introducing previous threads off the coast of Trondheim (Norway), Vietnam, and the fictional Soviet city of Stalsk-12, which appear onscreen for the first time at this point in the film. Many of these scenes develop in places with special statuses which carry out operations away from the scrutiny of the rest of society, such as free ports, ships at sea, and secret cities, presenting economic elites as people who operate at the fringes of society and the law. In this sense, *Tenet* can be read as a film that suggests that the unchecked drive towards profitability requires not only operating from spaces of exception but also generating temporal exceptions. That is, the neoliberalism of the future literally requires reshaping time/history to suit the needs of global elites. Through its action-packed scenes, *Tenet* shows the present as a testing ground for the limits of an economic system that depends on its constant expansion across space and time.

Although *Arrival* may not immediately come to mind as a time-travel film, establishing connections across time is central to the development of its storyline. After the alien Costello meets Dr. Banks (Amy Adams) individually and tells her about the applications of the alien language, she starts realizing that the conception of time that this language gives allows those who understand it to see the future. Unlike human languages, this one offers a non-linear perspective of time. This knowledge allows Dr. Banks, a US citizen, to use the alien language to her and humanity's advantage by briefly but decisively taking part in global geopolitics. In a world in which most countries have become extremely wary and have ceased cooperation after the tensions following the arrival of the aliens, she decides to share her knowledge about the potential of the alien language with General Shang from China (Tzi Ma). In order to do so, Louise sees into a future conversation with Shang at a gala event in which he gives her his phone number and also tells her his wife's dying words—two elements that allow Louise to convey the discovery she has made in the past and change Shang's mind towards the aliens and other countries. Crosscutting between past and future conversations between both characters—sometimes for just a few seconds—allows viewers to experience an alternative sense of time. In *Arrival*, mentally experiencing the future entails incorporating part of the alien other into one's mind. In this way, the film uses editing, spatiotemporal links, and the premise of the non-linear language to highlight the importance of reshaping mental frameworks in order to make the most of interactions with the other. The next scene reinforces this idea, as several miniature frames of newscasts from different parts of the world light up against a black background forming a mosaic and showing the swift evolution of global geopolitics after's Louise's intervention, as they first inform of China's decision to share their intelligence and then about other countries following suit. Such responses present processes of cosmopolitan openness as contagious, as Louise and the aliens' initially reluctant trust and knowledge-sharing eventually give way to a cascade of similar reactions. However, the cosmopolitan ambivalence of sf cinema is yet again confirmed in this part of the film by the centrality of China and the US as global superpowers and the fact that the only understandable language heard in the newscasts is English. Despite this, both *Arrival* and *Tenet* evince the increasing relevance of world locations and transnational links in storylines about temporal connections.

A remarkable number of films also focus on how spaces change through time or establish often-unnoticed connections between distant times. In the two versions of *The Time Machine* (Pal 1960s; Wells 2002) and in *Lucy* (Besson 2014), the protagonist develops the technology or acquires the ability to go forward or backward in time across centuries, witnessing how spaces and their inhabitants radically transform with the passing of time. Such revisions of spatial configurations open paths to interrogate discourses that defend the *supposed* cultural and ethnic purity and homogeneity of a given place. In the case of *Lucy*, the film shows—within the scope of two minutes—radically different versions of Times Square: from the present, to its original construction, to a time where Native Americans roamed un-urbanized plains, to an era when dinosaurs lived, and, finally, to pre-*Homo sapiens* times. Offering a similar perspective on the passing of time, the protagonist in *The Man from Earth* (who has traveled across centuries) notes that "you can't go home again because it isn't the same." These films, along with other examples that I mention later such as *Cloud Atlas* and *The Fountain* (Aronofsky 2006), show a different approach to the relationship between time and space from that of films from the immediately preceding decades. Vivian Sobchack notes that 1980s films in general and even time-travel films such as *Back to the Future* or *The Philadelphia Experiment* (Raffill 1984) often "conflate past, present, and future," offering homogenized and nostalgic portraits of time (274–6). In contrast, the aforementioned twenty-first-century films emphasize the heterogeneous configurations that a given space may adopt through time.

While these films suggest that places do not have a static essence, other films use similar concepts to highlight the interconnectedness (but not the conflation) of time. The famous graphic match in *2001: A Space Odyssey* (Kubrick 1968) bridges four million years of technological evolution, presenting humans as part of an evolving continuum that persistently verges on the dystopian. *The Tree of Life* (Malick 2011) goes a step further. As William Brown notes, it takes viewers "from the present moment right back to the origins of the universe, and from the present moment forward to the 'end of time'" (101). While more modest in scope, the mockumentary *The Age of Stupid* (Armstrong 2009) also establishes links between past and present human actions and future scenarios of global environmental apocalypse by using real images of environmental damage from the past and the present in different continents. Conceptually, all of these examples emphasize the interdependence of different moments across time and the perpetual mutability of cultures and peoples.

Although spatiotemporal connections across different historical periods and countries have been present in the cinema from the outset—for instance, in *Intolerance* (Griffith 1916)—such links have proliferated in recent sf films. These films often stress that characters happen to live in a given place at one time, but they or a version of them may have also lived or could live in a different place at a different past or future time, thus raising questions about strict understandings of cultural and biological belonging. An early, anachronistic example of this trend is *Slaughterhouse Five* (Hill 1972), which revolves around the protagonist's traumatic experience of World War II by following his mind as it jumps between different episodes of his life during the War in Germany, back home in the US after the war, and on planet Tralfamadore (after supposedly being abducted by aliens). Later films such as *The Fountain*, *The Man from Earth*, and *Portable Life* (Boonman 2011) also tend to focus on one or two actors moving across time and continents, sometimes as the same person and other times as different characters. While *The Fountain* and *Portable Life* feature a range of different locations, films do not always resort to introducing their actors in different spatiotemporal contexts on screen. That is, actors do not always move around in the plot, although they always do in the story. For instance, *The Man from Earth* takes place in a cottage where a mysterious man tells a group of friends about his long and highly mobile life. The film revolves around Professor John Oldman (David Lee Smith), a person who has lived 14,000 years and is an eternal migrant who has dwelled, among other places, in Mesopotamia, the UK, France, Belgium, the US, Sumer, Babylonia, Phoenicia, and India. Even though he eventually turns out to be an alternative version of the Christian figure of Jesus, he also praises Buddha's teachings. As a person who is regularly on the move and who appreciates different cultures, his figure questions monolithic notions of local, regional, or national identities.

In spite of the early example of *Intolerance*, which connects different humans across different times and places through their shared encounters with the colliding forces of hatred and love, films in general and sf films in particular have rarely connected such a vast array of circumstances and personal experiences. One exception is *The Philosophers/After the Dark* (Huddles 2013), which shows how a group of students and their teacher imagine and shape a range of alternative worlds from a classroom at an international high school in Indonesia. As in the case of *The Man from Earth*, *The Philosophers* shows that films can draw connections using a single room as the only location in the real world of the film and still offer thought-provoking scenarios in which different temporal, spatial, and social configurations drive the narrative. This film offers a range of scenarios in which characters consider questions related to biopolitics and intersectionality (including race, gender, sexuality, occupation, skills, and disability), often through a cosmopolitan glass. Yet, as products of characters' imaginations, their projected futures ultimately remain grounded in the characters' present. A more remarkable example is *Cloud Atlas*, which weaves a web of stories influenced by a range of (neo)colonial and cosmopolitan influences across different continents and centuries. Moving between the Chatham Islands in the Pacific, San Francisco, England, Scotland, the fictional and futuristic city of Neo Seoul, a post-apocalyptic Hawaii, and an unknown planet, and between the years 1849, 1936, 1973, 2012, 2144, and 2346, the film addresses interrelated concerns about oppression, race, greed, sexuality, age, sentience, beliefs, and environmental exploitation. In this sense, *Cloud Atlas* virtually channels all the main cosmopolitan discourses in contemporary sf cinema. *Cloud Atlas* also stands out because of the way in which it explores the borders of editing and narrative conventions. Constantly juggling times and places, the film establishes strong connections between characters by pushing the limits of intensified continuity, casting, performance, and makeup. More generally, by directing viewers' attention towards the connections between its six storylines, the film practices cosmopolitan intersectionality in both conceptual and formal terms.

Cloud Atlas also represents a so far unmentioned phenomenon in contemporary sf cinema: several recent films articulate discourses on cosmopolitan connectivity by introducing reincarnation in their narratives. Apart from *Cloud Atlas*, recent sf reincarnation movies include stories about spatiotemporal mobility such as those in *The Fountain* and *Portable Life* and other more time-bound stories such as those in *I Origins* and *Jupiter Ascending*. In general, these films embrace cosmopolitanism by suggesting that, while human souls seemingly vanish when death arrives, they actually find a new body to start a new life. As a natural process (following the logic of these films), the reincarnation of these souls may happen anywhere. Reincarnation then challenges established borders and blurs the line between self and other. *I Origins* devotes most of its story to tracking the connection between the eyes of Sofi (Àstrid Bergès-Frisbey), a white and probably European woman who lives in New York, and Salomina (Kasish), an Indian girl. While the moment in which both characters connect is brief and appears at the end of the film, by establishing such a link, the film invites viewers to question their notion of national belonging. In addition, this connection is made at a climatic point in the film, after most of the plot revolves around the circumstances surrounding such a link. Through this connection, the film appears to wonder whether human beings would care more about others if we knew that we might become someone else in our next life. Although *Jupiter Ascending* may not come readily to mind as a reincarnation movie, it relies on the premise that its protagonist, Jupiter Jones (Mila Kunis), a Russian immigrant who works as a cleaner in Chicago, was a Queen of the Abrasax royal family on another planet in her past life. In this way, the film looks beyond nationality in its attempt to develop a cosmopolitan critique of belonging: it suggests that cultural essentialism also relies on the enforcement of borders that maintain class and income inequalities.

Some films further interrogate the limits between self and other by drawing links between humans and other beings. For instance, *The Fountain* suggests that Izzi (Rachel Weisz) becomes a tree after her death and *Uncle Boonmee Who Can Recall His Past Lives* (Weerasethakul 2010) features an ape-like being who was a human in a past life. *Uncle Boonmee* also shows a princess (Wallapa Mongkolprasert) having sex with a catfish, suggesting that they have some kind of past connection. More recently, *Annihilation* (Garland 2018) has also engaged with the trope of transspecies connection and individual transformation. The film explores the connection between humans and other species by imagining a scenario in which a contagious alien agent causes all beings (plants, humans, animals) to adopt features of other species they come into contact with, literally merging with them. This produces multiple cross-species combinations, something which the protagonist (Natalie Portman) comes to see as not intrinsically positive or negative, as she explains at the end of the film. The development of *Annihilation*'s narrative then questions differences and hierarchies between species and, by extension, notions of national belonging. In general, the reincarnation and transformation elements in these films blur the line between self and other in an attempt to make viewers aware of the lives of other beings with whom they share the world.

"There Is a Method to This Tale of Madness": Putting the Pieces of *Cloud Atlas* Together

Cloud Atlas has an interlocking structure that constantly jumps across time and space. For purposes of clarity, I start by summarizing each of the six storylines chronologically. The first story begins in the Chatham Islands in Polynesia in 1849, where Adam Ewing (Jim Sturgess) signs a contract through which he buys some slaves. Most of the story takes place on a ship that takes him back home to San Francisco, where he is poisoned by Dr. Goose (Tom Hanks) and saved by the stowaway Autua (David Gyasi). The next story takes viewers to Scotland in 1936, where Robert Frobisher (Ben Wishaw) works as an amanuensis for the famous composer Vivian Ayrs (Jim Broadbent) while he corresponds with his lover Rufus Sixsmith (James D'Arcy), who is a student in Cambridge. Frobisher's story revolves around this long-distance relationship and his constant clashes with Ayrs, some because of the latter's homophobia. The film then jumps to 1970s San Francisco, where inquisitive journalist Luisa Rey (Halle Berry) unveils—with the help of an older Rufus Sixmixth, the scientist Isaac Sachs (Tom Hanks), and security guard Joe Napier (Keith David)—the conspiracy of an oil company to make a nuclear reactor fail. In the year 2012, viewers meet Timothy Cavendish (Jim Broadbent), a vanity editor, who teams up with other seniors to escape the elderly home where his brother has locked him up in Scotland.

Forward into 2144, *Cloud Atlas* sketches a cyberpunk Neo Seoul in which identical-looking fabricants (clones) work at the service of pureblood consumers (humans) under the rule of a corpocracy. The story focuses on the life of "fabricant" Sonmi-451 (Donna Bae) who works as a waitress for the fast-food chain Papa Song and later becomes a revolutionary leader with the help of Hae Jo Chang (Jim Sturgess), the Rebellion's First Science Officer. The last story transports viewers to Big Isle (Hawaii)[1] in the year 2346, where some humans (Valleymen) live in technology-free communities, others (the Kona) have become cannibalistic soldiers, and other humans (Prescients) are a technologically advanced civilization who can no longer survive in their territory and need the help of the Valleymen to search for a new place to call home. This post-apocalyptic story focuses on the collaboration between Valleyman Zachry (Tom Hanks) and Prescient Meronym (Halle Berry). There are two significant changes regarding story locations with respect to the novel. First, in the film's 1936 storyline, Robert Frobisher works as an amanuensis in a Scottish castle instead of a Belgian one, probably because of shooting and/or budget limitations. Second, at the end of the film, Zachry and Meronym have left Big Isle and moved to a different planet where they are raising a racially diverse family.

Although the film approaches the same themes and includes more or less the same characters as the novel, their narratives develop in radically different ways. The novel first presents the six stories in chronological order, from 1849 to a post-apocalyptic Ha-Why in the future. After the chapter set in future Hawaii ("Sloosha's Crossin' an' Ev'rythin' After"), the novel returns to the other stories in reverse chronological order, ending in 1850. The novel therefore develops a Russian-doll structure (Selisker 454) that constitutes a palimpsest in which all the stories form "a bundle of several different textual strands held together by porous seams" (Dix 119). The film, in contrast, constantly juggles times and spaces and links personal experiences through editing, sound, and casting, multiplying the novel's "porous seams" exponentially. The film alters the structure of the novel from the very beginning, as it opens with a series of short scenes from each of the stories in non-chronological order: from the twenty-fourth century to 1849, 1973, 2012, 1936, and finally 2144. These opening scenes are then followed by two or three longer scenes per storyline (this time in chronological order) in which the film establishes the contexts for each of the times more clearly. In addition, another significant change in the film is that Zachry's yarn frames the whole film. The only two sequences in which he appears as a narrator on another planet open and close the film. In the novel, in contrast, Zachry's yarn functions as an anchoring point in the middle of the narrative, allowing it to reverse its so far linear perspective of time. In general, the film version of *Cloud Atlas* presents a much more fragmented form, temporality, and spatiality.

The film retains and develops some of the strategies that the novel employs to interlink the different storylines. It connects characters through their birthmarks, embeds bits of media from previous stories in the stories that follow them, and includes similar or identical objects that establish casual links between characters. Both in the film and in the novel, one character from each of the storylines (Adam Ewing, Robert Frobisher, Luisa Rey, Tim Cavendish, Sonmi-451, and Meronym) has a birthmark in the shape of a comet, suggesting that the same soul reincarnates as these different characters. The fact that the birthmark has the shape of a comet situates human life in a cosmic context wider than localities, nations, and continents and appears to embrace the idea of boundless mobility. By connecting the different traits of these characters under the umbrella of a single soul, both the novel and the film present disparate kinds of gender, sexuality, race, nationality, age, beliefs, religion, profession, skills, personality, and even biological origin as part of a continuum. The different kinds of media that *Cloud Atlas* features (a journal, letters, a novel, a film, a recorded interrogation, a yarn) also establish a chain of connections, influences, and inspiration across time and space. While the novel develops the narrative through different narrative forms (an actual journal, epistolary chapters, third-person narration, first-person narration, and an interview), the film introduces the different media as objects rather than as means of narration. Instead, the film signals the different styles of the stories through the different film sub-genres in which each of the stories participates (period drama, thriller, comedy, dystopian sf, post-apocalyptic sf/fantasy). As in the novel, the film embeds media from the past in future times. Frobisher reads Ewing's journal; Frobisher's music permeates—in multiple forms—all of the stories; Rey reads the correspondence between Frobisher and Sixmith; Cavendish edits a novel based on Rey's investigation; the rebellion that Cavendish inspires at the elderly home becomes the subject of a reference film for fabricants; Sonmi becomes a Goddess in 2346 Hawaii, and her ideas circulate both in video form and in a book made of fabric onto which words are sewn. The film also connects stories in more 'banal' ways, mostly through objects. For instance, Dr Goose steals a pair of blue buttons from Adam Ewing in 1849, which reappear in Zachry's hands in 2346. Similarly, Ewing burns a contract on a fireplace in 1849 and old Zachry tells his story by a fire in one of the last scenes in the film. In this way, the film recycles and expands some of the novel's strategies to bring a wide range of experiences, styles, and tones together.

Most scholarship on *Cloud Atlas* has focused on the novel, the differences between it and the film, or on a specific story or set of stories in the novel or the film. Analyses of any of the two media often highlight the interconnection between the six storylines but often fail to investigate the relationship between the different kinds of links that appear, the way they operate, and the discourses that they develop. For instance, Jo Alyson Parker notes that "doors and bridges often [serve] as links" (127) and yet she does not consider what the film achieves by adding such connections to the stories. Instead, Parker underlines the disparate forms of the novel and the film, arguing that the fact that Zachry's yarn frames the rest of the film radically changes the open-endedness of the novel (123, 132–3). Cáel M. Keegan, however, reads this change in a more positive light, arguing that the film eventually moves towards a utopian future in which Meronym and Zachry escape the reach of colonial racism by moving to a distant planet (88, 99). Another common way of approaching *Cloud Atlas* is by concentrating on a limited set of stories. For example, in an article on the film, Gabriel Estrada analyzes the representation of the indigenous nations of the Moriori and

Māori in the Polynesian Chatham Islands in 1849 and the (supposedly) Kanaka Maoli in 2346 Hawaii. Drawing on evidence from these two storylines, Estrada surprisingly argues that *Cloud Atlas* develops a discourse based on "heterosexist settler colonialism" (1). Yet, such an argument loses weight when the connections between the different stories are considered, as I argue later.

Cáel M. Keegan's book *Lana and Lilly Wachowski* (2018) is one of the analyses that more clearly foregrounds the connections between the different storylines in the film. He primarily focuses on the ways in which the film draws links across gender and race. More specifically, Keegan reads the film through the notion of trans★, which he defines as "a force characterized by unpredictable flows across discrete forms" and as a way of "expressing unrealized bodies" (3-4). Through this lens, Keegan offers an insightful reading of the trans★ dimension of the film—a dimension that is generally overlooked. Yet, at the same time, this approach leads him to largely focus on the Neo Seoul and Big Isle storylines. From a different perspective, Kristian Shaw applies the cosmopolitan perspective that *Cloud Atlas* seems to cry for. He emphasizes that the novel revolves around "an interconnected global multitude that escapes the cyclical entropy of history" (57). However, in spite of his emphasis on interconnection and the concept of multitude throughout the chapter that he devotes to *Cloud Atlas*, Shaw does not pay much attention to the 2349, 1936, and 1973 stories. While scholars tend to privilege certain storylines for a variety of legitimate reasons, *Cloud Atlas* calls for analyses that treat the film or the novel as the narrative networks that they are. The analysis of the film in this chapter attempts to mirror the relatively equal treatment all the storylines are given in it.

Probably the most relevant scholarly contribution from the point of view that I am applying here is Donna Peberdy's article on performance and the multi-protagonist cast of the film. Focusing on one of the most innovative aspects of the film (the casting of the same actors as different characters in all or most of the stories), Peberdy sheds light on the network of human relations across time and space that the film builds. She notes:

> [T]he multi-role performances not only see the actors perform across time, space and genre but also, with the help of makeup and prosthetics, across gender, sexuality, race and ethnicity. For example, Berry plays a native African woman, a Caucasian Jewish woman, an Indian woman and an aged Korean man; Sturgess, Weaving, D'Arcy, Grant and Broadbent also play Asian characters in the Neo Seoul storyline; Whishaw and Weaving appear as women in the present-day story; and Bae plays Caucasian and Mexican women in two of the storylines.
>
> *(169)*

Apart from the categories that Peberdy mentions, actors also transcend class and power dynamics and experience shifts in the relevance of their characters from one story to the next. For instance, Keith David—who plays secondary and minor roles in the film—goes from being a servant in 1849, to a security guard in 1973, to the leader of a resistance group in 2144, to the leader of the Prescients in 2346. In some cases, viewers have perceived some of these performances as instances of whitewashing (e.g., Sturgess playing a Korean character) (Perberdy 170). Yet, to see whitewashing in a film that so explicitly foregrounds characters' rebirth across borders is to miss the point, specially bearing in mind the role of actors such as Donna Bae, who plays a Latino character in the 1973 and an Anglo-American-looking woman in 1849. As Peberdy emphasizes, by relying on multi-role performances, the film challenges boundaries (177). At the same time, the cosmopolitan discourse of the film does not only rely on the fact that actors play multiple roles. If that were so, a single actor may have been enough for the movie to get its message across. The film shows souls moving and evolving across time, but also establishes connections between the protagonists' souls and other characters who are generally from different times. Thus, *Cloud Atlas*' cosmopolitan discourse depends not only on performances but on its multi-protagonist structure.

The theory of the multi-protagonist film genre that María del Mar Azcona has developed serves to define many of the stylistic resources that *Cloud Atlas* employs. Azcona identifies a set of visual conventions that also helps me to explain how *Cloud Atlas* weaves a cosmopolitan network between characters. As she notes, multi-protagonist films often gather "a broad spectrum of characters [with similar narrative weight] who get involved in different storylines" (2010, 37). Films with several protagonists tend to synchronize stories, establish parallels, and find unexpected connections between them. For these purposes, they draw connections through camera movement and often employ graphic matches, matches on action, montage sequences, or a recognizable soundtrack that link the experiences of different characters (Azcona 2010, 37–44). Azcona also observes that global thrillers like *Syriana* (Gaghan 2005) rely on the juxtaposition of similar activities. As the typology of these linking techniques suggests, multi-protagonist films establish connections governed by randomness and chance. In addition, these films are particularly useful vehicles to explore questions related to globalization: through their form and subject matter, they both show and embody the difficulty of making sense of global puzzles (Azcona 2010, 130–1, 143).

Cloud Atlas exploits all these conventions of the multi-protagonist film and takes them a step further than similar transnational ensembles. While many of its visual and aural strategies coincide with those employed in *Syriana*, *Babel* (Iñárritu 2006), and similar films, *Cloud Atlas* multiplies its reliance on the aforementioned techniques and experiments with additional ways of drawing connections. In this sense, *Cloud Atlas* is not only a film about characters that cross spatiotemporal boundaries but also a film that crosses and reshapes several cinematic borders. *Cloud Atlas* matches storylines by cutting between two parts played by the same actor at two different times or between the similar facial expressions of two different characters/actors, by juxtaposing similar actions, objects, and situations, or by editing together two shots that use the same kind of framing (e.g., angle) in two different periods. The movement of the camera sometimes continues a movement initiated by a character in a different storyline. Further contributing to the film's quest for spatiotemporal fragmentation, graphic matches may occur several minutes after the first shot appears. For instance, the almost visually identical train rides of Frobisher and Cavendish to Scotland in 1936 and 2012 appear 40 minutes away from each other (Figures 4.1 and 4.2). Visual strategies like this invite viewers to actively look for connections beyond neighboring shots or scenes and between all storylines.

The film also creates similar effects through the mise-en-scène. As Lana Wachowski points out in the special features of the *Cloud Atlas* Blu-Ray, the chateau where Vyvian Ayrs lives in Scotland reappears later on as a home for the elderly. Similarly, the layout of the Papa Song restaurant and the London roof bar in the 2012 story are the same. Zachry's left-shoulder tattoo also replicates the pattern of Vivian Ayrs' nightdress. By using different film genres for each of the periods, the film also transcends generic boundaries each time it establishes

FIGURES 4.1 AND 4.2 In *Cloud Atlas* (Tykwer and The Wachowskis 2012), two shots separated by 40 minutes of screen time form a graphic match that stretches editing conventions and invites viewers to look for connections in the film's spatiotemporal cocktail.

a visual link between two or more stories. In addition, *Cloud Atlas* regularly includes montage sequences in which a character from a given time speaks as the film crosscuts between her/his time and other periods. Sometimes, the reaction of a character appears after a sound from a different time that could have triggered that reaction (but in reality does not). Characters also utter words that are edited together with related actions from other times and that appear to inspire and help other characters or simply describe their experiences. Just as characters reincarnate themselves into other characters, so does "The Cloud Atlas Sextet" composed by Robert Frobisher mutate into different diegetic and non-diegetic versions (Peberdy 177). In one instance, it becomes a slightly different tune that fabricants sing as the film crosscuts between their Xultation (execution) ceremony and Frobisher composing the original song. These examples show that the film makes the most out of Mitchell's original story by exploiting the possibilities that cinematic language offers. Through this array of strategies, *Cloud Atlas* constantly encourages viewers to look for additional ways in which the different pieces of its spatiotemporal puzzle may fit together. In this sense, the film encourages viewers to put into practice the cosmopolitan habit of paying attention to what unites rather than what divides humans.

The Multiple Iterations of Coloniality in *Cloud Atlas*

In the film's five-minute-long trailer, Isaac Sachs (Tom Hanks) suggests that *Cloud Atlas* revolves around forces such as fear, belief, and love, which "begin long before we are born and continue after we perish." While these phenomena are at the center of all the narrative strands, Sachs does not mention two other interrelated forces that also mutate across time and pervade all the stories in the film: greed and coloniality. Before addressing any racial and religious issues related to colonialism in the first story, *Cloud Atlas* features the signing of a contract between two men, which establishes the purchase of some slaves. Thus, the film emphasizes the economic dimension of coloniality from the very beginning. Indeed, it seems no coincidence that the first story in *Cloud Atlas* is set in 1849, a time to which Robert Holton refers as "High Empire" (2008, 133). Yet, the film channels its most obvious critique of greed through the neoliberal version of coloniality in 2144, when Neo Seoul has become a city with an ever-rising skyline. Extreme long shots convey a sense of overdevelopment, as multiple objects and details flood shots of industrial facilities and of buildings mounting on each other. Sonmi's description of fabricants' "24-hour cycle" suggests that she lives in a system that operates non-stop. It is also a system that economizes on the material resources that its labor force uses to the maximum extent. Workers live in corporate facilities, shower by walking in and out of a room in a queue, and sleep on rows of individual pods piled on walls, saving space. When they wake up, the doors of these cabins pop out automatically and slide the bodies of the fabricants out. In this way, fabricants appear to emerge from an oven, as if they were manufactured bread rolls. Ironically, the film later reveals that the clones are a cheap source of food for themselves. The "soap" that they eat is made from the bodies of older fabricants, echoing the dietary nightmares of the 1973 film *Soylent Green* (Fleischer), in which the main food supply for the population is also made from human corpses. Although corporate actors barely appear in *Cloud Atlas*, these details suggest that neoliberalism has been carefully tweaked to optimize corporate profits.

Previous stories also reflect different iterations of the relentless force of greed. Vyvyan Ayrs seeks to steal and profit from the work of his amanuensis, Robert Frobisher. The 1970s thriller revolves around Big Oil's attempts to trigger a major failure in a nuclear plant in order to manipulate public opinion and eliminate competitors in energy markets. In 2012, Timothy Cavendish's brother (Hugh Grant) gleefully notes that Aurora House is "incredibly lucrative." Finally, Meronym says that the "hunger for more" of previous civilizations caused their fall. Indeed, all of the stories revolve around humans' hunger for money and power.

All the stories couple economic coloniality, greed, and exploitation with other kinds of colonial and imperial difference, including categories such as race, species-belonging, religion, gender, sexuality, age, and nature. As I show later, the film relies on different kinds of coloniality to articulate its defense of cosmopolitan ideals. Given its emphasis on colonial divisions, *Cloud Atlas* grounds its cosmopolitan discourse in a similar way to the approaches to cosmopolitanism that Walter Mignolo, David Harvey, and Gurminder Bhambra have proposed. They argue that any attempt to explore cosmopolitan possibilities should account for the influence and impact of (neo)colonial designs through time (Mignolo 2000, 723; Harvey 2009, 283; Bhambra 320). Following the observations of these scholars and *Cloud Atlas'* own discourse, in the following pages I try to map the range of colonial relations that the film presents.

In the two storylines that foreground coloniality most obviously (1849 and 2144), the characters played by Hugo Weaving note: "there is a natural order to this world," hinting at the centrality of pseudo-scientific racial, national, and genetic hierarchies within colonial logic. In the first case, the scene in which Adam Ewing formalizes a contract with Reverend Horrox (Hugh Grant) is followed by a scene in which they discuss slavery, another scene in which native slaves are working on a plantation, and finally, another one in which a man whips Autua, a Moriori man, savagely. The role of fabricants within the economic system of the twenty-second century is compounded by the construction of a biological order. Fabricants call humans "purebloods," a name that signposts the inferior status of the clones. In addition, love and sex between purebloods and fabricants is forbidden, replicating earlier miscegenation laws. Both in 1849 and 2144, predominant religions (Christianity and the Consumer Catechisms, respectively) become another means of supporting pseudo-scientific differentiations between humans. In-between, the film includes other references to racial and national difference, although it does not relate them clearly to economic coloniality. In 1936, Vyvyan Ayrs lets Robert Frobisher know that Jocasta

(Hale Berry) and a German composer had feelings towards each other, but their relationship was doomed because of the sociopolitical environment in Germany. In the 1970s storyline, a Latina woman knocks a racist hired assassin down and tells him: "don't call me a fucking wetback." The twenty-fourth-century ghost Old Georgie (Hugo Weaving) misleadingly warns Zachry about Meronym's intentions, saying: "She ain't your tribe, ain't your color." In this manner, *Cloud Atlas* connects all of its storylines thematically by showcasing different kinds of economic, racial, national, religious, and genetic colonialities and drawing parallels between them.

The list of colonial connections does not stop there. Although coloniality may not appear to be related to sexual, gender, age, and species hierarchies at first sight, Walter Mignolo notes that the colonial matrix of power (a term coined by Aníbal Quijano) consists of four interrelated domains: "control of the economy, of authority, of gender and sexuality, and of knowledge and subjectivity" (2011, 8). To this matrix, Mignolo also adds nature. Control over these domains was originally exercised through theological differences and later through racial and gender/sexual distinctions as well (Mignolo 2011, 8–10). Yet, these differences do not replace each other, but rather pile up and produce evolving versions of the logic of coloniality. In like manner, *Cloud Atlas* shows how colonial differences can adopt a wide range of configurations. In the first story, Madame Horrox (Susan Sarandon) points at the absence of women in the theological/racial designs that several men discuss during dinner. Characters from the 1970s story also draw attention (in both hopeful and derogatory terms) to the historical exclusion of women from higher education institutions and to chauvinist remarks that value women's looks over their professionalism. The film also suggests that the arrow of time does not necessarily bring about improvements for women: The Neo Seoul story foregrounds the misogyny of its futuristic society. Apart from the fact that the whole of the exploited workforce is female (something that is also obvious in the 1970s maquila-style factory), purebloods touch fabricants' bodies as they please and a male customer uses a bottle of mustard to simulate that he is ejaculating on a fabricant's back as she bends over to pick up some trays. In addition, Seer Rhee (Hugh Grant), the restaurant's manager, sexually abuses Yoona-939 (Xun Zhou) and terminates her life in a later scene by pressing a button when she attempts to run away from the restaurant. The Chatham Islands, San Francisco, and Neo Seoul storylines thus show that gender discrimination and abuse, greed, and genetic and racial hierarchies are part of the same colonial matrix.

Although in a less obvious manner, *Cloud Atlas* also establishes connections between coloniality and sexuality, age, and nature. Ayrs' condescending attitude towards Robert Frobisher is not just a matter of age and expertise, but sexuality. The composer tells Robert that, before his arrival, an acquaintance wrote about the latter in the following terms: "he is a prostitute whose liaison with perverts and sodomites were commonplace [...]. Lock up the silverware." Apart from being demeaning, Ayrs' words point at the practice of baseless criminalization of homosexual people. After these comments, Ayrs goes on to threaten Robert with ruining his career, showing a direct relationship between notions of value and success and sexual hierarchies. By making homophobia the main source of oppression in one of its storylines, *Cloud Atlas* charts a connection between heteronormativity and the wider network of colonial difference—a relationship that several writers and scholars have noted (Anzaldúa 41; Mignolo 2011, 18; Schoonover and Galt 37, 240–1). In more general terms, the 2012 storyline suggests that the system also profits from the mistreatment of the elderly and the privation of some of their rights. Finally, the film shows that a system geared towards even-increasing economic accumulation does not hesitate to encroach on and abuse nature, disregarding that a whole community will be exposed to nuclear disaster in 1973 and letting sea levels rise to the pace of economic profit in 2144. In the end, *Cloud Atlas* draws attention to the multiple layers that constitute coloniality. As Mignolo argues, the colonial matrix of power "operates in a series of interconnected heterogeneous historico-structural nodes crossed by colonial and imperial differences and by the underlying logic that secures those connections: the logic of coloniality" (2011, 17). The ability of the film to map several strands and nodes of the logic of coloniality across time is one of the key features that make it unique. *Cloud Atlas* manages to pull together different instances of oppression and to regularly connect most of them to other key features of the colonial matrix of power such as authority and economic control.

Apart from connecting all the storylines thematically through different kinds of colonial hierarchies, *Cloud Atlas* strengthens its colonial network by establishing visual links between different pairs of storylines, often in the form of matches on action and conceptual matches. Through the term 'conceptual match,' I refer to shots that show characters immersed in two similar situations without relying on the explicit replication of an image. The film also draws heavily on conceptual matches that connect sound (the words that a character utters) with a related image or situation in another storyline. Regarding matches on action, one of the most obvious is a delayed match between Hae Jo Chang walking on a footbridge on the Neo Seoul skyline and Autua walking on the ship mast. In both cases, characters fall down (tripping and jumping, respectively). In addition, they are both shot at by other people who have a higher position in the colonial hierarchy. *Cloud Atlas* establishes another clear parallel through a conceptual match in which Hae Jo and Sonmi, and later Luisa Rey, find themselves under a mass of water. In the first case, Hae Jo and Sonmi take refuge below a trapdoor after making an underwater tunnel explode in order to get rid of the police forces that chase them. In the second case, a hired assassin pushes Rey off a bridge with his car, making Rey's car sink into the water. In both cases, water fills the whole frame and links characters who are targeted by corporate actors. Although these matches are not edited directly together (as graphic matches and matches on action are), the scenes in which they appear do indeed follow one another and it is therefore easy for viewers to appreciate the similarity of both situations. Several other conceptual matches also establish connections between

1973 and 2012 and between 2012 and 2144 through scenes involving cars and characters who are locked, respectively. By multiplying connections related to oppression and persecution through editing and several kinds of visual matches, *Cloud Atlas* reinforces its presentation of coloniality as a continuum. Although the film revolves, as I show later, around characters' efforts to challenge coloniality, the presence of it in all of the stories suggests that ethical progress is not linear. Cosmopolitanism therefore does not always gain ground along with the passing of time in the film.

Connecting Humans across Time and Space: Cosmopolitan Reincarnations and Shared Experiences

Although *Cloud Atlas* frames coloniality in critical terms and channels cosmopolitan discourses through its depiction of it, coloniality also serves as a backdrop against which to build cosmopolitan alternatives. The film does this in two main ways: (1) by questioning and reversing the aforementioned colonial discourses (mostly through personal connections between characters and storylines) and (2) by engaging characters in individual and collaborative struggles against coloniality. Regarding the first strategy, *Cloud Atlas* draws on the main theme of reincarnation as cosmopolitan metaphor, the use of doors as a metaphorical reference to transmigration, and a range of editing combinations that draw attention to the experiences and feelings that characters share. In all these cases, the film questions colonial discourses by pointing at characters' shared humanity. The emphasis of the film on this aspect is not anecdotal or trivial. Several scholars see the notion of common humanity as one as central to cosmopolitanism (Nussbaum xii, 7; Appiah 111, 134-5; Fine 2007, xvii). These theorists do not claim that all humans are or should be identical or have the same habits and beliefs. Rather, they point out that all people should be respected and valued as human beings that share similar feelings, emotions, and abilities and deserve the same basic rights. Despite the simplicity of this argument, this is an idea that many people do not share or care about, especially in the current climate of nostalgia for national identities and calls for a staunch defense of national borders.

   Cloud Atlas' concept of intersectional, transnational, and cross-temporal reincarnation exposes the fabricated nature of the hierarchical differences that the logic of coloniality breeds. Where coloniality draws borders, reincarnation builds cosmopolitan bridges. The title of the film itself points at the relationship between these two dimensions. The word "cloud" hints at the shape-shifting, fluid character of reincarnated identities. "Atlas" alludes both to the planetary dimension of the story and, through its cartographic undertones, to the link between the drawing of the first maps of the entire world and the emergence of coloniality (Mignolo 2011, 185–7; Mezzadra and Neilson 2013, 30–5). As the animated intertitle at the beginning of the film suggests, clouds (traveling souls) redraw the lines that trace the map of the colonial world. Of course, reincarnation is not necessarily cosmopolitan per se. Indeed, some cultures have used the concept of reincarnation to justify social inequalities and maintain the state of things as they are and others have limited its scope to the family or to privileged groups such as royalty, saints, or heroes (Bernabé and Mendoza 556, 562–4). Yet, *Cloud Atlas'* ability to bring intersectionality into most of the afore-mentioned references to reincarnation in the film clearly offers a cosmopolitan view of transmigration. In this sense, the film presents a cosmopolitan image of reincarnation that is close to the idea of universal solidarity at the center of the Pythagorean concept of reincarnation or to Buddhist and Jain beliefs, which see reincarnation as a phenomenon that transcends castes and social divides (Bernabé and Mendoza 558, 568–9).

Although I have already mentioned that the main ways in which *Cloud Atlas* points at its reincarnation theme are the appearance of the birthmarks in a group of characters and the multi-role, intersectional performances of most of its cast, the film employs additional strategies to make the transmigration theme more obvious. *Cloud Atlas* regularly draws explicit visual connections between two characters played by the same actors through editing choices: the same actor appears in two scenes (sometimes shots) from different times edited together or as part of a montage that includes other storylines. While Frobisher, Sachs, Cavendish, and Sonmi say lines that directly refer to reincarnation, Sonmi pro-nounces the words with the most obvious cosmopolitan implications. She says: "from womb to tomb we are bound to others, past and present." Apart from the explicit cosmopolitanism of Sonmi's reference to "others," her line appears three times through different media, bringing her message to the foreground through its repetition (53, 110, and 153 minutes into the film). Finally, the end credits further reinforce the intersectional cosmopolitanism of the film by showing the names of each of the actors that play different roles along with images of each of the characters that they play framed in an oval against a black background. In this way, the end credits compress and underline the transnational and cross-tempo-ral connections that develop throughout the film. Despite *Cloud Atlas'* multiple references to reincarnation, its cosmopolitanism is not restricted to this concept. As I explain later, the film provides examples of characters' shared humanity by establishing connections between different actors too.

Cloud Atlas also uses doors as a conceptual and visual metaphor of reincarna-tion and cosmopolitan possibilities. For instance, when Cavendish comes across the house where his former girlfriend Ursula (Susan Sarandon) lives, he says: "I could slink off and continue as planned, or I could go boldly to the *door* and discover what hope, if any, lay within" (my emphasis). After he utters this sentence, the film instantly cuts to a different scene in which Zachry (a rein-carnation of Cavendish [both have birthmarks]), knocks on the door of a house where a character played by Susan Sarandon is healing a girl. By connecting these two scenes through a door, the film reinforces the idea that the same soul has been present in these two moments despite their temporal, geographical, and cultural remoteness. The most obvious example of the connection between doors and reincarnation appears at the end of the film when Sonmi explains: "I believe death is a door. When it closes, another one opens." Sonmi (Bae) pronounces these words just after Hae Jo Chang (Sturgess), the person she loves, is killed. Immediately after she pronounces these words, the film introduces a scene in which Ewing (Sturgess) opens a door and embraces his wife Tilda (Bae) (Figure 4.3). This metaphorical use of doors allows Sonmi to imagine an alternative iteration of her life in which she does not lose Jim Sturgess. The last scene in *I Origins* also relies on the metaphorical potential of doors. After being certain that part of Sofi's consciousness has transmigrated to Salomina's body, Ian (Michael Pitt) goes down the stairs of a hotel holding Salomina in his arms and goes out through a doorway. As he pushes the doors open, an almost-blinding source of light beaming in the middle of the frame suggests that both characters are walking into a new world (Figure 4.4): a world in which people may change their ways of seeing and relating to other nations, cultures, and races after knowing that they can become anyone else, anywhere else in the world. *I Origins*, like

FIGURES 4.3 AND 4.4   *Cloud Atlas* (Tykwer and The Wachowskis 2012) (top) and *I Origins* (Cahill 2014) (bottom) use doors as a symbol of the cosmopolitan potential of reincarnation.

Cloud Atlas, draws on doors both to point at the interconnectedness of human lives and to hint at the possibility of cosmopolitan change.

Some of the strategies that *Cloud Atlas* uses to present a cosmopolitan view of reincarnation have also been recently deployed in other media as ways of channeling cosmopolitan discourses. The web version of *Human* (Arthus-Bertrand 2015), a documentary that offers a cosmopolitan look at human emotions across 60 countries and 63 languages, is a clear example of this. In a similar way to *Cloud Atlas*' ending, Arthus-Bertrand's documentary begins with a montage of human faces of different genders, ages, races, religions, and sexualities against a black background. Despite the variety of facial features and emotions that the opening moments show, they convey a sense of these people's shared humanity through the bodies that stand out against the black background and their shared ability to show their feelings through their facial expressions. Similarly, *I Origins* includes a montage of extreme close-ups of different kinds of eyes at the very beginning, bringing all the humans to whom those eyes belong together through the same kind of visual concept and frame composition. Using a similar temporal perspective to that of *Cloud Atlas*, "The DNA Journey," a 2017 advertising campaign by the travel search engine Momondo points at the multiple ethnic influences that most people have by looking at the genetic information that their ancestry has passed onto them. In a set of reality-show-style videos, a variety of individuals from different countries give a sample of their saliva to find out about the ethnic groups that form their DNA mix over the last 500–2000 years. The videos then show that participants typically share genetic information with rival ethnic groups and nationalities that they sometimes despise. In addition, the campaign shows that, on average, people tend to belong to between four and six ethnic groupings. In this way, the ad emphasizes the multiple origins that people have, especially when considering the evolution of their DNA across time. While this campaign is not about reincarnation, it adopts a similar temporal perspective to that of *Cloud Atlas* to highlight the constructed nature of the social borders that often separate human beings. The shared visual and temporal strategies that *Cloud Atlas*, *I Origins*, *Human*, and "The DNA Journey" share hint at the emergence of common, cross-genre strategies that allow films and other media to establish cosmopolitan connections between humans.

Cloud Atlas also offers a cosmopolitan vision of humanity by presenting characters as part of a global community of humans that go through similar experiences and share similar emotions. Although many of the characters' shared experiences may appear to be primarily about the impact of coloniality in their lives, the visual and conceptual techniques that the film employs actually emphasize the feelings or experiences that characters share across time. Indeed, in several cases, characters' common reactions or emotions are not related to coloniality. One of the most obvious ways in which the film does this is by including montages that combine shots from different storylines while a single character from one of those stories talks about his/her experiences or makes generalizations about life. In many cases, what the chosen character says applies to or is illustrated by the other stories that appear in the montage. In addition, a melody (typically, "The Cloud Atlas Sextet") tends to accompany such pseudo-narrations. Sometimes, there is no character acting as a kind of narrator and only the Sextet brings together the similar experiences that the characters have. A clear example of this strategy is the montage that draws parallels between Frobisher's feelings and those of Sonmi and Dr. Sachs while Frobisher's voice-over hints at his infatuation with Vivian Ayrs. An eyeline match between Frobisher and Ayrs is followed by Frobisher narrating his experience over shots of the other storylines. While he says: "it was music that poured from his eyes and breathed from his lips," the film includes shots of Rey and Sachs about to meet for the first time and of Sonmi listening to Chang's heartbeats. In the next shots, both Sonmi and Chang and Rey and Sachs look at each other's eyes, signaling a potential romantic connection. By bringing these three looks together through editing and Frobisher's voice, *Cloud Atlas* suggests that many people have the ability to connect with other humans just by looking at their eyes—a notion that the film explores earlier through the first encounter between Ewing and Autua.

The film also employs different kinds of matches to underline that characters go through similar experiences and react in similar ways. These matches involve both main and secondary characters. There are manifold examples of these two strategies throughout the film. A conceptual match brings together Catkin (Raevan Lee Hanan)—who lives in the twenty-fourth century—and Sonmi as they both lie down in different beds. Frobisher and Jocasta have sex just before Cavendish and Ursula do in the next scene. A graphic match of the faces of the Mexican woman from the 1970s and Mr. Meeks (one of the people who run away from the elderly home) shows that they both feel overwhelmed. Filmed from their backs, Zachry and Sonmi see their communities being abused from a distance in extreme long shots which are respectively followed by close-ups of both characters' faces. Separated by just a minute of screen time, Sonmi and Sixsmith share their grief for the death of their lovers. And the list goes on. From these examples of visual matches and the aforementioned combination of narration/music and montages, it is clear that the narrative of *Cloud Atlas* is not only interested in colonial continuities across time. The film also provides multiple examples of shared emotions and experiences that go from the seemingly banal to what matters most in people's lives (e.g., freedom, love). Such an emphasis on similarities between humans across geographical locations and times indeed blurs the hierarchical distinctions that the logic of coloniality establishes. Eventually, the constant inclusion of connections between characters foregrounds a cosmopolitan sense of shared human sentience.

Cloud Atlas' discourse on shared humanity has at least two limitations. First, it may appear obvious or unnecessary to point at the fact that every person is equally human. At the same time, the recent spread of populisms based on the reinforcement of borders and national, racial, sexual, and income divisions show that the cosmopolitan notion of a common humanity cannot be taken for granted. A more substantial limitation to the film's discourse is that, despite its convoluted structure, it eventually presents an easy cosmopolitanism that overlooks contro-versial differences between disparate ways of understanding human rights. The concept of shared humanity addresses cosmopolitan challenges, but mostly on a superficial level. Despite its intersectional discourse, *Cloud Atlas* barely tackles questions related to cosmopolitan conflicts between particular approaches to cul-ture, forms of social organization, and social norms. Such conflicts often—but not only—concern sexuality and women's and LGBTQ rights (Appiah 77–84; Plummer 131–43; Schoonover and Galt 49–78). These tensions are not always directly related to coloniality. A clear example of these conflicts is the opposite views on female genital mutilation that people have wherever it is practiced and wherever it is outlawed (Appiah 72–3). *Cloud Atlas'* discourse of shared human-ity and its avoidance of thorny cosmopolitan conflicts hinder the possibility of negotiating radical differences between humans. As Robert Fine argues, cosmo-politanism can be a tool to bridge "the dualisms of our age" (2012, 384). *Cloud Atlas* bridges some of those dualisms, but mostly imagines easy negotiations of the less controversial cosmopolitan tensions.

A Multitude of Drops: The Relevance of Ordinary Cosmopolitanism

Despite the aforementioned limitations, the cosmopolitan discourse of *Cloud Atlas* goes beyond the mere denunciation of coloniality and its emphasis on charac-ters' shared feelings and humanity. The film also features characters who engage in local struggles against oppressive hierarchies and regulations. Throughout the film, characters often transcend physical and more abstract social borders. Although these borders sometimes are not explicitly transnational or transcul-tural, they often articulate concerns that are related to those of cosmopolitan-ism such as human rights and well-being. The presence of these borders in the film also highlights characters' attempts to contest—sometimes symbolically and other times literally—(neo)colonial forms of domination. Regarding borders with a more physical and visual presence, the most obvious example is perhaps the moment when a group of retirees manage to break out of the elderly house by driving a car through the gates of the facility. The film also presents Sonmi's escape as the crossing of a border in a shot in which Chang's hand invites her to walk out of a completely blue room through a white threshold. The white opening in the room's blue walls breaks the chromatic monotony of the space and presents Sonmi's escape as a transition between two spaces: one of enslave-ment and one of potential freedom. Borders are also particularly present when Sonmi and Chang sneak into a restricted area and she discovers the bleak meat-processing industry that runs on fabricants' bodies. The film first foregrounds the presence of a fence by filming Sonmi through it as she sees the industrial facility from the outside. In a later scene, Sonmi is filmed through a glass wall as she sees other fabricants hanging from their feet as if they were pigs in a slaughter-house. The transition from the fence to the glass suggests that Sonmi has crossed a knowledge barrier. Yet, the border is still there, as she has not figured out yet how to challenge the boundaries between purebloods and fabricants. Further examples appear in these and other storylines. Even though these visual examples are not explicitly transnational, the discourse that the film develops through its regular references to borders is, in broad terms, a cosmopolitan one. In a film that constantly jumps between local realities and draws countless connections between them, the seemingly local character of some border transgressions is not such. In the film's overall discourse, love, kindness, and cosmopolitanism emerge from the tensions that all kinds of borders channel.

A montage that appears two hours into the film further emphasizes the centrality of borders in *Cloud Atlas'* discourse and the cosmopolitan dimension of borders in the film. The montage brings together three couples (two of them interracial and intercultural and one of them queer) to the tune of "The Cloud Atlas Sextet" and a pseudo-narration by Robert Frobisher. In the three cases, at least a member of the couple transcends social borders. The montage opens with a shot of Sonmi framed through window railings, connecting with the overarching theme of her entrapment and liberation throughout the film. In the next shots, Sonmi approaches Chang, says "I know it is forbidden" (referring to the rule that forbids human–fabricant sex and relationships), and kisses him. In this way, Sonmi and Chang transcend a border that is not visible and yet present in the words of Sonmi. After this, Frobisher's narration begins as the film crosscuts between shots of him at the Scott Monument in Edinburgh and of Ewing and Autua on the ship as they all contemplate different sunsets. A new scene in a room full of china pieces begins as Frobisher says: "I understand now that boundaries between noise and sound are conventions." As he pronounces the word "conventions," a close-up shows a china figure shattering against the floor, suggesting that Frobisher and Sixsmith (who has just entered the room) are also challenging conventions. Frobisher continues his speech with the words: "all boundaries are conventions waiting to be transcended" as the next shot cuts to Sonmi and Chang having sex. Frobisher continues to talk about conventions as the next shots cut to Zachry wrapping Meronym up with his blanket as she sleeps—showing his solidarity and his potential romantic interest in her. This seemingly irrelevant act is of particular significance because Zachry and Meronym belong to different civilizations and Zachry is highly suspicious of Meronym initially. Frobisher's monologue continues by noting that "separation is an illusion" as Sonmi and Chang continue to have sex. In addition, the film sandwiches a shot of a vase being smashed in the 1936 scene between shots of the 2144 sex scene, further interweaving these moments of transgression. The montage concludes with a couple of shots of Frobisher and Sixsmith throwing shelves down and breaking most of the plates and china in the room, and thus, metaphorically breaking most conventions. In this figurative manner, Frobisher and Sixsmith—like the other two couples—transgress the norms that hamper their relationship.

This montage sequence stands out among the moments that foreground the presence of borders in the film and the rest of the montage sequences because of the range of strategies that it uses to connect the different storylines and to draw viewers' attention towards the cosmopolitan attitude of questioning and transgressing borders. Frobisher's discourse regularly mentions conventions, boundaries, and divisions while shots of other lives and his own appear. All of the characters in these shots challenge social borders related to their personal relationships in one way or another. Even though there is no action in Ewing and Autua's shots in the montage sequence, the presence of both characters quietly watching the sunset shows that they have transcended a boundary that the film had signaled much earlier. When Autua looks Ewing in the eye while the former is being whipped, he breaks the shell that isolates the white man's feelings from the atrocities that accompany the contract that he has just signed. As Autua later tells him, by looking him in the eye, he is able to break that barrier, establish a connection with the lawyer, and plant the seed for their later friendship. The montage described in the last paragraph forges further connections between the different transgressions of boundaries by crosscutting within the montage and blurring the border between Frobisher and Sonmi's stories specifically. Unlike other borders that appear in the film, the ones in this montage sequence clearly mediate transcultural divisions and hierarchies constructed by the colonial matrix of power. Ironically, despite *Cloud Atlas'* emphasis on transcending borders, its cosmopolitan discourse depends on them. One of the main ways in which the film articulates its defense of cosmopolitanism is by pointing at the presence of borders. In this sense, it is evident that, as Cooper and Rumford suggest, borders do not only divide but also connect (262–3). All the personal connections between the characters involved in the montage sequence are indeed mediated by a border.

The previous account of borders in *Cloud Atlas* may give the impression that the film naively suggests that borders are easy to cross. Indeed, the montage sequence contributes to this effect by bringing together several moments of transgression and masking the more violent and repressive dimension of borders. Yet, other scenes in the film introduce the bleaker side of borders, as I have argued in my account of the evolution of the colonial matrix of power in the film. For instance, (neo)colonial actors attempt to kill Autua, Luisa, Sonmi, and Hae Jo when they cross different kinds of systemic borders. The 2144 storyline also includes several examples of the ugly and overwhelming side of borders: Yoona's attempt to escape Papa Song ends in her death, Sonmi hesitates whether to cross the threshold that separates Papa Song from the outside world, and Sonmi's discovery of the truth behind the Xultation ceremony traumatizes her. However, the fact that most of these examples come from the Neo Seoul storyline indicate that, in general terms, the film is reluctant to draw attention to the difficulty of crossing borders. In addition, the film just offers glimpses of the aforementioned moments in its crosscutting spree. This suggests that the film is not as interested in showing the challenging experience of crossing a border as in drawing attention to the logic of coloniality. In *Cloud Atlas*, crossing borders often appears to require little effort. This is particularly evident in the escape from the elderly home and in the shots in which Zachry leaves his prejudice behind and lends his blanket to Meronym. The film's celebration of frequent and effortless crossings of borders and barriers builds a discourse based on an easy cosmopolitanism. This kind of engagement with borders provides further evidence of the general reluctance of the film to deal with challenging cosmopolitan conflicts.

Despite the easy cosmopolitanism that certain aspects of the aforementioned montage sequence project, *Cloud Atlas* generally offers a nuanced image of cosmopolitan processes. It makes clear something that the individual appearances of other borders in the film imply: cosmopolitan impulses in *Cloud Atlas* emerge from everyday experiences and small actions, an aspect that Raffaella Baccolini has also noted (76). In this sense, *Cloud Atlas* presents what Skrbiš and Woodward would call "ordinary cosmopolitanism" (99–102). This does not mean that characters transcend these borders on a daily basis (although some do). Rather, ordinary cosmopolitanism refers to actions that impact personal lives and local realities. The film indicates that actions driven by cosmopolitan thoughts or feelings do not always attempt to modify large global schemes. In addition, ordinary cosmopolitanism does not necessarily emerge from exposition to other cultural forms or from a disposition or interest in other cultures. In *Cloud Atlas*, characters exercise what Skrbiš and Woodward call the "reflexive style" of ordinary cosmopolitanism (104). As they explain, reflexive cosmopolitanism is a "process of political and ethical reasoning" that allows people to "[step] outside power categories" (104). By transgressing a variety of physical and symbolic borders configured by specific local and historical circumstances, *Cloud Atlas'* characters hint at the cosmopolitan potential of small actions.

Throughout the film, actions, cultural objects, and ideas from other times influence and inspire characters from the future in their struggles against the matrix of colonial power. Although some actions appear to be local and ordinary at first sight, they transmit cosmopolitan impulses and generate transnational impacts. For instance, the British composer Robert Frobisher compares his experiences to those in the diary written by Adam Ewing on his journey through the Pacific and seems to get part of the inspiration to write his sextet from them. Frobisher's letters to his lover Sixsmith accidentally lead Luisa Rey to the next clue in her risky investigation in San Francisco. A phrase from the film based on Timothy Cavendish's Scottish odyssey—"I will not be subjected to criminal abuse"—inspires Yoona and Sonmi to reveal against the system that exploits them. The transcription of Sonmi's revelations into a book influence Valleymen's peaceful beliefs in 2346 Hawaii. In all of these cases, characters' actions are influenced by the texts, films, or video recordings from other times and places that come across their ways. From a cosmopolitan perspective, the transnational circulation and influence of cultural objects and ideas that *Cloud Atlas* maps shows that cultures are not static entities. Indeed, cultural borders are permeable and what some may see as the essence of a culture is often a mix of other influences (Appiah 107–11; Holton 2008, 135–9). *Cloud Atlas* does not stop here: it presents influences across time and space as cosmopolitan agents.

The impact of the aforementioned actions and the circulation of the things that characters create present cosmopolitan efforts as cumulative. *Cloud Atlas* infuses the butterfly effect—one of the conventions of multi-protagonist films—with cosmopolitan potential. As Azcona notes, multi-protagonist films often show how minor actions or events can create snowball effects that affect other characters. These effects are not necessarily positive. Indeed, they often have a negative impact on characters' lives (2010, 34–5, 141). In contrast, cumulative effects in *Cloud Atlas* often contribute to the advancement of cosmopolitan causes. The metaphor of the ocean as "a multitude of drops" illustrates this. After Ewing and Tilda announce that they are going to work with the abolitionists, Tilda's father (Hugo Weaving) warns them: "no matter what you do, it will never amount to more than a single drop in a limitless ocean." To this, Ewing replies: "What is an ocean but a multitude of drops?" This exchange of opinions reinforces the film's discourse on the relevance of small-scale, ordinary actions for the advancement of cosmopolitan causes. A drop may just change a small detail in the present or even get lost in a sea of colonial currents, but that small action may also trigger a chain of personal reactions or unforeseeable impacts across geographical and temporal distances. Although drops may vary in their number and shape, *Cloud Atlas* suggests that every little action contributes to making cosmopolitan currents stronger. At the end of *X-Men: Days of Future Past*, Charles Xavier offers a similar reflection. He says: "countless choices define our fate. Each choice, each moment: a ripple in the river of time. Enough ripples and you change the tide." With these discourses, *Cloud Atlas* and *Days of Future Past* seem to step out of a convention of multi-protagonist films. Azcona notes that global multi-protagonist stories often present solutions to global problems as "extremely difficult to come by" and human agency as futile (2010, 124–6). While *Cloud Atlas*, like *Days of Future Past*, does not necessarily envision cosmopolitan utopias, it suggests that human actions are far from futile.

Characters also undertake cosmopolitan endeavors and face coloniality through collaboration within and across storylines. This kind of connection has noteworthy implications from a formal and theoretical point of view. Through these collaborations, *Cloud Atlas* imagines a social web that resembles Mignolo's concept of decolonial cosmopolitanism. As Mignolo explains: "the cosmopolis of the future would be composed of 'communal nodes' around the planet cooperating rather than competing with each other" (2011, 283). Similarly, the film foregrounds collaborations across civilizational divides and sometimes even across times. Apart from the aforementioned examples of characters sharing experiences or emotions (which develop a communal discourse), *Cloud Atlas* exploits the possibilities that editing and multi-role performances offer to reveal instances of extradiegetic collaboration between characters from different storylines. For instance, while Zachry is considering whether to stab Meronym (Halle Berry) at the space center in the twenty-fourth century, in the 1970s storyline Joe Napier (Keith David) warns Luisa Rey (Berry) that some people will attempt to kill her. Seconds later, Meronym (Berry) turns around and discovers Zachry carrying a knife on his hand—as if she had been listening to Napier's warning. Through this kind of connection, *Cloud Atlas* advances a strategy that is common in the television series *Sense8* (The Wachowskis and Straczynski 2015–18). The series revolves around a group of mentally connected characters who frequently draw on the abilities of other characters who are hundreds of miles away to deal with challenging situations. Apart from collaboration across time and space, *Cloud Atlas* also shows Autua and Ewing and Zachry and Meronym helping each other despite the cultural conventions that initially prevent them from doing so. In this way, *Cloud Atlas* explicitly shows the emergence of communal nodes across civilizational and temporal borders. In broader terms, the equal weight and the slight variations in theme across the different storylines suggest that *Cloud Atlas* does not privilege a specific cosmopolitan vision but the communal nodes that the different stories weave against coloniality.

Kristian Shaw also points at the relevance of cooperation within the novel's cosmopolitan discourse and in Mitchell's work in general. More specifically, Shaw notes similarities between these cosmopolitan connections and Michael Hardt and Antonio Negri's notion of the multitude (11–13). Quoting Hardt and Negri, Shaw argues that *Cloud Atlas* pictures "'a network that provides the means of encounter so that we can work and live in common' (2004, xiv)" (12). While cooperation and communality are certainly at the core of *Cloud Atlas*' narrative, it must also be acknowledged that the film privileges a certain kind of node within that network. It focuses on a group of nodes that are predominantly Western. Of the six stories in the film, two take place in the UK, and three on current US soil (at least partially). While this set of geographical locations contributes to draw attention to the origin of colonial actors in some cases, in general, it distances the film from struggles in large parts of the world such as Latin America, Africa, and Central and Western Asia. Moreover, by doing so, the film—like the novel—overlooks that these are precisely the regions that have endured the roughest consequences of (neo)coloniality. In this sense, the film engages with diversity in an ambivalent manner, producing a kind of diversity that is more homogeneous than those envisioned in the concepts of the multitude and decolonial cosmopolitanism. Even though *Cloud Atlas* appears to present an image of cosmopolitanism that offers room for a variety of decolonial projects, the invisibility of the regions and people that have been most deeply affected by coloniality ultimately weakens the cosmopolitan potential of the nodes that the film connects.

Although the last lines may give the impression that *Cloud Atlas*' emphasis on interconnections and cosmopolitan impulses presents a linear conception of time, this is not the case. *Cloud Atlas* does not present history as the path towards a predetermined future, nor does it present cosmopolitanism as an ethical force that advances steadily through time. Writing about the novel, Kristian Shaw notes that "later chapters impact on the actions of earlier chapters—a reminder that futures are still open and subject to individual agency" (59). In contrast, Jo Alyson Parker argues that the film alters the temporal discourse of the novel and presents a more linear view of history. In Parker's view, by opening and closing with a scene in which old Zachry tells a story, "the film shifts its emphasis from a future in flux to a future that is fixed—as in a frame" (123). While the 2346 storyline certainly frames the other stories, Parker overlooks that in several scenes past actions reverse future actions and future actions influence the past. Some pairs of actors meet again in a past storyline after one of them passes away in a future storyline. Through a conversation between Ayrs and Frobisher, the film also suggests that the future influences the past. Before Frobisher begins composing "The Cloud Atlas Sextet," Ayrs goes to his room in the middle of the night, telling him that he has had a dream in which he listened to a beautiful melody "in a nightmarish café [with] blaring, bright light, but underground, [with] no way out" where all the waitresses "had the same face"—obviously, the Papa Song restaurant. In a letter to Sixsmith, Frobisher notes that although Ayrs could not remember the melody, "music poured from his eyes." Later on, when Frobisher plays the sextet for the first time, Ayrs notes that that was the music from his dream. The film then opens up the possibility that Frobisher may have gotten his inspiration to write the sextet from the future through Ayrs' dream.

Regarding the presentation of cosmopolitan advances through time, the film suggests that cosmopolitan ethics and rights are not part of a project that develops automatically with the passing of time. For instance, the situation of women's rights in Neo Seoul is actually worse than that of Luisa Rey and the female workers of the maquila-style factory in 1970s San Francisco. The same holds for the way humans treat the environment in both storylines. The fact that the future is not intrinsically more cosmopolitan than the past is particularly evident in the film's celebration of love in its last 20 minutes. While *Cloud Atlas* offers a utopian ending in which several romantic couples get together (Ewing and Tilda, Cavendish and Ursula, Zachry and Meronym), from a chronological perspective, one of these couples of actors does not end together. Sonmi-451 (Bae) sees Hae-Joo Chang (Sturgess) die in 2346. However, in the next scene, the same actors reunite and hold each other after Ewing comes home from the Pacific in 1850. Something similar happens in the case of Frobisher and Sixsmith's love story. Although a hired assassin shoots Sixsmith 47 minutes into the film in the 1970s storyline, he joins Frobisher an hour and thirteen minutes later in the dream-like scene in which they break china pieces in an alternative 1936. The use of non-chronological editing then suggests that cosmopolitanism is not something that comes along with the passing of time. In *Cloud Atlas*, the past sometimes seems to offer more pathways to pursue utopian, cosmopolitan goals than the future. Despite the fact that Meronym, Zachry, and their family seem to have escaped the stronghold of coloniality on Earth in the last scene of the film (Keegan 99-100), the film's spatiotemporal cocktail and its constant process of imagining movement towards and away from cosmopolitan ideals seem to prevent us from seeing the passing of time in the film as a journey towards cosmopolitan futures—even if the last scene is indeed utopian.

Although the future may not always be brighter in *Cloud Atlas*, most of the stories have an optimistic ending in which cosmopolitan ethics gain ground to colonial forces in the individual lives of the main characters. Two exceptions are the love stories between Frobisher and Sixsmith and Sonmi and Chang, which end with the death of all these characters at different times. In the case of the latter, the film revises the development of its narrative by showing Bae and Sturgess' reunion in 1850. The fact that Frobisher and Sixsmith are the only couple who is denied a happy, optimistic ending has led Gabriel Estrada to argue that *Cloud Atlas* denies any hope of "queer futurity" (7). Yet, Frobisher and Sixsmith's singularity as the only couple that does not get a happy ending can be read through a different light. By singling out this couple, the film underlines their suffering and the potentially fatal consequences of homophobia. In addition, the film hints, as Frobisher writes in his farewell letter, that he and Sixsmith will meet again in "a better world." Although Frobisher eventually commits suicide and the couple does not reappear in any other storyline, the film offers a peek into queer futurity earlier. As I mentioned before, the scene in which Frobisher and Sixsmith smash vases and plates suggests that they are symbolically breaking colonial borders and homophobic restraints (Figure 4.5). At the end of the scene, Sixsmith wakes up on a train car, signaling that this scene is a product of his imagination. The fact that the action happens in an unlikely room full of china pieces also suggests that the action is taking place in an alternative, timeless reality and enhances the utopian connotations of Frobisher's words. Following this line of thought, the scene brings to mind José Esteban Muñoz's notion of queer utopia: the transgression of boundaries in it remains abstract enough to indicate that both characters desire something that is "not yet here" (26). At the same time, the scene depicts a moment of queer ecstasy in which both characters step out of "the temporal stranglehold [of] straight time" (32). Ironically, this scene also embodies the ambivalent nature of cosmopolitanism in twenty-first century sf cinema. Despite imagining a queer future, the metaphorical character of the scene downplays its queerness. After all, apart from the half-cunning, half-desiring looks between both men, sexuality does not play any role in the scene.

FIGURE 4.5 In *Cloud Atlas* (Tykwer and The Wachowskis 2012), a room full of china pieces about to be smashed presents an alternative reality: a queer utopia.

Like many cosmopolitan sf movies, *Cloud Atlas* displays a certain degree of ambivalence in its defense of cosmopolitanism. Throughout the chapter, I have pointed at the film's reliance on easy cosmopolitanism, its reluctance to explore controversial cosmopolitan conflicts, and its privileging of Western nodes within its seemingly decolonial cosmopolitanism. Apart from that, *Cloud Atlas'* celebration of diversity is based on the self: the idea that we should care about others because we may reincarnate into them dilutes the ethical strength of the film's advocacy of cosmopolitan empathy and solidarity. This is not exclusively a limitation of *Cloud Atlas*. *I Origins* and Momondo's "The DNA Journey" also base their cosmopolitanism on the transnational dimension of the genetic configuration of the self. In addition, Gabriel Estrada has rightly criticized the unproblematized depiction of the Mauna Kea Mountain in the film as the grounds for an observation center. As he points out, such depiction dismisses indigenous spiritualties by disregarding the sacred character of the mountain (2014, 24). Finally, despite *Cloud Atlas'* attempt to present a variety of identities and geographical and racial origins through its multi-role casting, the cast is itself predominantly Western. Except for Donna Bae and Zhou Xun, who are South Korean and Chinese, respectively, all the major actors are from the UK, the US, or Australia.

Despite these weaknesses, *Cloud Atlas* undoubtedly develops one of the most powerful cosmopolitan discourses in sf cinema to date. Although the cast is surprisingly homogeneous in terms of nationality, the characters that these actors embody paint an altogether different picture. The film takes every opportunity to show human heterogeneity and to draw intersectional connections across a wide range of aspects of human life. Moreover, while the film's celebration of diversity through reincarnation may seem limited, it also establishes transnational connections between characters who are not reincarnated. By emphasizing characters' shared experiences, emotions, and humanity against the multiple faces of coloniality, *Cloud Atlas* draws attention to the "universalist aspiration for moral connectedness," which is one of the cornerstones of cosmopolitanism, as Nikos Papastergiadis notes (136). At the same time, through its depiction of future colonialities and its exploration of reverse causality, the film shows that cosmopolitanism cannot be taken for granted. *Cloud Atlas* equally underscores the relevance of small actions and ordinary cosmopolitanism as a way of building communal nodes across geographical and temporal borders. Thus, in spite of its ambivalent elements, as a whole, *Cloud Atlas* offers one of the most unflinching defenses of cosmopolitan ideals and practices in sf cinema.

Note

1 The film does not specify the location of the Big Isle with respect to contemporary geography. According to Gabriel Estrada, Big Isle is Hawaii (4). Estrada probably infers this from the fact that the last story is set in "Ha-Why" in the novel. In addition, the space observation center at the top of a mountain in Big Isle recalls similar observatories in contemporary Hawaii. I will refer to Estrada's analysis of the presence of this observation center in the film later.

CONCLUSION

This book has shown how recent sf films bring to the surface elements of the genre that are particularly useful to channel transnational issues and have been part of science fiction for a long time. Sf has historically been interested in exploitative forms of government, abusive corporations, apocalyptic landscapes, disasters, planetary events, aliens, alternative civilizations and life forms, and travels across time and space. Given the intensification of globalization since the 1990s and 2000s, it is indeed no wonder that sf has begun to develop discourses on cosmopolitanism. At the turn of the twenty-first century, systemic dystopias have begun to show a clear interest in border zones, walled cities, and dispersed borders that replicate the hierarchies established by larger territorial configurations. These films pay particular attention to the ways in which transnational asymmetries between cities, countries, imagined geographical formations, planets, or space stations offer opportunities to generate more profit. Many systemic dystopias include virtual meetings, calls, holograms, and maps that emphasize the transnational ties of corporate managers. Through different combinations of these and other tropes, contemporary sf films draw attention to the radical divide between global elites and those who are at the margins of neoliberal societies. Other films situate their barren landscapes, extreme temperatures, or rising sea levels in a larger context of global ecological crisis. Sometimes they transform intergalactic exploration into a necessity through scenarios in which life is no longer possible on Earth. Several of the films mentioned in this book also address cosmopolitan concerns by relying on montage sequences that offer a glimpse of the transnational scope of disasters. In recent years, some films have also begun to develop stories in which protagonists and secondary characters travel to other world locations trying to avoid disaster scenarios but end up encountering disasters in other places too. All these narratives

DOI: 10.4324/9781003164517-6

contribute to building a cosmopolitan sense of planet and raise awareness of the deeply unequal situations that climate change generates.

Twenty-first century sf films also seem eager to imagine humans and aliens who manage to negotiate their differences, live peacefully, and even collaborate. Although sf continues to feature menacing, destructive, and unintelligible aliens, many films depict humans and aliens who communicate successfully. Unlike in most 1980s romantic sf films, aliens often stay on Earth or humans move to the alien planet. In addition, the interaction between humans and aliens tends to lead to the interrogation of some social norms and borders. Several recent dystopias also imagine couples that challenge the belief systems that prevent them from loving a person who is different in genetic, national, or ethnic terms. Many contemporary sf films also embrace openness by grounding their narratives in supernatural concepts that blur the line between self and other. To do so, they present individuals as part of a global, cross-temporal network of humans and suggest that belonging to a particular nation, race, gender, class, sexual orientation, or species is purely coincidental. Such films often revolve around immortal characters, migrant souls, or time travel beyond local and national environments. Sometimes, they deal with individuals who are destined to occupy the place of another human, an animal, or a tree in their next life. Through this kind of narrative, films emphasize that human souls and spaces mutate through time and thereby challenge essentialist notions of national and cultural belonging. In this context, a cosmopolitan approach to sf cinema can be particularly useful to make transnational phenomena more visible and shed light on the ways in which sf films perform cosmopolitanism. In general, the use of cosmopolitan theory helps turn the spotlight on conviviality and absence thereof, the equal right of individuals to have access to natural and economic resources, and their right to live beyond the rigid structures that the logic of coloniality (in its multiple forms) mandates.

Contemporary sf films revolve around a variety of cosmopolitan concerns. By focusing on transnational "relations of domination, dispossession, and exploitation" that develop around borders (Mezzadra and Neilson 2013, 18), my analysis of *In Time* and *Elysium* has explored the ways in which economic powers shape abusive structures of extraction. The systems depicted in these films allow elites to maximize their revenue while encroaching on the well-being of the rest of the population. Following David Harvey, the cosmopolitan approach employed in this book has also paid special attention to the social actors that contribute to that situation and their reasons for doing so (2009, 57–8). In a similar vein, the cosmopolitan focus on the right to live a decent life has led me to analyze the biopolitical logics that govern the apocalyptic scenario that *2012* presents. In this respect, the film shows a seemingly critical awareness of the importance of nationality and wealth in establishing biopolitical hierarchies and exposes the unequal value of human lives. *2012* also points to an equally relevant aspect of eco-cosmopolitanism: the development of a sense of planet. By replicating some environmental processes through spectacle and connecting its disaster scenes in a more logical way than it seems, the film draws attention to the chain of trans-national impacts that characterize climate change. The focus on processes of personal cosmopolitan transformation in *The Host* has shown that cosmopolitan ways of thinking and acting, in contrast to the universal connotations of the term, do not tend to develop with ease and are often partial and intermittent. The border-as-method approach adopted in this book has also led me to consider what still remains at the margins of the genre's cosmopolitan imaginary. In this sense, I have explored the centrality of queer issues to cosmopolitanism through the example of *Codependent Lesbian Space Alien Seeks Same*. This film evinces the utopian potential of sf camp to celebrate sexual, affective, and national other-ness and to envision queer worlds beyond the West. Finally, I have described the complex web of spatiotemporal connections in *Cloud Atlas* to analyze the film's articulation of the tensions between cosmopolitanism and the different iterations of coloniality through time. In spite of this, *Cloud Atlas* does not present cos-mopolitanism as a grand scheme. Instead, cosmopolitanism in the film emerges from small, ordinary actions that challenge oppressive regulations and borders.

Formally, sf films use a wide range of strategies to deal with cosmopolitan-ism. The films analyzed in this book show that some of the strategies that con-temporary sf cinema uses include: inventive concepts or premises that ask to be explored, spectacular disasters, bare and detail-crammed spaces that channel cos-mopolitan concerns and possibilities, spaces that show the development of char-acters' psychology, shoestring camp, and editing choices that push beyond the supposed limits of intensified continuity, multi-role performances, and multi-protagonist conventions. There are, then, no specific film techniques or styles that are essential to channel cosmopolitan concerns. However, some of the films analyzed in the previous chapters rely on some common strategies. For instance, the endings of *2012*, *The Host*, *Codependent Lesbian*, *Cloud Atlas*, and other exam-ples draw a connection between the seemingly cosmopolitan realities of their protagonists and the planet or galaxy in which they live. In this sense, these films transport viewers from individual stories to the wider context in which they take place. María del Mar Azcona notes that this is a common feature in film end-ings. At the same time, she observes that when multi-protagonist films rely on this strategy, they tend to point at the small part characters play in a bigger social structure that requires the appreciation of many other small details and actors to be understood (2010, 43). Cosmopolitan sf films use this common technique in their own way. Although sf films rely on this strategy in slightly different con-texts, they all use it to draw attention to the extended cosmopolitan potential of the story that they have developed. These endings could certainly be criticized for their totalizing moves. However, in general, they tend to reflect a utopian impulse, inviting viewers to consider the wider implications of the stories that these films present.

Although the former account suggests that the films under scrutiny envi-sion societies in which cosmopolitanism is bound to spread, my analysis has also pointed at the ambivalent side of cosmopolitan discourses—an aspect that other scholars have also observed (Skrbiš and Woodward 116; Papastergiadis 116–31; Plummer 89; Azcona 2019, 185). The cosmopolitan approach employed in this book has attempted to make the ambivalent dimension of cosmopolitan discourses in sf more visible. The ambivalence of the films analyzed in the previous pages is evident in their exploration of systems of global exploitation. *Elysium* celebrates universal access to healthcare, but masks the rest of the economic problems that, in all likelihood, continue to affect Earth's inhabitants at the end of the film. *2012* fails to point at the ways in which affluent individuals and industrial nations contribute to the depletion of natural resources, the degradation of ecosystems, and to triggering disasters. *Cloud Atlas* regularly presents situations in which characters successfully face cosmopolitan tensions and challenge borders. However, the film also develops an easy cosmopolitanism that avoids thorny conflicts.

All the films analyzed in the previous chapters celebrate the weakening of borders and the development of more open positions towards the other. Yet, at the same time, many of them redirect their focus towards the heroism of the white protagonists or imagine alien others who are white. Even when characters are more racially diverse (as in *Cloud Atlas*), the actors that play them are often from the US or the UK. In addition, *Cloud Atlas* and *The Host* build their discourses about openness on the idea that the other is a different version of the self. *Codependent Lesbian* illustrates the tension between abstract ideas and specific realities of acute suffering that Ken Plummer finds in discourses on cosmopolitan sexualities in general (89, 97). Through its abstract, camp depiction of the aliens, the film presents a weird and different civilization that is likable and easy to empathize with. Yet, the lack of details about the personal experiences of aliens on their planet fails to draw attention to the actual, sometimes life-threatening, challenges that sexually oppressed minorities face. In general, ambivalence is a pervasive element in the cosmopolitan discourses that science fiction films have developed at the beginning of the twenty-first century. Despite the ample room for improvement in the genre's engagement with certain realities and possibilities, sf films often invite us to think about key and often urgent cosmopolitan issues. As science fiction cinema continues to thrive and adopt new forms, the genre is likely to keep offering journeys and visions that, despite their ambivalence, invite us to critically reflect on the world we inhabit and consider ways to improve it.

WORKS CITED

"2004 Worldwide Grosses." *Box Office Mojo*, 2005, http://www.boxofficemojo.com/yearly/chart/?view2=worldwide&yr=2004&p=.htm. Accessed 30 January 2018.

"2008 Worldwide Grosses." *Box Office Mojo*, 2009, http://www.boxofficemojo.com/yearly/chart/?view2=worldwide&yr=2008&p=.htm. Accessed 30 January 2018.

"2009 Worldwide Grosses." *Box Office Mojo*, 2010, http://www.boxofficemojo.com/yearly/chart/?view2=worldwide&yr=2009&p=.htm. Accessed 30 January 2018.

2012. Directed by Roland Emmerich. Columbia Pictures, Centropolis Entertainment, Farewell Productions, and The Mark Gordon Company, 2009.

"2014 Worldwide Grosses." *Box Office Mojo*, 2015, http://www.boxofficemojo.com/yearly/chart/?view2=worldwide&yr=2014&p=.htm. Accessed 30 January 2018.

Adamson, Joni. "Indigenous Literatures, Multinaturalism, and *Avatar*: The Emergence of Indigenous Cosmopolitics." *American Literary History*, vol. 24, no. 1, 2012, pp. 153–162.

Agamben, Giorgio. *Homo Sacer: Sovereign Power and Bare Life*. Translated by Daniel Heller-Roazen. Stanford University Press, 1998.

Amilhat-Szary, Anne Laure and Frédéric Giraut. "Borderities: The Politics of Contemporary Mobile Borders." *Borderities and the Politics of Contemporary Mobile Borders*, edited by Anne Laure Amilhat-Szary and Frédéric Giraut. Palgrave Macmillan, 2015, pp. 1–22.

Amoore, Louise. "Biometric Borders: Governing Mobilities in the War on Terror." *Political Geography*, vol. 25, no. 3, 2006, pp. 336–351.

Anderson, Christopher Todd. "Post-Apocalyptic Nostalgia: *WALL-E*, Garbage, and American Ambivalence toward Manufactured Goods." *Literature Interpretation Theory*, vol. 23, no. 3, 2012, pp. 267–282.

Anglin, Sallie. "Generative Motion: Queer Ecology and Avatar." *The Journal of Popular Culture*, vol. 48, no. 2, 2015, pp. 341–354.

Anzaldúa, Gloria. *Borderlands/La Frontera: The New Mestiza*. 1987. Aunt Lute Books, 2012.

Appiah, Kwame Anthony. *Cosmopolitanism: Ethics in a World of Strangers*. Penguin, 2006.

Archer, Neil. "Transnational Science Fiction at the End of the World: Consensus, Conflict, and the Politics of Climate Change." *JCMS: Journal of Cinema and Media Studies*, vol. 58, no. 3, 2019, pp. 1–25.

Azcona, María del Mar. *The Multi-Protagonist Film*. Wiley-Blackwell, 2010.

Azcona, María del Mar. "Matt Damon: A Cosmopolitan Hero for the Mainstream." *Celebrity Studies*, vol. 10, no. 2, 2019, pp. 174–190. Published online on 13 March 2018.

Baccolini, Raffaella. "Utopia in Dystopia: *Cloud Atlas*." *Science Fiction Film and Television*, vol. 9, no. 1, 2016, pp. 73–76.

Bahng, Aimee. *Migrant Futures: Decolonizing Speculation in Financial Times*. Duke UP, 2018.

Baker, Brian. "'Here on the Outside': Mobility and Bio-politics in Michael Winterbottom's *Code 46*." *Science Fiction Studies*, vol. 42, no. 1, 2015, pp. 115–131.

Balibar, Étienne. *Politics and the Other Scene*. Verso, 2002.

Bauman, Zygmunt. *Globalization: The Human Consequences*. Columbia UP, 1998.

Beck, Ulrich. "World Risk Society as Cosmopolitan Society? Ecological Questions in a Framework of Manufactured Uncertainties." *Theory, Culture and Society*, vol. 13, no. 4, 1996, pp. 1–32.

Beck, Ulrich. "The Cosmopolitan Manifesto." *New Statesman*, March 20, 1998.

Beck, Ulrich. "The Cosmopolitan Society and its Enemies." *Theory, Culture & Society*, vol. 19, no. 1–2, 2002, pp. 17–44.

Beck, Ulrich. *The Cosmopolitan Vision*. Polity, 2006.

Beck, Ulrich. *World at Risk*. 2007. Polity, 2009.

Beck, Ulrich. "Remapping Social Inequalities in an Age of Climate Change: For a Cosmopolitan Renewal of Sociology." *Global Networks*, vol. 10, no. 2, 2010, pp. 165–181.

Beck, Ulrich and Beck-Gernsheim, Elizabeth. *Fernliebe: Lebensformen im Globalen Zeitalter*. Suhrkamp, 2011.

Beck, Ulrich. "Global Inequality and Human Rights: A Cosmopolitan Perspective." *The Routledge Handbook of Cosmopolitanism Studies*, edited by Gerard Delanty. Routledge, 2012, pp. 302–315.

Belloni, Matthew and Tatiana Siegel. "*Total Recall*: Did Sony Appease China with Scene Changes?" *The Hollywood Reporter*, 16 August 2012, https://www.hollywoodreporter.com/movies/movie-news/total-recall-sony-china-colin-farrell-363326/. Accessed 15 May 2021.

Bergthaller, Hannes. "A Sense of No-Place." *European Journal of English Studies*, vol. 16, no. 2, 2012, pp. 151–162.

Bernabé, Alberto and Mendoza, Julia. "Analogías y Diferencias entre las Doctrinas de la Transmigración." *Reencarnación: La Transmigración de las Almas entre Oriente y Occidente*, edited by Alberto Bernabé, Madayo Kahle and Marco Antonio Santamaría. Abada Editores, 2011, pp. 555–572.

Bhambra, Gurminder. "Cosmopolitanism and Postcolonial Critique." *The Ashgate Reseach Companion to Cosmopolitanism*, edited by María Rovisco and Magdalena Nowicka. Ashgate Publishing, 2011, pp. 313–328.

Biskind, Peter. *Seeing Is Believing: How Hollywood Taught Us to Stop Worrying and Love the Fifties*. Pantheon Books, 1983.

Bordun, Troy. "What Becomes of Endings on Film? *Elysium, Mad Max: Fury Road, Snowpiercer*." *Science Fiction Film and Television*, vol. 9, no. 1, 2016, pp. 76–79.

Bordwell, David. *The Way Hollywood Tells It: Story and Style in Modern Movies*. University of California Press, 2006.

Bould, Mark. "We're Not in Kansas any More: Some Notes on Camp and Queer Sf Movies." *Foundation*, vol. 86, 2002, pp. 40–50.

Bould, Mark. *Science Fiction: Routledge Film Guidebooks*. Routledge, 2012.

Bould, Mark. *The Anthropocene Unconscious: Climate Catastrophe Culture*. Verso, 2021.

Boyle, Kirk and Dan Mrozowski. "Screening Cosmos-Politanism: The Anthropocenic Politics of Outer Space Media." *Science Fiction Film and Television*, vol. 12, no. 3, 2019, pp. 343–63.

Braasch, Gary, editor. *Earth under Fire: How Global Warming Is Changing the World*. University of California Press, 2007.

Branston, Gill. "The Planet at the End of the Word." *New Review of Film and Television Studies*, vol. 5, no. 2, 2007, pp. 211–229.

Brereton, Pat. *Hollywood Utopia: Ecology in Contemporary American Cinema*. Intellect, 2005.

Brown, Wendy. *Walled States, Waning Sovereignty*. Zone Books, 2010.

Brown, William. *Supercinema: Film-Philosophy for the Digital Age*. Berghahn, 2013.

Buckley, Ross. "Introducing a 0.05% Financial Transactions Tax as an Instrument of Global Justice and Market Efficiency." *Asian Journal of International Law*, vol. 4, no. 1, 2013, pp. 153–167.

Bukatman, Scott. *Terminal Identity: The Virtual Subject in Postmodern Science Fiction*. Duke University Press, 1993.

Butler, Andrew. "Heteronormative Futures" in "SFS Symposium: Sexuality in Science Fiction." *Science Fiction Studies*, vol. 36, no. 3, 2009, pp. 388–389.

Butler, Andrew. "Human Subjects—Alien Objects? Abjection and the Constructions of Race and Racism in *District 9*." *Alien Imaginations: Science Fiction and Tales of Transnationalism*, edited by Ulrike Küchler, Silja Maehl, and Graeme Stout. Bloomsbury, 2015, pp. 95–112.

Canavan, Gerry. ""If the Engine Ever Stops, We'd All Die": *Snowpiercer* and Necrofuturism." *Paradoxa: Sf Now*, vol. 26, edited by Mark Bould and Rhys Williams. Paradoxa, 2014a, pp. 41–66.

Canavan, Gerry. "Introduction: If This Goes On." *Green Planets: Ecology and Science Fiction*, edited by Gerry Canavan and Kim Stanley Robinson. Wesleyan University Press, 2014b, pp. 1–24.

Castells, Manuel. *The Rise of the Network Society*. Wiley-Blackwell, 2nd ed., with new preface, 2010.

Castle, Stephen and Barbara Surk. "Migrants Diverted to Slovenia after Hungary Closes Border." *The New York Times*, 17 October 2015, http://www.nytimes.com/2015/10/18/world/europe/hungary-closes-border-changing-refugees-path.html?hp&action=click&pgtype=Homepage&module=   second-column-region&region=top-news&WT.nav=top-news. Accessed 21 March 2016.

Chung, Hye Jean. *Media Heterotopias Digital Effects and Material Labor in Global Film Production*. Duke UP, 2018.

Cloud Atlas. Directed by The Wachowskis and Tom Tykwer. Cloud Atlas Productions, X-Filme Creative Pool, Anarchos Pictures, A Company Filmproduktionsgesellschaft, ARD Degeto Film, Ascension Pictures, Dreams of Dragon Picture, Five Drops, and Media Asia Group, 2012.

Codependent Lesbian Space Alien Seeks Same. Directed by Madeleine Olnek. Madeleine Olnek, Laura Terruso, Melissa Finell, Lucy Sexton, and Cynthia Fredette, 2011.

Collins, Marscha. "Echoing Romance: James Cameron's *Avatar* as Ecoromance." *Mosaic: A Journal for the Interdisciplinary Study of Literature*, vol. 47, no. 2, 2014, pp. 104–119.

Cooper, Anthony and Chris Rumford. "Cosmopolitan Borders: Bordering as Connectivity." *The Ashgate Reseach Companion to Cosmopolitanism*, edited by María Rovisco and Magdalena Nowicka. Ashgate Publishing, 2011, pp. 261–275.

Cooper, Mark Garrett. "Narrative Spaces." *Screen*, vol. 43, no. 2, 2002, pp. 139–157.

Cornea, Christine. *Science Fiction Cinema: Between Fantasy and Reality*. Edinburgh UP, 2007.

Crespo, Inês and Ângela Pereira. "Climate Change Films: Fear and Agency Appeals." *Transnational Ecocinema: Film Culture in an Era of Ecological Transformation*, edited by Pietari Kääpä and Tommy Gustafsson. Intellect, 2013, pp. 165–186.

Crutzen, Paul and Eugene Stoermer. "The Anthropocene." *IGBP Global Change Newsletter*, vol. 41, 2000, pp. 17–18.

Csicsery-Ronay, Istvan. "Dis-Imagined Communities: Science Fiction and the Future of Nations." *Edging into the Future: Science Fiction and Contemporary Cultural Transformation*, edited by Veronica Hollinger and Joan Gordon. University of Pennsylvania Press, 2002, pp. 217–238.

Csicsery-Ronay, Istvan. "Some Things We Know about Aliens." *The Yearbook of English Studies*, vol. 37, no. 2, 2007, pp. 1–23.

Csicsery-Ronay, Istvan. "What Do We Mean When We Say "Global Science Fiction"? Reflections on a New Nexus." *Science Fiction Studies*, vol. 39, no. 3, 2012, pp. 478–494.

Cubitt, Sean. "Always Take the Weather: Green Media in a Global Context." *Eco Media*. Rodopi, 2005, pp. 117–132.

Cupples, Julie. "Wild Globalization: The Biopolitics of Climate Change and Global Capitalism on Nicaragua's Mosquito Coast." *Antipode*, vol. 44, no. 1, 2012, pp. 10–30.

Dalby, Simon. "Biopolitics and Climate Security in the Anthropocene." *Geoforum*, vol. 49, 2013, pp. 184–192.

Dargis, Manohla. "When the World Hangs in the Balance, a Reliable Calendar Is Needed." *The New York Times*, 12 November 2009, http://www.nytimes.com/2009/11/13/movies/13twentytwelve.html?_r=0. Accessed 20 July 2017.

Davis, Robert. "The Instantaneous Worldwide Release: Coming Soon to Everyone, Everywhere." *Transnational Cinema: The Film Reader*, edited by Elizabeth Ezra and Terry Rowden. Routledge, 2006, pp. 73–80.

De Ville, Ferdi and Gabriel Siles-Brügge. *The Truth about the Transatlantic Trade and Investment Partnership*. Polity, 2016.

Decker, Erica, Jared Sabovitch, and Jason Edmonson. "Canada Fires: Amateur Footage Shows Resident's Terror." In Cook, James. "Canada Wildfire: Images Show McMurray Devastation." *BBC News*, 6 May 2016, http://www.bbc.com/news/world-us-canada-36224767. Accessed 12 June 2016.

Delanty, Gerard. "The Cosmopolitan Imagination: Critical Cosmopolitanism and Social Theory." *British Journal of Sociology*, vol. 57, no. 1, 2006, pp. 25–47.

Delanty, Gerard. *The Cosmopolitan Imagination*. Cambridge UP, 2009.

Delanty, Gerard. "The Idea of Critical Cosmopolitanism." *The Routledge Handbook of Cosmopolitanism Studies*, edited by Gerard Delanty. Routledge, 2012, pp. 38–46.

Deleuze, Gilles and Félix Guattari. *A Thousand Plateaus*. Translated by Brian Massumi. University of Minnesota Press, 1987.

Deleyto, Celestino and María del Mar Azcona. *Alejandro González Iñárritu*. University of Illinois Press, 2010.

Deleyto, Celestino. "The Beauty of the Gated Community." *Cinema, Culture and Society*, 24 August 2013, http://ccs.unizar.es/ccsblog/139-the-beauty-of-the-gated-community. Accessed 31 May 2021.

Deleyto, Celestino. "Looking from the Border: A Cosmopolitan Approach to Contemporary Cinema." *Transnational Cinemas*, vol. 8, no. 2, 2017, pp. 95–112.

dell'Agnese, Elena. "The US–Mexico Border in American Movies: A Political Geography Perspective." *Geopolitics*, vol. 10, no. 2, 2005, pp. 204–221.

Desser, David. "Race, Space and Class: The Politics of Cityscapes in Science-Fiction Films." *Alien Zone II: The Spaces of Science Fiction Cinema*, edited by Annette Kuhn. Verso, 1999, pp. 80–96.

Dickens, Peter and James Ormrod. "Globalization of Space: From the Global to the Galactic." *The Routledge International Handbook of Globalization Studies*, edited by Bryan Turner. Routledge, 2010, pp. 531–553.

Dix, Hywel. *Postmodern Fiction and the Break-Up of Britain*. Continuum, 2010.

Dyer, Richard. "White." *Screen*, vol. 29, no. 4, 1988, pp. 44–65.

Dyer, Richard. *White*. Routledge, 1997.

Echeverría, Julia. *The Viral Screen: Viruses, Zombies, and Infectious Diseases in Post-Millennial Films*. 2017. University of Zaragoza, PhD Dissertation.

Ellsworth, William. "Injection-Induced Earthquakes." *Science*, vol. 341, no. 6142, 15 July 2013, pp. 1–7, https://www.science.org/doi/10.1126/science.1225942. Accessed 18 October 2020.

Elysium. Directed by Neill Blomkamp. TriStar Pictures, Media Rights Capital, QED International, Alpha Core, Simon Kinberg Productions, Genre Films, and Sony Pictures Entertainment, 2013.

Epstein, Gerald. "Introduction: Financialization and the World Economy." *Financialization and the World Economy*, edited by Gerald Epstein. Edward Elgar Publishing, 2005, pp. 3–16.

Estrada, Gabriel S. "'Cloud Atlas' Queer Tiki Kitsch: Polynesians, Settler Colonialism, and Sci-Fi Film." *Journal of Religion & Film*, vol. 18, no. 2, 2014, pp. 1–32.

Felix, David. "Financial Globalization and the Tobin Tax." *Challenge*, vol. 38, no. 3, 1995, pp. 56–59.

Fine, Robert and Robin Cohen. "Four Cosmopolitanism Moments." *Conceiving Cosmopolitanism: Theory, Context and Practice*, edited by Steven Vertovec and Robin Cohen. Oxford UP, 2002, pp. 137–162.

Fine, Robert. *Cosmopolitanism*. Routledge, 2007.

Fine, Robert. "The Idea of Cosmopolitan Solidarity." *The Routledge Handbook to Cosmopolitanism Studies*, edited by Gerard Delanty. Routledge, 2012, pp. 376–386.

Fisher, Mark. *Capitalist Realism: Is There No Alternative?* Zero Books, 2009.

Fisher, Mark. "Precarious Dystopias: *The Hunger Games, In Time*, and *Never Let Me Go*." *Film Quarterly*, vol. 65, no. 4, 2012, pp. 27–33.

Fiskio, Janet. "Apocalypse and Ecotopia: Narratives in Global Climate Change Discourse." *Race, Gender & Class*, vol. 19, no. 1–2, 2012, pp. 12–36.

Fojas, Camila. *Border Bandits: Hollywood on the Southern Frontier*. University of Texas Press, 2008.

Foucault, Michel. *The History of Sexuality. Volume I: An Introduction*. Translated by Robert Hurley. 1976. Pantheon Books, 1978.

Frame, David and Myles R. Allen. "Climate Change and Global Risk." *Global Catastrophic Risks*, edited by Nick Bostrom and Milan M. Cirkovic. Oxford UP, 2008, pp. 265–286.

Freedman, Carl. "Utopianism and Bong Joon-Ho's *Snowpiercer*." *Science Fiction Film and Television*, vol. 9, no. 1, 2016, pp. 84–86.

García Canclini, Néstor. "Culturas Híbridas y Estrategias Comunicacionales." *Estudios sobre las Culturas Contemporáneas*, Época II, vol. 3, no. 5 (junio), 1997, pp. 109–128.

Geraghty, Lincoln. *American Science Fiction Film and Television*. Berg, 2009.

Gibson, Suzie. "Stop the Ships: *Elysium*, Asylum Seekers and the Battle over Sovereign Borders." *Screen Education*, vol. 78, 2015, pp. 78–85.

Giddens, Anthony. *The Politics of Climate Change*. Polity, 2009.

Girgus, Sam B. *The Films of Woody Allen*. Cambridge UP, 2nd ed., 2007.

Golub, Philip S. and Jean-Paul Maréchal. "Overcoming the Planetary Prisoner's Dilemma: Cosmopolitan Ethos and Pluralist Cooperation." *Ethics and Global Environmental Policy: Cosmopolitan Conceptions of Climate Change*, edited by Paul G. Harris. Edward Elgar Publishing, 2011, pp. 150–174.

Gomel, Elana. "Everyday Apocalypse: The Ethics and Aesthetics of the End of Time." *Postmodern Science Fiction and Temporal Imagination*. Continuum, 2010, pp. 118–146.

Gómez-Muñoz, Pablo. "The Alien as a Vehicle for Cosmopolitan Discourses: The Case of *The Day the Earth Stood Still* (2008)." *Atlantis: Journal of the Spanish Association for Anglo-American Studies*, vol. 40, no. 2, 2018, pp. 123–144.

Grant, Barry Keith. *Invasion of the Body Snatchers*. Palgrave Macmillan/British Film Institute, 2010.

Grant, Barry Keith. *100 Science Fiction Films*. Palgrave Macmillan/British Film Institute, 2013.

Gunning, Tom. "The Cinema of Attractions: Early Film, Its Spectator and the Avant-Garde." *Wide Angle*, vol. 8, no. 3–4, 1986, pp. 63–70.

Hamner, Everett. "Virtual Immigrants: Transfigured Bodies and Transnational Spaces in Science Fiction Cinema." *Simultaneous Worlds: Global Science Fiction Cinema*, edited by Jennifer Feeley and Sarah Ann Wells. University of Minnesota Press, 2015, pp. 154–170.

Hardt, Michael and Antonio Negri. *Multitude: War and Democracy in the Age of Empire*. Hamish Hamilton, 2004.

Harris, Paul G. *World Ethics and Climate Change: From International to Global Justice*. Edinburgh UP, 2010.

Harvey, David. "Cosmopolitanism and the Banality of Geographical Evils." *Public Culture*, vol. 12, no. 2, 2000, pp. 529–564.

Harvey, David. *Cosmopolitanism and the Geographies of Freedom*. Columbia UP, 2009.

Haupts, Tobias. "Dystopien in Blau, Grau und Weiß: Zur Ausformung von Eis und Kälte in Bong Joon-hos *Snowpiercer*." *Die Zukunft Ist Jetzt*, edited by Aidan Power et al. Bertz und Fischer, 2016, pp. 181–191.

Heise, Ursula. *Sense of Place and Sense of Planet: The Environmental Imagination of the Global*. Oxford UP, 2008.

Higbee, Will and Song Hwee Lim. "Concepts of Transnational Cinema: Towards a Critical Transnationalism in Film Studies." *Transnational Cinemas*, vol. 1, no. 1, 2010, pp. 7–21.

Higgins, David. "Toward a Cosmopolitan Science Fiction." *American Literature*, vol. 83, no. 2, 2011, pp. 331–354.

Hjort, Mette. "On the Plurality of Cinematic Transnationalism." *World Cinemas: Transnational Perspectives*, edited by Natasa Durovicová and Kathleen Newman. Routledge, 2009, pp. 12–33.

Holton, Robert. "Foreword." *Performing Global Networks*, edited by Karen Fricker and Ronit Lentin. Cambridge Scholars Publishing, 2007, pp. vii–viii.

Holton, Robert. *Global Networks*. Palgrave MacMillan, 2008.

Hudson, Dale. "Vampires of Color and the Performance of Multicultural Whiteness." *The Persistence of Whiteness: Race and Contemporary Hollywood Cinema*, edited by Daniel Bernardi. Routledge, 2008, pp. 127–156.

Hughey, Matthew. *The White Savior Film: Content, Critics, and Consumption*. Temple UP, 2014.

I Origins. Directed by Mike Cahill. Verisimilitude, WeWork Studios, Bersin Pictures, Penny Jane Films, 2014.

In Time. Directed by Andrew Niccol. New Regency Productions and Strike Entertainment, 2011.

"*In Time* Filming Locations. Part 7." *Seeing Stars*, http://www.seeing-stars.com/Locations/InTime7.shtml. Accessed 25 March 2014.

IPCC. *Climate Change 2014: Synthesis Report*, edited by The Core Writing Team, Rajendra Pachauri, and Leo Meyer. Intergovernmental Panel on Climate Change, 2015, pp. 1–151.

IPCC. "Summary for Policymakers." *Climate Change 2021: The Physical Science Basis. Contribution of Working Group I to the Sixth Assessment Report of the Intergovernmental Panel on Climate Change*, edited by Valérie Masson-Delmotte, Panmao Zhai et al., 2021, https://www.ipcc.ch/report/ar6/wg1/downloads/report/IPCC_AR6_WGI_SPM_final.pdf. Accessed 28 March 2022.

Ivakhiv, Adrian. *Ecologies of the Moving Image: Cinema, Affect, Nature*. Wilfrid Laurier UP, 2013.

Johnston, Keith. *Science Fiction Film: A Critical Introduction*. Berg, 2011.

Keane, Stephen. *Disaster Movies: The Cinema of Catastrophe*. 2001. Wallflower, 2006.

Keegan, Cáel M. *Lana and Lilly Wachowski*. University of Illinois Press, 2018.

Kendall, Gavin, Ian Woodward, and Zlatko Skrbiš. *The Sociology of Cosmopolitanism: Globalization, Identity, Culture and Government*. Palgrave Macmillan, 2009.

Klein, Naomi. *This Changes Everything: Capitalism vs. The Climate*. Simon and Schuster, 2014.

Küchler, Ulrike, Silja Maehl, and Graeme Stout. "Introduction." *Alien Imaginations: Science Fiction and Tales of Transnationalism*, edited by Ulrike Küchler, Silja Maehl, and Graeme Stout. Bloomsbury, 2015, pp. 1–12.

Landon, Brooks. *The Aesthetics of Ambivalence: Rethinking Science Fiction Film in the Age of Electronic (Re)production*. Greenwood Press, 1992.

Langley, Alison. "Austria Streamlines Slovenia Border to Process Refugees." *Deutsche Welle*, 22 January 2016, http://www.dw.com/en/austria-streamlines-slovenia-border-to-process-refugees/a-18999606. Accessed 21 March 2016.

Lebovic, Nitzan. "The Biopolitical Film (A Nietzschean Paradigm)." *Postmodern Culture*, vol. 23, no. 1, 2012.

Lim, Song Hwee. "Concepts of Transnational Cinema Revisited." *Transnational Screens*, vol. 10, no. 1, 2019, pp. 1–12.

Lothian, Alexis. *Old Futures: Speculative Fiction and Queer Possibility*. NYU Press, 2018.

Loza, Susana. "Playing Alien in Post-Racial Times." *Monster Culture in the 21st Century*, edited by Marina Levina and Diem-My T. Bui. Bloomsbury, 2013, pp. 53–72.

Marazzi, Christian. *The Violence of Financial Capitalism*. Semiotext(e), 2010.

McCabe, Felicity. "Dead Animals near Kalawleh, Somaliland." In Clár Ní Chonghaile "In Somaliland, Climate Change Is Now a Life-or-Death Challenge." *The Guardian*, 23 November 2015, https://www.theguardian.com/globaldevelopment/2015/nov/23/somaliland-climate-change-drought-cyclones-life-or-death-challenge. Accessed 23 November 2017.

McClintock, Pamela. "Global Box Office: *Jupiter Ascending* Finds Redemption in China." *Hollywood Reporter*, 8 March 2015, http://www.hollywoodreporter.com/news/global-box-office-jupiter-ascending-779980. Accessed 13 March 2015.

McFate, Sean. *The Modern Mercenary: Private Armies and What They Mean for World Order.* Oxford University Press, 2014.

McGrath, Matt. "'Perfect Storm' of El Niño and Warming Boosted Alberta Fires." *BBC News*, 5 May 2016, http://www.bbc.com/news/science-environment-36212145. Accessed 8 May 2017.

McGuire, Bill. *Waking the Giant: How a Changing Climate Triggers Earthquakes, Tsunamis, and Volcanoes.* Oxford UP, 2012.

McLeod, John. *Life Lines: Writing Transcultural Adoption.* Bloomsbury, 2015.

Melzer, Patricia. "The Coming Future" in "SFS Symposium: Sexuality in Science Fiction." *Science Fiction Studies*, vol. 36, no. 3, 2009, pp. 397–398.

Mennel, Barbara. *Queer Cinema: Schoolgirls, Vampires and Gay Cowboys.* Wallflower, 2012.

Meyer, Stephenie. *The Host: A Novel.* Little, Brown and Company, 2008.

Mezzadra, Sandro and Brett Neilson. *Border as Method, or, the Multiplication of Labor.* Duke UP, 2013.

Mezzadra, Sandro and Brett Neilson. "Operations of Capital." *South Atlantic Quarterly*, vol. 114, no. 1, 2015, pp. 1–9.

Mignolo, Walter. "The Many Faces of Cosmo-polis: Border Thinking and Critical Cosmopolitanism." *Public Culture*, vol. 12, no. 3, 2000, pp. 721–748.

Mignolo, Walter. *The Darker Side of Western Modernity: Global Futures, Decolonial Options.* Duke UP, 2011.

Miller, Cynthia and Bowdoin Van Riper. "The Future, in Bed with the Past: Miscegenation in Science Fiction Film and Television." *The Sex Is Out of this World: Essays on the Carnal Side of Science Fiction*, edited by Sherry Ginn and Michael Cornelius. McFarland, 2012, pp. 17–33.

Milner, Andrew. "Science Fiction and Climate Change." Science Fiction Research Association Conference, 28–30 June 2016, University of Liverpool. Keynote Address.

Mitchell, David. *Cloud Atlas.* Sceptre/Hodder and Stoughton, 2004.

Morton, Timothy. "Pandora's Box: *Avatar*, Ecology, Thought." *Green Planets: Ecology and Science Fiction*, edited by Gerry Canavan and Kim Stanley Robinson. Wesleyan UP, 2014, pp. 206–225.

Muñoz, José Esteban. *Cruising Utopia: The Then and There of Queer Futurity.* NYU Press, 2009.

Naficy, Hamid. "Situating Accented Cinema." *Transnational Cinema: The Film Reader*, edited by Elizabeth Ezra and Terry Rowden. Routledge, 2006, pp. 111–130.

Nagib, Lúcia. "Towards a Positive Definition of World Cinema". *Remapping World Cinema*, edited by Song Hwee Lim and Stephanie Dennison. Wallflower Press, 2006, pp. 30–37.

Nama, Adilifu. *Black Space: Imagining Race in Science Fiction Film.* University of Texas Press, 2008.

Neyrat, Frédéric. "The Biopolitics of Catastrophe, or How to Avert the Past and Regulate the Future." *South Atlantic Quarterly*, vol. 115, no. 2, 2016, pp. 247–265.

Nussbaum, Martha. "Introduction: Cosmopolitan Emotions" and "Patriotism and Cosmopolitanism." *For Love of Country*, edited by Joshua Cohen, 1996. Beacon Press, 2002, pp. ix–xiv and 3–20.

Ong, Aihwa. *Neoliberalism as Exception: Mutations in Citizenship and Sovereignty.* Duke UP, 2006.

Ortega, Bob and Rob O'Dell. "Deadly Border Agent Incidents Cloaked in Silence." *The Arizona Republic*, 16 December 2013, http://www.azcentral.com/news/politics/articles/20131212arizona-border-patrol-deadly-force-investigation.html. Accessed 28 September 2015.

Ortega, Bob. "Border Patrol Checkpoints Stir Public Backlash." *USA Today*, 7 June 2014, http://www.usatoday.com/story/news/nation/2014/06/07/border-patrol-checkpoints-stir-public-backlash/10113693/. Accessed March 21, 2016.

Oxford Analytica. "International Trade Partnerships: Deal or No Deal?" *Oxford Analytica*, 31 July 2014, http://www.oxan.com/analysis/dailybrief/samples/InternationalTradeTreaties.aspx?WT.mc_id=TWT. Accessed October 30, 2016.

Padilla, Mark B. et al. "Introduction: Cross-Cultural Reflections on an Intimate Intersection." *Love and Globalization: Transformations of Intimacy in the Contemporary World*, edited by Mark B. Padilla et al. Vanderbilt UP, 2007, pp. ix–xxxi.

Papastergiadis, Nikos. *Cosmopolitanism and Culture*. Polity, 2012.

Parizot, Cédric et al. "The AntiAtlas of Borders, A Manifesto." *Journal of Borderlands Studies*, vol. 29, no. 4, 2014, pp. 503–512.

Parker, Jo Alyson. "From Time's Boomerang to Pointillist Mosaic: Translating *Cloud Atlas* into Film." *SubStance*, vol. 44, no. 1, 2015, pp. 123–135.

Pearson, Wendy. "Alien Cryptographies: The View from Queer." *Science Fiction Studies*, vol. 26, no. 1, 1999, pp. 1–22.

Pearson, Wendy. "Towards a Queer Genealogy of SF." *Queer Universes: Sexualities in Science Fiction*, edited by Wendy Pearson, Veronica Hollinger, and Joan Gordon. Liverpool UP, 2008, pp. 72–100.

Pearson, Wendy. "Queer Theory." *The Routledge Companion to Science Fiction*, edited by Mark Bould et al. Routledge, 2009, pp. 298–307.

Peberdy, Donna. "Narrative Trans-Actions: *Cloud Atlas* (2012) and Multi-Role Performance in the Global Ensemble." *Transnational Cinemas*, vol. 5, no. 2, 2014, pp. 167–180.

Pierson, Michelle. *Special Effects: Still in Search of Wonder*. Columbia UP, 2002.

Piketty, Thomas. *Capital in the Twenty-First Century*. Harvard UP, 2013.

Pirro, Robert. "Aesthetic Legacies and Dashed Political Hopes: Caspar David Friedrich Motifs in Roland Emmerich's Post-9/11 Popcorn Message Movies." *The Germanic Review*, vol. 88, 2013, pp. 400–417.

Plummer, Ken. *Cosmopolitan Sexualities: Hope and the Humanist Imagination*. Polity, 2015.

Popescu, Gabriel. *Bordering and Ordering the Twenty-First Century: Understanding Borders*. Rowman and Littlefield, 2012.

Potzch, Holger. "The Emergence of iBorder: Bordering Bodies, Networks, and Machines." *Environment and Planning D: Society and Space*, vol. 33, 2015, pp. 101–118.

Pratt, Vic. "Cheap Thrills: Sci-fi on a Shoestring." *Sci-fi: Days of Fear and Wonder*, edited by James Bell. British Film Institute, 2014, pp. 52–57.

Quijano, Aníbal and Immanuel Wallerstein. "Americanity as a Concept, or the Americas in the Modern World-System." *International Social Science Journal*, vol. 29, 1992, pp. 549–557.

Ramírez Berg, Charles. "Immigrants, Aliens, and Extraterrestrials: Science Fiction's Alien "Other" as (Among Other Things) New Latino Imagery." *Film Genre Reader IV*, edited by Barry Keith Grant. University of Texas Press, 2012, pp. 402–32. First published in *CineAction*, vol. 18, Fall 1989, pp. 3–17.

Reber, Dierdra. *Coming to Our Senses: Affect and an Order of Things for Global Culture*. Columbia UP, 2016.

Rehling, Nicola. *Extra-Ordinary Men: White Heterosexual Masculinity and Contemporary Popular Cinema*. Lexington Books, 2009.

Reusswig, Fritz and Anthony Leiserowitz. "The International Impact of *The Day After Tomorrow*." *Environment: Science and Policy for Sustainable Development*, vol. 47, no. 3, 2005, pp. 41–44.

Rieder, John. *Colonialism and the Emergence of Science Fiction*. Wesleyan UP, 2008.

Rivera, Lysa. "Future Histories and Cyborg Labor: Reading Borderlands Science Fiction after NAFTA." *Science Fiction Studies*, vol. 39, no. 3, 2012, pp. 415–436.

Rodríguez Ortega, Vicente. *La Ciudad Global en el Cine Contemporáneo: Una Perspectiva Transnacional*. Shangrila Textos Aparte, 2012.

Rovisco, María. "Towards a Cosmopolitan Cinema: Understanding the Connection between Borders, Mobility and Cosmopolitanism in the Fiction Film." *Mobilities*, vol. 8, no. 1, 2013, pp. 148–165.

Rumford, Chris. "Bordering and Connectivity: Cosmopolitan Opportunities." *The Routledge Handbook of Cosmopolitanism Studies*, edited by Gerard Delanty. Routledge, 2012, pp. 245–253.

Rust, Stephen. "Hollywood and Climate Change." *Ecocinema: Theory and Practice*, edited by Stephen Rust, Salma Monani, and Sean Cubitt. Routledge, 2013, pp. 191–211.

Sands, Peter. "Global Cannibal City Machines: Recent Visions of Urban/Social Space." *Global Cities: Cinema, Architecture and Urbanism in a Digital Age*, edited by Linda Krause and Patrice Petro. Rutgers UP, 2003, pp. 129–141.

Santirso, Jaime. "China, ante el espejo de la ciencia ficción." *El País*, 16 February 2021, https://elpais.com/cultura/2021-02-15/china-ante-el-espejo-de-la-ciencia-ficcion.html?event_log=oklogin&o=cerrcult&prod=REGCRARTCULT

Sassen, Saskia. *Globalization and Its Discontents*. The New Press, 1998.

Sassen, Saskia. *Territory, Authority, Rights: From Medieval to Global Assemblages*. 2006. Princeton UP, 2008.

Sassen, Saskia. "Expelled: Humans in Capitalism's Deepening Crisis." *Journal of World-Systems Research*, vol. 19, no. 2, 2013a, pp. 198–201.

Sassen, Saskia. "When the Center No Longer Holds: Cities as Frontier Zones." *Cities*, vol. 34, 2013b, pp. 67–70.

Sassen, Saskia. *Expulsions: Brutality and Complexity in the Global Economy*. Harvard UP, 2014.

Schoonover, Karl and Rosalind Galt. *Queer Cinema in the World*. Duke UP, 2016.

Sedgwick, Eve Kosofsky. *Epistemology of the Closet*. University of California Press, 1990.

Selisker, Scott. "The Cult and the World System: The Topoi of David Mitchell's Global Novels." *Novel: A Forum on Fiction*, vol. 47, no. 3, 2014, pp. 443–459.

Shaviro, Steven. *Connected, or What It Means to Live in the Network Society*. University of Minnesota Press, 2003.

Shaw, Deborah. "Transnational Cinema: Mapping a Field of Study." *The Routledge Companion to World Cinema*, edited by Rob Stone et al. Routledge, 2018, pp. 290–298.

Shaw, Kristian. *Cosmopolitanism in Twenty-First Century Fiction*. Palgrave Macmillan, 2017.

Singer, P. W. *Corporate Warriors: The Rise of the Privatized Military Industry*. Cornell UP, 2003.

Skillington, Tracey. "Cosmopolitan Justice and Global Climate Change: Toward Perpetual Peace or War in a Resource-Challenged World?" *Irish Journal of Sociology*, vol. 20, no. 2, 2012, pp. 132–152.

Skrbiš, Zlatko and Ian Woodward. *Cosmopolitanism: Uses of the Idea*. Sage, 2013.

Smith, Adam. "Days of Reckoning." *Empire*, no. 325, July 2016, pp. 62–69.

Sobchack, Vivian. *Screening Space: The American Science Fiction Film*. 1980. Ungar, 1987.

Solnit, Rebecca. *A Paradise Built in Hell: The Extraordinary Communities that Arise in Disaster*. Penguin, 2009.

Stacey, Jackie. "The Uneasy Cosmopolitans of *Code Unknown*." *Whose Cosmopolitanism? Critical Cosmopolitanism, Relationalities and Discontents*, edited by Andrew Irving and Nina Glick Schiller. Berghahn, 2015a, pp. 160–171.

Stacey, Jackie. "Whose Cosmopolitanism? The Violence of Idealizations and the Ambivalence of Self." *Whose Cosmopolitanism? Critical Cosmopolitanism, Relationalities and Discontents*, edited by Andrew Irving and Nina Glick Schiller. Berghahn, 2015b, pp. 34–36.

Steffen, Will, Paul Crutzen, and John McNeill. "The Anthropocene: Are Humans Now Overwhelming the Great Forces of Nature?" *Ambio*, vol. 36, no. 8, 2007, pp. 614–621.

Stiglitz, Joseph. *The Price of Inequality*. W.W. Norton & Company, 2012.

Strange, Michael. "Implications of TTIP for Transnational Social Movements and International NGOs." *The Politics of Transatlantic Trade Negotiations: TTIP in a Globalized World*, edited by Jean-Frédéric Morin et al. Ashgate, 2015, pp. 81–91.

Strauss, Michael. "Nations Outside Their Borders: How Extraterritorial Concessions Reinforce Sovereignty." *Borderities and the Politics of Contemporary Mobile Borders*, edited by Anne Laure Amilhat-Szary and Frédéric Giraut. Palgrave Macmillan, 2015, pp. 53–67.

Suparak, Astria. "Virtually Asian." *Vimeo*, 23 January 2021, https://vimeo.com /503907394.

Suvin, Darko. *Metamorphoses of Science Fiction: On the Poetics and History of a Literary Genre*. Yale UP, 1979.

Svodoba, Michael. "Cli-fi on the Screen(s): Patterns in the Representation of Climate Change in Fictional Films." *WIREs Climate Change*, vol. 7, 2016, pp. 43–64.

Telotte, Jay P. *Science Fiction Film*. Cambridge UP, 2001.

Telotte, Jay P. "*F.P.1* and the Language of Global Science Fiction Cinema." *Simultaneous Worlds: Global Science Fiction Cinema*, edited by Jennifer Feeley and Sarah Ann Wells. University of Minnesota Press, 2015, pp. 103–118.

The Associated Press. "It's Not Just Alberta: Fires Fueled by Warming Climate Are Increasing." *CBC News*, 11 May 2016, http://www.cbc.ca/news/technology/climate -change-fires-1.3576682. Accessed May 11, 2017.

The Host. Directed by Andrew Niccol. Chockstone Pictures, Nick Wechsler Productions, and Silver Reel, 2013.

"The Robin Hood Tax Campaign." *Oxfam International*, 2010, http://www.oxfam.org/ en/campaigns/health-education/robin-hood-tax. Accessed February 17, 2014.

Thompson, Kirsten Moana. *Apocalyptic Dread: American Film at the Turn of the Millenium*. State University of New York Press, 2007.

Tinkcom, Matthew. *Working Like a Homosexual: Camp, Capital, Cinema*. Duke UP, 2002.

Tonkin, Hannah. *State Control over Private Military and Security Companies in Armed Conflict*. Cambridge UP, 2011.

United States Census Bureau, 2010, http://quickfacts.census.gov/qfd/states/06/0644000 .html. Accessed March 5, 2014.

Van Houtum, Henk and Ton van Naersen. "Bordering, Ordering, Othering." *Tijdschrift voor Economische en Sociale Geografie*, vol. 93, no. 2, 2002, pp. 125–136.

Vanderheiden, Steve. "Climate Justice as Globalized Responsibility: Mitigation, Adaptation and Avoiding Harm to Others." *Ethics and Global Environmental Policy: Cosmopolitan Conceptions of Climate Change*, edited by Paul G. Harris. Edward Elgar Publishing, 2011, pp. 20–41.

Varin, Caroline. *Mercenaries, Hybrid Armies, and National Security*. Routledge, 2015.

Vertovec, Steven and Robin Cohen, editors. *Conceiving Cosmopolitanism: Theory, Context and Practice*. Oxford UP, 2002.

Vertovec, Steven. *Transnationalism*. Routledge, 2009.

Vint, Sherryl. "Thinking Sex in SF" in "SFS Symposium: Sexuality in Science Fiction." *Science Fiction Studies*, vol. 36, no. 3, 2009, pp. 402–3.

Vint, Sherryl. "Introduction: Science Fiction and Biopolitics." *Science Fiction Film and Television*, vol. 4, no. 2, 2011, pp. 161–172.

Vint, Sherryl. "The Biopolitics of Globalization in Damir Lukačevic's *Transfer.*" *Red Alert! Marxist Approaches to SF Cinema*, edited by Ewa Mazierska and Alfredo Suppia. Wayne State UP, 2016, pp. 98–120.

von Burg, Ron. "Decades Away or *The Day After Tomorrow?* Rhetoric, Film, and the Global Warming Debate." *Critical Studies in Media Communication*, vol. 29, no. 1, 2012, pp. 7–26.

Walters, William. "Secure Borders, Safe Haven, Domopolitics." *Citizenship Studies*, vol. 8, no. 3, 2004, pp. 237–260.

Whitley, David. *The Idea of Nature in Disney Animation: From Snow White to WALL-E*. Ashgate, 2012.

Wilkinson, Bruce. "Humans as Geologic Agents: Deep-Time Perspective." *Geology*, vol. 33, no. 3, 2005, pp. 161–164.

Williams, Linda. *Playing the Race Card: Melodramas of Black and White from Uncle Tom to O. J. Simpson*. Princeton UP, 2001.

Woodward, Ian and Zlatko Skrbiš. "Performing Cosmopolitanism." *Routledge Handbook of Cosmopolitan Studies*, edited by Gerard Delanty. Routledge, 2012, pp. 127–137.

Zalasiewicz, Jan et al. "The Anthropocene: A New Epoch of Geological Time?" *Philosophical Transactions of the Royal Society A*, vol. 369, 2011, pp. 835–841.

INDEX

Page numbers in *italics* indicate figures, **bold** indicate tables in the text, and references following "n" refer endnotes.

Printed in the United States
by Baker & Taylor Publisher Services